AF553511

MARKETING MANAGEMENT

MARKETING MANAGEMENT

Dr. Sudhir Gupta

CENTRUM PRESS
NEW DELHI-110002 (INDIA)

CENTRUM PRESS
H.O.: 4360/4, Ansari Road, Daryaganj,
New Delhi-110002 (India)
Tel: 23278000, 23261597, 23255577, 23286875
B.O.: No. 1015, Ist Main Road, BSK IIIrd Stage,
IIIrd Phase, IIIrd Block, Bangalore-560085 (INDIA)
Tel: 080-41723429
Email: centrumpress@gmail.com
Visit us at: www.centrumpress.com

Marketing Management

First Edition, 2011

ISBN 978-93-80921-18-1

PRINTED IN INDIA

Printed at Balaji Offset, Delhi.

Contents

Preface

As we all know that marketing management is one of the most important topics in MBA. Marketing management is a business discipline which is focused on the practical application of marketing techniques and the management of a firm's marketing resources and activities. Rapidly emerging forces of globalisation have compelled firms to market beyond the borders of their home country making International marketing highly significant and an integral part of a firm's marketing strategy.

This book is designed to be a comprehensive text on marketing management for students in Punjab Technical University. This book covers a whole syllabus of marketing management, and attempt to introduce the subject in a comprehensive way. It avoids the narrow focus and considerable complexity of many other books in this area where in depth treatment is required, students are recommended to read relevant texts by leading contributors to idea about marketing thinking and practice.

The objective of the book is to bring together a balanced selection of core concepts as well as new perspectives that collectively articulate a knowledge-based view of marketing. We hope that the discussion made in this book will help the readers to understand and learnt about the different aspects of "Marketing Management" in a most comprehensive way to face the present and future challenges which are occurred in this field. Any suggestion for improving the content of the book will be warmly appreciated.

Author

Preface

1

Marketing Concepts and Orientation

NATURE OF MARKETING

Marketing is the process by which companies determine what products or services may be of interest to customers, and the strategy to use in sales, communications and business development. It is an integrated process through which companies create value for customers and build strong customer relationships in order to capture value from customers in return.

Marketing is used to identify the customer, to keep the customer, and to satisfy the customer. With the customer as the focus of its activities, it can be concluded that *marketing management* is one of the major components of business management. The evolution of marketing was caused due to mature markets and overcapacities in the last 2-3 centuries. Companies then shifted the focus from production to the customer in order to stay profitable.

The term *marketing concept* holds that achieving organizational goals depends on knowing the needs and wants of target markets and delivering the desired satisfactions. It proposes that in order to satisfy its organizational objectives, an organization should anticipate the needs and wants of consumers and satisfy these more effectively than competitors.

Marketing: Several definitions have been proposed for the term marketing. Each tends to emphasize different issues. Memorizing a definition is unlikely to be useful; ultimately, it makes more sense to thinking of ways to benefit from creating customer value in the most effective way, subject to ethical and other constraints that one may have. The 2006 and 2007 definitions offered by the American Marketing Association are relatively similar, with the 2007 appearing a bit more concise.

Note that the definitions make several points:

- A main objective of marketing is to create customer value.
- Marketing usually involves an exchange between buyers and sellers or between other parties.
- Marketing has an impact on the firm, its suppliers, its customers, and others affected by the firm's choices.
- Marketing frequently involves enduring relationships between buyers, sellers, and other parties.
- Processes involved include "creating, communicating, delivering, and exchanging offerings."

Delivering customer value. The central idea behind marketing is the idea that a firm or other entity will create something of value to one or more customers who, in turn, are willing to pay enough to make the venture worthwhile considering opportunity costs. Value can be created in a number of different ways. Some firms manufacture basic products but provide relatively little value above that. Other firms make products whose tangible value is supplemented by services.

It is not necessary for a firm to physically handle a product to add value—e.g., online airline reservation systems add value by:

- Compiling information about available flight connections and fares,
- Allowing the customer to buy a ticket,
- Forwarding billing information to the airline, and
- Forwarding reservation information to the customer.

It should be noted that value must be examined from the point of view of the customer. Some customer segments value certain product attributes more than others. A very expensive product—relative to others in the category—may, in fact, represent great value to a particular customer segment because the benefits received are seen as even greater than the sacrifice made. Some segments have very unique and specific desires, and may value what—to some individuals—may seem a "lower quality" item—very highly.

SOME FORMS OF CUSTOMER VALUE

The marketing process involves ways that value can be created for the customer. *Form utility* involves the idea that the product is made available to the consumer in some form that is more useful than any commodities that are used to create it. A customer buys a chair, for example, rather than the wood and other components used to create the chair. Thus, the customer benefits from the specialization that allows the manufacturer to more efficiently create a chair than the customer could do himself or herself. *Place utility* refers to the idea that a product made available to the customer at a preferred location is worth more than one at the place of manufacture.

It is much more convenient for the customer to be able to buy food items in a supermarket in his or her neighbourhood than it is to pick up these from the farmer. *Time utility* involves the idea of having the product made available when needed by the customer. The customer may buy a turkey a few days before Thanksgiving without having to plan to have it available. Intermediaries take care of the logistics to have the turkeys—which are easily perishable and bulky to store in a freezer—available when customers demand them. *Possession utility* involves the idea that the consumer can go to one store and obtain a large assortment of goods from different manufacturers during one shopping occasion. Supermarkets combine food and other household items from a number of different suppliers in one place. Certain "superstores" such as the European *hypermarkets* and the Wal-Mart "super centres" combine even more items into one setting.

MARKETING VS. THE SELLING CONCEPT

Two approaches to marketing exist. The traditional *selling* concept emphasizes selling existing products. The philosophy here is that if a product is not selling, more aggressive measures must be taken to sell it—e.g., cutting price, advertising more, or hiring more aggressive sales-people. When the railroads started to lose business due to the advent of more effective trucks that could deliver goods right to the customer's door, the railroads cut prices instead of recognizing that the customers ultimately wanted *transportation* of goods, *not* necessarily *railroad* transportation. Smith Corona, a manufacturer of typewriters, was too slow to realise that consumers wanted the ability to process documents and *not* typewriters per se. The *marketing* concept, in contrast, focuses on getting consumers what they seek, *regardless of whether this entails coming up with entirely new products.*

The 4 *Ps*—*product, place, promotion,* and *price*—represent the variables that are within the control of the firm. In contrast, the firm is faced with uncertainty from the environment.

SCOPE OF MARKETING

Marketing people are involved in marketing 10 types of entities: Goods, services, experiences, events, persons, places, properties, organizations, information, and ideas.

Goods: Physical goods constitute the bulk of most countries' production and marketing effort. The United States produces and markets billions of physical goods, from eggs to steel to hair dryers. In developing nations, goods—particularly food, commodities, clothing, and housing—are the mainstay of the economy.

Services: As economies advance, a growing proportion of their activities are focused on the production of services. The U.S. economy today consists of a 70–30 services-to-goods mix. Services include airlines, hotels, and maintenance and repair people, as well as professionals such as accountants, lawyers,engineers, and doctors. Many market offerings consist of a variable mix of goods and services.

Experiences: By orchestrating several services and goods, one can create, stage,and market experiences. Walt Disney World's Magic Kingdom is an experience;so is the Hard Rock Cafe.

Events: Marketers promote time-based events, such as the Olympics, trade shows, sports events, and artistic performances.

Persons: Celebrity marketing has become a major business. Artists, musicians,CEOs, physicians, high-profile lawyers and financiers, and other professionalsdraw help from celebrity marketers.

Places: Cities, states, regions, and nations compete to attract tourists, factories,company headquarters, and new residents.5 Place marketers include economicdevelopment specialists, real estate agents, commercial banks, local businessassociations, and advertising and public relations agencies.

Properties: Properties are intangible rights of ownership of either real property or financial property. Properties are bought and sold, and this occasions a marketing effort by real estate agents and investment companies and banks.

Organizations: Organizations actively work to build a strong, favourable image in the mind of their publics. Philips, the Dutch electronics company, advertises with the tag line, "Let's Make Things Better." The Body Shop and Ben and Jerry's also gain attention by promoting social causes. Universities, museums, andperforming arts organizations boost their public images to compete more successfully for audiences and funds.

Information: The production, packaging, and distribution of information is one of society's major industries.6 Among the marketers of information are schools and universities; publishers of encyclopedias, and specialized magazines; makers of CDs; and Internet Web sites.

Ideas: Every market offering has a basic idea at its core. In essence, products and services are platforms for delivering some idea or benefit to satisfy a core need.

MARKETING MANAGEMENT

Marketing Management is a business discipline which is focused on the practical application of marketing techniques and the management of a firm's marketing resources and activities. Rapidly emerging forces of globalization have compelled firms to market beyond the borders of their home country making International marketing highly significant and an integral part of a firm's marketing strategy. Marketing managers are often responsible for influencing the level, timing, and composition of customer demand accepted definition of the term. In part, this is because the role of a marketing manager can vary significantly based on a business' size, corporate culture, and industry context.

For example, in a large consumer products company, the marketing manager may performance as the overall general manager of his or her assigned product To create an effective, cost-efficient Marketing management strategy, firms must possess a detailed, objective understanding of their own business and the market in which they operate. In analyzing these issues, the discipline of marketing management often overlaps with the related discipline of strategic planning.

STRUCTURE

Traditionally, marketing analysis was structured into three areas: Customer analysis, Company analysis, and Competitor analysis. More recently, it has become fashionable in some marketing circles to divide these further into certain five "Cs": Customer analysis, Company analysis, Collaborator analysis, Competitor analysis, and analysis of the industry Context.

Department analysis is to develop a schematic diagram for market segmentation, breaking down the market into various constituent groups of customers, which are called customer segments or market segmentations. Marketing managers work to develop detailed profiles of each segment, focusing on any number of variables that may differ among the segments: demographic, psychographic, geographic, behavioural, needs-benefit, and other factors may all be examined. Marketers also attempt to track these segments' perceptions of the various products in the market using tools such as perceptual mapping.

In company analysis, marketers focus on understanding the company's cost structure and cost position relative to competitors, as well as working to identify a firm's core competencies and other competitively distinct company resources. Marketing managers may also work with the accounting department to analyse the profits the firm is generating from various product lines and customer accounts. The company may also conduct periodic brand audits to assess the strength of its brands and sources of brand equity.

The firm's collaborators may also be profiled, which may include various suppliers, distributors and other channel partners, joint venture partners, and others. An analysis of complementary products may also be performed if such products exist.

Marketing management employs various tools from economics and competitive strategy to analyse the industry context in which the firm operates. These include Porter's five forces, analysis of strategic groups of competitors, value chain analysis and others. Depending on the industry, the regulatory context may also be important to examine in detail.

In competitor analysis, marketers build detailed profiles of each competitor in the market, focusing especially on their relative competitive strengths and weaknesses using SWOT analysis. Marketing managers will examine each competitor's cost structure, sources of profits, resources and competencies, competitive positioning and product differentiation, degree of vertical integration, historical responses to industry developments, and other factors.

Marketing management often finds it necessary to invest in research to collect the data required to perform accurate marketing analysis. As such, they often conduct market research to obtain this information.

Marketers employ a variety of techniques to conduct market research, but some of the more common include:

- Qualitative marketing research, such as focus groups
- Quantitative marketing research, such as statistical surveys
- Experimental techniques such as test markets
- Observational techniques such as ethnographic observation

Marketing managers may also design and oversee various environmental scanning and competitive intelligence processes to help identify trends and inform the company's marketing analysis.

Marketing Strategy

If the company has obtained an adequate understanding of the customer base and its own competitive position in the industry, marketing managers are able to make their own key strategic decisions and develop a marketing strategy designed to maximize the revenues and profits of the firm. The selected strategy may aim for any of a variety of specific objectives, including optimizing short-term unit margins, revenue growth, market share, long-term profitability, or other goals.

To achieve the desired objectives, marketers typically identify one or more target customer segments which they intend to pursue. Customer segments are often selected as targets because they score highly on two dimensions: 1) The segment is attractive to serve because it is large, growing, makes frequent purchases, is not price sensitive, or other factors; and 2) The company has the resources and capabilities to compete for the segment's business, can meet their needs better than the competition, and can do so profitably. In fact, a commonly cited definition of marketing is simply"meeting needs profitably."

The implication of selecting target segments is that the business will subsequently allocate more resources to acquire and retain customers in the target segment(s) than it will for other, non-targeted customers. In some cases, the firm may go so far as to turn away customers who are not in its target segment.The doorman at a swanky nightclub, for example, may deny entry to unfashionably dressed individuals because the business has made a strategic decision to target the"high fashion" segment of nightclub patrons.

In conjunction with targeting decisions, marketing managers will identify the desired positioning they want the company, product, or brand to occupy in the target customer's mind. This positioning is often an encapsulation of a key benefit the company's product or service offers that is differentiated and superior to the benefits offered by competitive products. For example, Volvo has traditionally positioned its products in the automobile market in North America in order to be perceived as the leader in"safety", whereas BMW has traditionally positioned its brand to be perceived as the leader in"performance."

Ideally, a firm's positioning can be maintained over a long period of time because the company possesses, or can develop, some form of sustainable competitive advantage. The positioning should also be sufficiently relevant to the target segment such that it will drive the purchasing behaviour of target customers.

Implementation Planning

After the firm's strategic objectives have been identified, the target market selected, and the desired positioning for the company, product or brand has been determined, marketing managers focus on how to best implement the chosen strategy. Traditionally, this has involved implementation planning across the "4Ps" of marketing: Product management, Pricing, Place and Promotion. Taken together, the company's implementation choices across the 4Ps are often described as the marketing mix, meaning the mix of elements the business will employ to "go to market" and execute the marketing strategy. The overall goal for the marketing mix is to consistently deliver a compelling value proposition that reinforces the firm's chosen positioning, builds customer loyalty and brand equity among target customers, and achieves the firm's marketing and financial objectives.

In many cases, marketing management will develop a marketing plan to specify how the company will execute the chosen strategy and achieve the business' objectives.

The content of marketing plans varies from firm to firm, but commonly includes:

- An executive summary
- Situation analysis to summarize facts and insights gained from market research and marketing analysis

- The company's mission statement or long-term strategic vision
- A statement of the company's key objectives, often subdivided into marketing objectives and financial objectives
- The marketing strategy the business has chosen, specifying the target segments to be pursued and the competitive positioning to be achieved
- Implementation choices for each element of the marketing mix

Project, Process, and Vendor Management

Once the key implementation initiatives have been identified, marketing managers work to oversee the execution of the marketing plan. Marketing executives may therefore manage any number of specific projects, such as sales force management initiatives, product development efforts, channel marketing prigrammes and the execution of public relations and advertising campaigns. Marketers use a variety of project management techniques to ensure projects achieve their objectives while keeping to established schedules and budgets.

More broadly, marketing managers work to design and improve the effectiveness of core marketing processes, such as new product development, brand management, marketing communications, and pricing. Marketers may employ the tools of business process reengineering to ensure these processes are properly designed, and use a variety of process management techniques to keep them operating smoothly.

Effective execution may require management of both internal resources and a variety of external vendors and service providers, such as the firm's advertising agency. Marketers may therefore coordinate with the company's Purchasing department on the procurement of these services.

Organizational Management and Leadership

Marketing management may spend a fair amount of time building or maintaining a marketing orientation for the business. Achieving a market orientation, also known as "customer focus" or the "marketing concept", requires building consensus at the senior management level and then driving customer focus down into the organization. Cultural barriers may exist in a given business unit or functional area that the marketing manager must address in order to achieve this goal. Additionally, marketing executives often performance as a "brand champion" and work to enforce corporate identity standards across the enterprise.

In larger organizations, especially those with multiple business units, top marketing managers may need to coordinate across several marketing departments and also resources from finance, research and development, engineering, operations, manufacturing, or other functional areas to implement the marketing plan. In order to effectively manage these resources, marketing executives may need to spend much of their time focused on political issues and inte-departmental negotiations.

The effectiveness of a marketing manager may therefore depend on his or her ability to make the internal "sale" of various marketing prigrammes equally as much as the external customer's reaction to such prigrammes.

Reporting, Measurement, Feedback and Control Systems

Marketing management employs a variety of metrics to measure progress against objectives. It is the responsibility of marketing managers–in the marketing department or elsewhere–to ensure that the execution of marketing prigrammes achieves the desired objectives and does so in a cost-efficient manner.

Marketing management therefore often makes use of various organizational control systems, such as sales forecasts, sales force and reseller incentive prigrammes, sales force management systems, and customer relationship management tools. Recently, some software vendors have begun using the term "marketing operations management" or "marketing resource management" to describe systems that facilitate an integrated approach for controlling marketing resources. In some cases, these efforts may be linked to various supply chain management systems, such as enterprise resource planning, material requirements planning, efficient consumer response, and inventory management systems.

Measuring the return on investment of and marketing effectiveness various marketing initiatives is a significant problem for marketing management. Various market research, accounting and financial tools are used to help estimate the ROI of marketing investments. Brand valuation, for example, attempts to identify the percentage of a company's market value that is generated by the company's brands, and thereby estimate the financial value of specific investments in brand equity. Another technique, integrated marketing communications, is a CRM database-driven approach that attempts to estimate the value of marketing mix executions based on the changes in customer behaviour these executions generate.

MARKETING ENVIRONMENT

Elements of the environment. The marketing *environment* involves factors that, for the most part, are beyond the control of the company. Thus, the company must *adapt* to these factors. It is important to observe how the environment changes so that a firm can adapt its strategies appropriately.

Consider these environmental forces:

- *Competition*: Competitors often "creep" in and threaten to take away markets from firms. For example, Japanese auto manufacturers became a serious threat to American car makers in the late 1970s and early 1980s. Similarly, the Lotus Corporation, maker of one of the first commercially successful spreadsheets, soon faced competition from other software firms. Note that while competition may be frustrating for the firm, it is good for consumers. Note that competition today is increasingly global in scope. It is important to recognize that competition can happen at different "levels." At the brand level, two firms compete in providing a very similar product or service. Coca Cola and Pepsi, for example, compete for the cola drink market, and United and American Airlines compete for the passenger air transportation market. Firms also face less direct—but frequently very serious—competition at the product level. For example, cola drinks compete against bottled water. Products or services can serve as substitutes for each other even though they are very different in form. Teleconferencing facilities, for example, are very different from airline passenger transportation, but both can "bring together" people for a "meeting." At the budget level, different products or services provide very different benefits, but buyers have to make choices as to what they will buy when they cannot afford—or are unwilling to spend on—both. For example, a family may decide between buying a new car or a high definition television set. The family may also have to choose between going on a foreign vacation or remodeling its kitchen. Firms, too, may have to make choices. The firm has the cash flow either to remodel its offices or install a more energy efficient climate control system; or the firm can choose either to invest in new product development or in a promotional campaign to increase awareness of its brand among consumers.

- *Economics*: Two economic forces strongly affect firms and their customers:
  - *Economic Cycles*: Some firms in particular are extremely vulnerable to changes in the economy. Consumers tend to put off buying a new car, going out to eat, or building new homes in bad times. In contrast, in good times, firms serving those needs may have difficulty keeping up with demand. One important point to realise is that different industries are affected to different degrees by changes in the economy. Although families can cut down on the quality of the food

they buy—going with lower priced brands, for example—there are limits to the savings that can be made without greatly affecting the living standard of the family. On the other hand, it is often much easier to put off the purchase of a new car for a year or hold off on remodeling the family home. If need be, firms can keep the current computers—even though they are getting a bit slow—when sales are down. The economy goes through cycles. In the late 1990s, the U.S. economy was quite strong, and many luxury goods were sold. Currently, the economy fluctuates between increasing strength, stagnation, or slight decline. Many firms face consequences of economic downturns. Car makers, for example, have seen declining profit margins as they have had to cut prices and offer low interest rates on financing. Generally, in good economic times, there is a great deal of demand, but this introduces a fear of possible inflation. In the U.S., the Federal Reserve will then try to prevent the economy from "overheating." This is usually done by raising interest rates. This makes businesses less willing to invest, and as a result, people tend to make less money. During a recession, unemployment tends to rise, causing consumers to spend less. This may result in a "bad circle," with more people losing their jobs due to lowered demands. Some businesses, however, may take this opportunity to invest in growth now that things can be bought more cheaply.

- *Inflation*: Over time, most economies experience some level of inflation. Therefore, it is useful to explicitly state whether a reference to money over time involves the actual dollar amount exchanged at any point or an "inflation adjusted" figure that "anchors" a given amount of money to the value of that money at some point in time. Suppose, for example, that cumulative inflation between 1960 and 2007 has been 1,000%—that is, on the average, it costs ten times as much to buy the same thing in 2007 as it did 47 years earlier. If the cumulative inflation between 1960 and 1984 had been 500%, we could talk about one 1984 dollar being worth fifty 1960 cents or two 2007 dollars. It is important to note that inflation is uneven. Some goods and services—such as health care and college tuition—are currently increasing in cost much higher than the average rate of inflation. Prices of computers, actually decline both in absolute numbers and in terms of the value for money paid once an adjustment has been made for the improvement in quality. That is, two years later, the computer has not only declined in price by 20%, but it may also be 30% better. In that case, then, there has actually been, over the period, a net deflation of 38.5% for the category.

- *Political*: Businesses are very vulnerable to changes in the political situation. For example, because consumer groups lobbied Congress, more stringent rules were made on the terms of car leases. The tobacco industry is currently the target of much negative attention from government and public interest groups. Currently, the desire to avoid aiding the enemy may result in laws that make it more difficult for American firms to export goods to other countries. Many industries have a strong economic interest in policies that benefit the industry may have a negative impact on the nation as a whole but enhance profits for the industry. For example, regulations that limit the amount of sugar that can be imported into the United States is estimated to cost each American approximately $10.00 a year. The total increase in profits to the sugar industry is difficult to estimate because many of the large producers of refined sugar are privately held corporations, but it is likely that the net gain to the industry is as much as the roughly $3 billion lost by Americans a whole. However, the interests of the industry are much more concentrated. The industry can rally its stockholders, unions and employees, and suppliers together to lobby for their special interests. In turn, the industry can join forces with other agricultural interests which each support each other's prigrammes.

- *Legal:* Firms are very vulnerable to changing laws and changing interpretations by the courts. Firms in the U.S. are very vulnerable to lawsuits. McDonald's, for example, is currently being sued by people who claim that eating the chain's hamburgers caused them to get fat. Firms are significantly limited in what they can do by various laws—some laws, for example, require that disclosures be made to consumers on the effective interest rates they pay on products bought on installment. A particularly interesting group of laws relate to antitrust. These laws basically exist to promote fair competition among firms. As suggested, consider such laws when we cover pricing later in the term.
- *Technological:* Changes in technology may significantly influence the demand for a product. For example, the advent of the fax machine was bad news for Federal Express. The Internet is a major threat to travel agents. Many record stores have been wiped out of business by the trend toward downloading songs. Although technological change eliminates or at least greatly diminishes some markets, it creates opportunities for others. For example, although Federal Express has lost a considerable amount of business from documents that can now be faxed or sent by the Internet rather than having to be physically shipped, there has been a large increase

in demand for packages to be delivered overnight or "second day air." Just-in-time manufacturing techniques, in addition to online sales, have dramatically increased the market for such shipments. Online sites such as eBay now makes it possible to sell specialty products that, in the old days, would have been difficult to distribute. Although it has been possible for more than a hundred years to sell merchandise by catalog, buyers of these specialty products often had no easy access to the catalogs.

- *Social*: Changes in customs or demographics greatly influence firms. Fewer babies today are being born, resulting in a decreased demand for baby foods. More women work outside the home today, so there is a greater demand for prepared foods. There are more unmarried singles today. This provides opportunities for some firms but creates problems for others. Today, there are more "blended" families that result as parents remarry after divorce. These families are often strapped for money but may require "duplicate" items for children at each parent's residence.

INDIAN MARKETING ENVIRONMENT

India is the second most populated country in the world, with nearly one billion people. It has a reasonably favourable pro-business environment that aims to attract multinational companies. Because of this enormous market size and positive business climate, scores of American firms—including General Electric, General Motors, McDonald's, Kellogg's, and Microsoft—have recently entered the Indian market. As a result, the country has forged strong commercial interests with the United States, with trade and business relations across many industrial sectors. In fact, the U.S. is India's leading source of technology and her most valuable investor.

However, any company that desires to enter the Indian market must realise the serious challenges of doing business there: segmenting the marketplace properly, understanding the country's economic and political situations, getting through the government bureaucracy, and understanding deep-seated cultural biases and attitudes. It is hoped that a discussion of the Indian marketplace in terms of market potential, culture, consumer behaviour, and selling aspects can add to other substances published recently in Business Horizons* and aid MNC executives in facing those challenges successfully. Sprinkled with numerous success tales and war stories, the discussion offers insights gleaned from a survey of Indian businesspeople—insights that can help provide a reality check on the Indian market potential.

TRUE MARKET POTENTIAL

A fairly large country, India is nearly 2,000 miles from north to south and some 1,800 miles from east to west. The current population of nearly one billion is growing at about 1.7 per cent per annum. Only about a quarter of the population live in an urban environment; the rest reside in rural settings.

When American executives reflect on the size and situation of India's potential customers, they erroneously conclude that the Indian middle class is analogous to the middle class in the United States or Europe. The reality, however, is that the income levels characterizing the Western middle class represent only a tiny upper class in India.

The Indian market can be divided into four levels in terms of purchasing power. The reality for American businesses is that only Level 1 customers are willing to purchase foreign-based firms' goods and services, with only a marginal hope of selling to Level 2 consumers. Hence, the Indian market potential for American firms is only 73 million consumers, not the almost one billion population of the country. Nevertheless, though only 7.5 per cent of the country's population, 73 million is still quite a large market when compared to many other developing nations.

Two particularly attractive segments are urban youth and the rural population. Krishna Rao Gowd, General Marketing Manager for India's Sunku Auto Ltd., stated in the survey that "the new generation is showing an inclination toward impulsive buying." However, he cautions,

Lots of purchase decisions of youngsters are still to be blessed by the elders. For example, buying a TV or a refrigerator is a collective decision, even though it is to be used by a newly married couple living 400 kilometres away from parents. Another survey respondent added, "Increasingly, India's rural market will become important."

MARKET DIVERSITY

A second reality of the Indian market structure is the fact that India has 17 official languages and an ethnic diversity as wide as that from Britain to the Middle East—not to mention 26 states, dozens of castes, and six major religions. The 5.7 million people in Chennai have vastly different tastes than the 8.5 million people from New Delhi, the 11.2 million in Calcutta, and the 12.8 million in Mumbai.

Such a diverse marketplace has a tremendous impact on product labeling, product variety, and where products can be sold successfully. McDonald's provides a good example of adapting to the diverse Indian marketplace. Though famous for its beef patty entrees, it has introduced vegetable burgers to the large Hindu population and mutton patties to Indian Muslims.

Tailoring goods and services to the local preferences is not a trivial undertaking. American firms must realise that much market research is needed to understand the regional consumer demands. And they must be willing to modify offerings at the local level.

ECONOMIC AND POLITICAL ENVIRONMENTS FOR DOING BUSINESS IN INDIA

To better understand the Indian marketplace, it is important to gain some perspectives on the country's economic and political environments. So our discussion will shift to India's political system, recent policies for opening the economy to foreign businesses, agreements with the United States, and strategies for getting through bureaucratic hurdles.

The Political System

India is a federal republic of 26 states and seven union territories. The country has a two-house parliamentary legislative system: the indirectly elected Upper House, the Rajya Sabha; and the directly elected Lower House, the Lok Sabha. The judicial system is an independent branch of government; the legal system is based on English common law. National and state legislatures are elected for five-year terms, although terms may be extended in a state of emergency and elections may be held early if the government loses Parliament's confidence. The Prime Minister is elected from the majority ruling party in Parliament.

MARKETING PLANNING

The area of marketing planning involves forging a plan for a firm's marketing activities. A marketing plan can also pertain to a specific product, as well as to an organization's overall marketing strategy. Generally speaking, an organization's marketing planning process is derived from its overall business strategy. Thus, when top management are devising the firm's strategic direction or mission, the intended marketing activities are incorporated into this plan. There are several levels of marketing objectives within an organization. The senior management of a firm would formulate a general business strategy for a firm. However, this general business strategy would be interpreted and implemented in different contexts throughout the firm.

MARKETING STRATEGY

Plans and Planning

Plans are needed to clarify what kinds of strategic objectives an organization would like to achieve and how this is to be done. Such plans must consider the amount of resources available. One critical resource is capital. Microsoft keeps a great deal of cash on hand to be able to "jump" on opportunities that come about. Small startup software firms, on the other hand, may have limited cash on hand. This means that they may have to forego what would have been a good investment because they do not have the cash to invest and cannot find a way to raise the capital.

Other resources that affect what a firm may be able to achieve include factors such as:

- *Trademarks/brand names*: It would be very difficult to compete against Coke and Pepsi in the cola market.
- *Patents*: It would be difficult to compete against Intel and AMD in the microprocessor market since both these firms have a number of patents that it is difficult to get around.
- *People*: Even with all of Microsoft's money available, it could not immediately hire the people needed to manufacture computer chips.
- *Distribution*: Stores have space for only a fraction of the products they are offered, so they must turn many away. A firm that does not have an established relationship with stores will be at a disadvantage in trying to introduce a new product.

Plans are subject to the choices and policies that the organization has made. Some firms have goals of social responsibility, for example. Some firms are willing to take a greater risk, which may result in a very large payoff but also involve the risk of a large loss, than others. Strategic marketing is best seen as an ongoing and never-ending process.

Typically:

- The organization will identify the *objectives* it wishes to achieve. This could involve profitability directly, but often profitability is a long term goal that may require some intermediate steps. The firm may seek to increase market share, achieve distribution in more outlets, have sales grow by a certain percentage, or have consumers evaluate the product more favourably. Some organizations have objectives that are not focused on monetary profit—e.g., promoting literacy or preventing breast cancer.
- An analysis is made, taking into consideration issues such as *organizational resources, competitors, the*

competitors' strengths, different types of customers, changes in the market, or *the impact of new technology.*

- Based on this analysis, a plan is made based on *tradeoffs between the advantages and disadvantages* of different options available.
- This strategy is then carried out. The firm may design new products, revamp its advertising strategy, invest in getting more stores to carry the product, or decide to focus on a new customer segment.
- After implementation, the results or outcome are evaluated. If results are not as desired, a change may have to be made to the strategy. Even if results are satisfactory, the firm still needs to monitor the environment for changes.

Levels of Planning and Strategies

Plans for a firm can be made at several different levels. At the *corporate* level, the management considers the objectives of the *firm as a whole.* For example, Microsoft may want seek to grow by providing high quality software, hardware, and services to consumers. To achieve this goal, the firm may be willing to invest aggressively.

Plans can also be made at the *business unit* level. For example, although Microsoft is best known for its operating systems and applications software, the firm also provides Internet access and makes video games. Different managers will have responsibilities for different areas, and goals may best be made by those closest to the business area being considered. It is also more practical to hold managers accountable for performance if the plan is being made at a more specific level. Boeing has both commercial aircraft and defence divisions. Each is run by different managers, although there is some overlap in technology between the two. Therefore, plans are needed both at the corporate and at the business levels.

Occasionally, plans will be made at the *functional* level, to allow managers to specialize and to increase managerial accountability. Marketing, for example, may be charged with increasing awareness of Microsoft game consoles to 55% of the U.S. population or to increase the number of units of Microsoft Office sold. Finance may be charged with raising a given amount of capital at a given cost. Manufacturing may be charged with decreasing production costs by 5%.

The firm needs to identify the business it is in. Here, a *balance* must be made so that the firm's *scope is not defined too narrowly or too broadly*. A firm may define its goal very narrowly and then miss opportunities in the market place. For example, if Dell were to define itself only as a computer company, it might miss an opportunity to branch into PDAs or Internet service. Thus, they might instead define themselves as a provider of "information solutions." A company should not define itself too broadly, however, since this may result in loss of focus. For example, a manufacturer of baking soda should probably not see itself as a manufacturer of all types of chemicals. Sometimes, companies can define themselves in terms of a customer need. For example, 3M sees itself as being in the business of making products whose surfaces are bonded together. This accounts for both Post-It notes and computer disks.

A firm's mission should generally include a discussion of the *customers served*, the kind of technology involved, and the markets served. Several issues are involved in selecting target customers.

As suggested, consider these in more detail within the context of segmentation, but for now, the firm needs to consider issues such as:

- The *size* of various market segments;
- How well these segments are being *served by existing firms*;
- *Changes* in the market—e.g., growth of segments or change in technology;
- How the firm should be *positioned*, or seen by customers. For example, Wal-Mart positions itself as providing value in retailing, while Nordstrom's defines itself more in terms of high levels of customer service.

The Boston Consulting Group matrix provides a firm an opportunity to assess *how well its business units work together*. Each business unit is evaluated in terms of two factors: *market share* and the *growth prospects* in the market. Generally, the larger a firm's share, the stronger its position, and the greater the growth in a market, the better future possibilities.

Four combinations emerge:

1. A *star* represents a business unit that has a high share in a growing market. For example, Motorola has a large share in the rapidly growing market for cellular phones.
2. A *question mark* results when a unit has a small share in a rapidly growing market. The firm's position, then, is not as strong as it would have been had its market share been greater, but there is an opportunity to grow. For example, Hewlett-Packard has a small share of the digital camera market, but this is a very rapidly growing market.
3. A *cash cow* results when a firm has a large share in a market that is not growing, and may even be shrinking. Brother has a large share of the typewriter market.
4. A *dog* results when a business unit has a small share in a market that is not growing. This is generally a somewhat unattractive situation, although dogs can still be profitable in the short run. For example, Smith Corona how has a small share of the typewriter market.

Firms are usually best of with a portfolio that has a *balance* of firms in each category. The cash cows tend to *generate cash but require little future investment*. On the other hand, stars generate some cash, but *even more cash is needed to invest in the future*—for research and development, marketing campaigns, and building new manufacturing facilities. Therefore, a firm may take excess cash from the cash cow and divert it to the star. For example, Brother could "harvest" its profits from typewriters and invest this in the unit making colour laser printers, which will need the cash to grow. If a firm has cash cows that generate a lot of cash, this may be used to try to improve the market share of a question mark. A firm that has a number of promising stars in its portfolio may be in serious trouble if it does not have any cash cows to support it. If it is about to run out of cash—regardless of how profitable it is—is becomes vulnerable as a takeover target from a firm that has the cash to continue running it.

A SWOT analysis is used to help the firm *identify effective strategies*. Successful firms such as Microsoft have certain strengths. Microsoft, for example, has a great deal of technology, a huge staff of very talented engineers, a great deal of experience in designing software, a very large market share, a well respected brand name, and a great deal of cash. Microsoft also has some weaknesses, however: The game console and MSN units are currently running at a loss, and MSN has been unable to achieve desired levels of growth. Firms may face opportunities in the current market.

Microsoft, for example, may have the opportunity to take advantage of its brand name to enter into the hardware market. Microsoft may also become a trusted source of consumer services. Microsoft currently faces several threats, including the weak economy. Because fewer new computers are bough during a recession, fewer operating systems and software packages. Rather than merely listing strengths, weaknesses, opportunities, and threats, a SWOT analysis should suggest how the firm may use its strengths and opportunities to overcome weaknesses and threats. Decisions should also be made as to how resources should be allocated. For example, Microsoft could either decide to put more resources into MSN or to abandon this unit entirely. Microsoft has a great deal of cash ready to spend, so the option to put resources toward MSN is available. Microsoft will also need to see how threats can be addressed. The firm can earn political good will by engaging in charitable acts, which it has money available to fund. For example, Microsoft has donated software and computers to schools. It can forego temporary profits by reducing prices temporarily to increase demand, or can "hold out" by maintaining current prices while not selling as many units.

Criteria for Effective Marketing Plans

Marketing plans should meet several criteria:

- The plan must be *specific* enough so that it can be implemented and communicated to people in the firm. "Improving profitability" is usually too vague, but increasing net profits by 5%, increasing market share by 10%, gaining distribution in 2,000 more stores, and reducing manufacturing costs by 2% are all specific.
- The plan must be *measurable* so that one can see if it has been achieved. The plans involve specific numbers.
- The goal must be *achievable* or realistic. Plans that are unrealistic may result in poor use of resources or lowered morale within the firm.
- The goals must be *consistent*. For example, a firm cannot ordinarily simultaneously plan improve product features, increase profits, and reduce prices.

MARKETING PROCESS

Under the marketing concept, the firm must find a way to discover unfulfilled customer needs and bring to market products that satisfy those needs.

The process of doing so can be modeled in a sequence of steps: the situation is analysed to identify opportunities, the strategy is formulated for a value proposition, tactical decisions are made, the plan is implemented and the results are monitored.

Table. The Marketing Process

Situation Analysis
I V
Marketing Strategy
I V
Marketing Mix Decisions
I V
Implementation & Control

SITUATION ANALYSIS

A thorough analysis of the situation in which the firm finds itself serves as the basis for identifying opportunities to satisfy unfulfilled customer needs. In addition to identifying the customer needs, the firm must understand its own capabilities and the environment in which it is operating.

The situation analysis thus can be viewed in terms an analysis of the external environment and an internal analysis of the firm itself. The external environment can be described in terms of macro-environmental factors that broadly affect many firms, and micro-environmental factors closely related to the specific situation of the firm.

The situation analysis should include past, present, and future aspects. It should include a history outlining how the situation evolved to its present state, and an analysis of trends in order to forecast where it is going. Good forecasting can reduce the chance of spending a year bringing a product to market only to find that the need no longer exists.

If the situation analysis reveals gaps between what consumers want and what currently is offered to them, then there may be opportunities to introduce products to better satisfy those consumers. Hence, the situation analysis should yield a summary of problems and opportunities. From this summary, the firm can match its own capabilities with the opportunities in order to satisfy customer needs better than the competition.

There are several frameworks that can be used to add structure to the situation analysis:

- *5 C Analysis*: Company, customers, competitors, collaborators, climate. Company represents the internal situation; the other four cover aspects of the external situation
- *PEST analysis*: For macro-environmental political, economic, societal, and technological factors. A PEST analysis can be used as the "climate" portion of the 5 C framework.
- *SWOT analysis*: Strengths, weaknesses, opportunities, and threats - for the internal and external situation.

A SWOT analysis can be used to condense the situation analysis into a listing of the most relevant problems and opportunities and to assess how well the firm is equipped to deal with them.

MARKETING STRATEGY

Once the best opportunity to satisfy unfulfilled customer needs is identified, a strategic plan for pursuing the opportunity can be developed. Market research will provide specific market information that will permit the firm to select the target market segment and optimally position the offering within that segment. The result is a value proposition to the target market.

The marketing strategy then involves:

- Segmentation
- Targeting
- Positioning the product within the target market
- Value proposition to the target market

MARKETING MIX DECISIONS

Detailed tactical decisions then are made for the controllable parametres of the marketing mix.

The action items include:

- Product development - specifying, designing, and producing the first units of the product.
- Pricing decisions
- Distribution contracts
- Promotional campaign development

IMPLEMENTATION AND CONTROL

At this point in the process, the marketing plan has been developed and the product has been launched. Given that few environments are static, the results of the marketing effort should be monitored closely. As the market changes, the marketing mix can be adjusted to accomodate the changes. Often, small changes in consumer wants can addressed by changing the advertising message. As the changes become more significant, a product redesign or an entirely new product may be needed. The marketing process does not end with implementation - continual monitoring and adaptation is needed to fulfill customer needs consistently over the long-term.

MODERN MARKETING CONTEXT

At all points of the modern marketing system people have formed associations and eliminated various middlemen in order to achieve more efficient marketing. Manufacturers often maintain their own wholesale departments and deal directly with retailers. Independent stores may operate their own wholesale agencies to supply them with goods. Wholesale houses operate outlets for their wares, and farmers sell their products through their own wholesale cooperatives. Recent years have seen the development of wholesale clubs, which sell retail items to consumers who purchase memberships that give them the privilege of shopping at wholesale prices. Commodity exchanges, such as those of grain and cotton, enable businesses to buy and sell commodities for both immediate and future delivery.

Methods of merchandising have also been changed to attract customers. The one-price system, probably introduced by A. T. Stewart in New York, saves sales clerks from haggling and promotes faith in the integrity of the merchant. Advertising has created an international market for many items, especially trademarked and labeled goods. In 1999 more than $308 billion was spent on advertising in the United States alone.

The number of customers, especially for durable goods, has been greatly increased by the practice of extending credit, particularly in the form of installment buying and selling installment buying and selling, buying and selling of goods on credit, with the stipulation that payments shall be made at specified intervals in set amounts. Customers also buy through mail-order catalogs by placing orders to specialized"home-shopping" television channels, and through on-line transactions on the Internet Internet, the, international computer network linking together thousands of individual networks at military and government agencies, educational institutions, nonprofit organizations, industrial and financial corporations of all sizes, and commercial enterprises.

Services are marketed in much the same manner as goods ana commodities. Sometimes a service, like that of a repair person or physician, is marketed through the same performance that produces it. Personal services may also be brokered by employment agencies, booking agents for concert or theatrical performers, travel agents, and the like. Methods of marketing now include market research, motivational research, and other means of determining consumer acceptability of a product before the producer decides to manufacture and market it on a large scale. Market research, often conducted by means of telephone interviews with consumers, is a major industry in itself, with the top 50 U.S. marketing firms tallying revenues of $5.9 billion in 1998.

EVOLUTION OF MODERN MARKETING

In a subsistence-level economy there is little need for exchange of goods because the division of labour is at a rudimentary level: most people produce the same or similar goods.

Interregional exchange between disparate geographic areas depends on adequate means of transportation. Thus, before the development of caravan travel and navigation, the exchange of the products of one region for those of another was limited. The village market or fair, the itinerant merchant or peddler, and the shop where customers could have such goods as shoes and furniture made to order were features of marketing in rural Europe. The general store superseded the public market in England and was an institution of the American country town.

In the United States in the 19th cent. the typical marketing setup was one in which wholesalers assembled the products of various manufacturers or producers and sold them to jobbers and retailers. The independent store store, commonly a shop or stall for the retail sale of commodities, but also a place where wholesale supplies are kept or sold. Retailing-the sale of merchandise to the consumer-is one of the oldest businesses in the world and was practiced in

In the 20th cent. that system met stiff competition from chain stores, which were organized for the mass distribution of goods and enjoyed the advantages of large-scale operation. Today large chain stores dominate the field of retail trade. The concurrent advent of the motor truck and paved highway, making possible the prompt delivery of a variety of goods in large quantities, still further modified marketing arrangement, and the proliferation of the automobile has expanded the geographic area in which a consumer can make retail purchases.

INDUSTRIAL MARKETING

Industrial marketing, which some marketing experts have described as a 'sleeping giant', has been the subject of very little research. This text is an attempt to create in the reader an interest in this challenging yet not much talked about subject.

Several developments have transformed industrial marketing in the last few years:

- Technology has become the cornerstone of industrial marketing. New product technologies are emerging and manufacturing processes are evolving. Information technology is being leveraged to develop new products and services, in addition to streamlining operations.
- The Internet has revolutionized industrial marketing. It has helped bring down the communication costs between the industrial marketers and other stakeholders drastically. E-procurement and e-marketplaces have gained popularity among organizational buyers.

The nature of competition has undergone a sea change in the industrial marketplace. "The Business Network is the Business Strategy." Today, competition is between value-chain partnerships rather than between industrial firms. From the 1990s, the Government of India has been supporting liberalization by taking various positive measures, including the permitting of foreign direct investments in capital intensive industries. In addition to setting up joint ventures and subsidiaries, many firms have adopted the outsourcing route. India's progress on both the domestic and export fronts has resulted in a growing demand for professionals to market industrial products, services, and solutions to a wide range of industries.

MARKET MEASUREMENT AND FORECASTING

Determining the potential of a market segment is indispensable for analysing the opportunities within a segment, and for deciding if it can possibly be chosen as a target market. It is not only the present market potential that is important and gives an indication of opportunities, but the firm must also be interested in market forecasts. The firm wants to survive in the long term and achieve its primary goal being to maximise profitability. Consequently market forecasting is also a very important aid for decision making by marketing management.

Measuring and forecasting requires an analysis of the market with an aim of expressing it in quantitative quantities both present and in the future. The quantitative measurement and forecasting of the market, together with its qualitative characteristics, are used as a basis for decision making by marketing management. Market measurement and forecasting can be seen as a subdivision of market research. This is a very superficial description of the important role market measurement and forecasting play.

THE IMPORTANCE OF MARKET MEASUREMENT AND FORECASTING

The main goal of market measurement and forecasting is to serve as an aid in the decisions that marketing management has to make. As has already been emphasised, the quality of decisions cannot be better than the information they are based on. Information gathered enables marketing management to make their decisions in a more objective and scientific manner and to lessen the risk and uncertainty that accompany subjective decisions and guesswork.

Naturally marketing management often make decisions which are not very important and/or do not hold a great risk. It would be ridiculous to arrange for the gathering of information by means of measurement and forecasting for all such small decisions of this nature. Thus it must be emphasised that just as with market research, the importance and risk of the decision must be weighed up against the cost and time involved in the gathering and processing of information. Luckily there are various secondary sources which contain information regarding market measurement and forecasting. These sources include various published research reports which can be bought at a fraction of the price of a new market research project, and other sources which, for example, are available on computer and can be processed for clients' needs.

KEY CONCEPTS IN PERSPECTIVE

You have probably often heard of the concept"market potential". In marketing terms this means the maximum potential demand for a certain product in a specific market as a whole. Market potential is relevant to a specific geographical area, a specific period of time, specific types of products, a specific market segment, and is expressed in terms of all of these.

Another concept that is relatively seldom used in colloquial language is"sales potential", which pertains to the maximum demand for a firm's product. Sales potential, in the same way as market potential, pertains to a specific geographical area, period, and market segment.

Sales potential, however, does not pertain to the types of products a firm deals with, but to a specific product of the firm. Potential market share is the difference between market potential and sales potential and actually gives an indication of which part of the potential market the firm expects to gain.

Market potential, sales potential and potential market share can pertain either to the present and/or the future. A firm strives to enjoy its sales potential to the full. Market measurement and forecasting, however, are not only relevant to potential demand, but also to actual present and future sales.

The actual sales of a type of product in a specific area, period and market segment can also be called the effective demand. The market share of one of a firm's products is calculated by the ratio of the actual sales of the product concerned to the actual sales in terms of that type of product. This ratio is expressed as a percentage. You have now learned the meaning of a few elementary concepts in terms of market measurement and forecasting. The marketer can compare these measurements to each other to gain insight into an important indicator of the success of the market offering in relation to other firms, the total market and the market potential.

MANAGEMENT OF MARKET MEASUREMENT AND FORECASTING

When you hear the management of market measurement and forecasting being expressed, by this stage you will already realise that it pertains to the planning, implementation and control of the market measurement and forecasting activities. Just as with any other scientific research, measurement and forecasting must be approached in a systematic and planned fashion to obtain the best value.

Problem and Information Needs

Seeing that it is very expensive to gather information, this step must be very carefully planned. The problem about which information should be gathered must be very clearly defined. Definition of the problem will determine which information must be clearly acquired so that only relevant data is gathered.

Gathering Relevant Information

Gathering information serves a dual purpose. Firstly, it provides sufficient data for the information need that is required to solve a problem, and secondly, it serves as a basis for the choice of particular methods of measurement and/or forecasting that are to be used.

Selecting the Methods of Market Measurement and Forecasting

The choice of measurement and forecasting methods begins with the evaluation of the data that has been gathered. There must be sufficient data of the right quality to provide a satisfactory answer to the problem by means of existing methods of analysis. Thereafter a suitable method can be selected by comparing the information needed and the abilities of the methods to meet the needs.

The method is selected by taking the following factors into account:

- The nature and availability of data. Is there sufficient data of the right nature that can be processed with the help of the specific method? What pattern does the data follow? Certain methods of forecasting can only handle some data patterns effectively. The following patterns can appear in the data: tendencies, seasonal fluctuations and conjuncture patterns.
- The accuracy that is required for decision making is influenced by the choice of methods, as some methods supply a much more accurate answer than others.
- Costs play a role here, in the same way as they do in most business activities. Just as in the case of marketing research, the costs involved in the chosen method must be weighed up against the accuracy and importance of the required information. Some methods are able to deliver very reliable information, but at extra cost and time.
- *Time*: Careful consideration is necessary in deciding whether the period of time needed for measurement or forecasting will provide the desired result. Furthermore, the application of certain methods takes much more time than others.
- *Application*: The results must be useful to the people who have to base their decisions thereon. This means that the results must be of a nature that will enable these people to interpret and understand it effectively.

There are several methods that can be selected for measuring and forecasting the market.

Execution and Evaluation

Once suitable methods have been selected, processing of the information can begin. The results of measuring and forecasting must be evaluated for their accuracy so that corrections can be made in the future. Market forecasting pertains to the long term and unpredictable changes are likely to necessitate an adaptation of the results.

VALUE CHAIN

To analyse the specific activities through which firms can create a competitive advantage, it is useful to model the firm as a chain of value-creating activities. Michael Porter identified a set of interrelated generic activities common to a wide range of firms.

The resulting model is known as the value chain and is depicted here:

Primary Value Chain Activities:

Inbound Logistics > Operations > Outbound Logistics > Marketing and Sales > Service

---

The goal of these activities is to create value that exceeds the cost of providing the product or service, thus generating a profit margin.

- Inbound logistics include the receiving, warehousing, and inventory control of input materials.
- Operations are the value-creating activities that transform the inputs into the final product.
- Outbound logistics are the activities required to get the finished product to the customer, including warehousing, order fulfillment, etc.
- Marketing and Sales are those activities associated with getting buyers to purchase the product, including channel selection, advertising, pricing, etc.
- Service activities are those that maintain and enhance the product's value including customer support, repair services, etc.

Any or all of these primary activities may be vital in developing a competitive advantage. For example, logistics activities are critical for a provider of distribution services, and service activities may be the key focus for a firm offering on-site maintenance contracts for office equipment.

These five categories are generic and portrayed here in a general manner. Each generic activity includes specific activities that vary by industry.

SUPPORT ACTIVITIES

The primary value chain activities are facilitated by support activities.

Porter identified four generic categories of support activities:

- *Procurement*: The function of purchasing the raw materials and other inputs used in the value-creating activities.
- *Technology Development*: Includes research and development, process automation, and other technology development used to support the value-chain activities.
- *Human Resource Management*: The activities associated with recruiting, development, and compensation of employees.
- *Firm Infrastructure*: Includes activities such as finance, legal, quality management, etc.

Support activities often are viewed as "overhead", but some firms successfully have used them to develop a competitive advantage, for example, to develop a cost advantage through innovative management of information systems.

VALUE CHAIN ANALYSIS

In order to better understand the activities leading to a competitive advantage, one can begin with the generic value chain and then identify the relevant firm-specific activities. Process flows can be mapped, and these flows used to isolate the individual value-creating activities. Once the discrete activities are defined, linkages between activities should be identified. A linkage exists if the performance or cost of one activity affects that of another. Competitive advantage may be obtained by optimizing and coordinating linked activities.

The value chain also is useful in outsourcing decisions. Understanding the linkages between activities can lead to more optimal make-or-buy decisions that can result in either a cost advantage or a differentiation advantage.

VALUE SYSTEM

The firm's value chain links to the value chains of upstream suppliers and downstream buyers. The result is a larger stream of activities known as the *value system*. The development of a competitive advantage depends not only on the firm-specific value chain, but also on the value system of which the firm is a part.

MARKETING RESEARCH

Managers need information in order to introduce products and services that create value in the mind of the customer. But the perception of value is a subjective one, and what customers value this year may be quite different from what they value next year. As such, the attributes that create value cannot simply be deduced from common knowledge. Rather, data must be collected and analysed. The goal of marketing research is to provide the facts and direction that managers need to make their more important marketing decisions.

To maximize the benefit of marketing research, those who use it need to understand the research process and its limitations.

MARKETING RESEARCH

These terms often are used interchangeably, but technically there is a difference.

Market research deals specifically with the gathering of information about a market's size and trends. *Marketing research* covers a wider range of activities. While it may involve market research, marketing research is a more general systematic process that can be applied to a variety of marketing

PROBLEMS IN VALUE OF INFORMATION

Information can be useful, but what determines its real value to the organization?

In general, the value of information is determined by:

- The ability and willingness to performance on the information.
- The accuracy of the information.
- The level of indecisiveness that would exist without the information.
- The amount of variation in the possible results.
- The level of risk aversion.
- The reaction of competitors to any decision improved by the information.
- The cost of the information in terms of time and money.

MARKETING RESEARCH PROCESS

Once the need for marketing research has been established, most marketing research projects involve these steps:

- Define the problem
- Determine research design
- Identify data types and sources
- Design data collection forms and questionnaires
- Determine sample plan and size
- Collect the data
- Analyse and interpret the data
- Prepare the research report

PROBLEM DEFINITION

The decision problem faced by management must be translated into a market research problem in the form of questions that define the information that is required to make the decision and how this information can be obtained. Thus, the decision problem is translated into a research problem. For example, a decision problem may be whether to launch a new product. The corresponding research problem might be to assess whether the market would accept the new product. The objective of the research should be defined clearly. To ensure that the true decision problem is addressed, it is useful for the researcher to outline possible scenarios of the research results and then for the decision maker to formulate plans of action under each scenario. The use of such scenarios can ensure that the purpose of the research is agreed uponbefore it commences.

RESEARCH DESIGN

Marketing research can classified in one of three categories:

- Exploratory research
- Descriptive research
- Causal research

These classifications are made just as to the objective of the research. In some cases the research will fall into one of these categories, but in other cases different phases of the same research project will fall into different categories.

- *Exploratory research:* Has the goal of formulating problems more precisely, clarifying concepts, gathering explanations, gaining insight, eliminating impractical ideas, and forming hypotheses. Exploratory research can be performed using a literature search, surveying certain people about their experiences, focus groups, and case studies. When surveying people, exploratory research studies would not try to acquire a representative sample, but rather, seek to interview those who are knowledgeable and who might be able to provide insight concerning the relationship among variables. Case studies can include contrasting situations or benchmarking against an organization known for its excellence. Exploratory research may develop hypotheses, but it does not seek to test them. Exploratory research is characterized by its flexibility.
- *Descriptive research:* Is more rigid than exploratory research and seeks to describe users of a product, determine the proportion of the population that uses a product, or predict future demand for a product. As opposed to exploratory research, descriptive research should define questions, people surveyed,

and the method of analysis prior to beginning data collection. In other words, the who, what, where, when, why, and how aspects of the research should be defined. Such preparation allows one the opportunity to make any required changes before the costly process of data collection has begun.

There are two basic types of descriptive research: Longitudinal studies and cross-sectional studies. Longitudinal studies are time series analyses that make repeated measurements of the same individuals, thus allowing one to monitor behaviour such as brand-switching. However, longitudinal studies are not necessarily representative since many people may refuse to participate because of the commitment required. Cross-sectional studies sample the population to make measurements at a specific point in time. A special type of cross-sectional analysis is a cohort analysis, which tracks an aggregate of individuals who experience the same event within the same time interval over time. Cohort analyses are useful for long-term forecasting of product demand.

- *Causal research:* Seeks to find cause and effect relationships between variables. It accomplishes this goal through laboratory and field experiments.

DATA TYPES AND SOURCES

Secondary Data

Before going through the time and expense of collecting primary data, one should check for secondary data that previously may have been collected for other purposes but that can be used in the immediate study. Secondary data may be internal to the firm, such as sales invoices and warranty cards, or may be external to the firm such as published data or commercially available data. The government census is a valuable source of secondary data. Secondary data has the advantage of saving time and reducing data gathering costs.

The disadvantages are that the data may not fit the problem perfectly and that the accuracy may be more difficult to verify for secondary data than for primary data. Some secondary data is republished by organizations other than the original source. Because errors can occur and important explanations may be missing in republished data, one should obtain secondary data directly from its source. One also should consider who the source is and whether the results may be biased.

There are several criteria that one should use to evaluate secondary data:

- Whether the data is useful in the research study.
- How current the data is and whether it applies to time period of interest.
- Errors and accuracy - whether the data is dependable and can be verified.
- Presence of bias in the data.
- Specifications and methodologies used, including data collection method, response rate, quality and analysis of the data, sample size and sampling technique, and questionnaire design.
- Objective of the original data collection.
- Nature of the data, including definition of variables, units of measure, categories used, and relationships examined.

Primary Data

Often, secondary data must be supplemented by primary data originated specifically for the study at hand.

Some common types of primary data are:

- Demographic and socioeconomic characteristics
- Psychological and lifestyle characteristics
- Attitudes and opinions
- Awareness and knowledge - for example, brand awareness
- *Antentions*: For example, purchase intentions. While useful, intentions are not a reliable indication of actual future behaviour.
- *Motivation*: A person's motives are more stable than

his/her behaviour, so motive is a better predictor of future behaviour than is past behaviour.

- Behaviour

Primary data can be obtained by communication or by observation. Communication involves questioning respondents either verbally or in writing. This method is versatile, since one needs only to ask for the information; however, the response may not be accurate.

Communication usually is quicker and cheaper than observation. Observation involves the recording of actions and is performed by either a person or some mechanical or electronic device. Observation is less versatile than communication since some attributes of a person may not be readily observable, such as attitudes, awareness, knowledge, intentions, and motivation.

Observation also might take longer since observers may have to wait for appropriate events to occur, though observation using scanner data might be quicker and more cost effective.

Observation typically is more accurate than communication. Personal interviews have an interviewer bias that mail-in questionnaires do not have. For example, in a personal interview the respondent's perception of the interviewer may affect the responses.

QUESTIONNAIRE DESIGN

The questionnaire is an important tool for gathering primary data. Poorly constructed questions can result in large errors and invalidate the research data, so significant effort should be put into the questionnaire design. The questionnaire should be tested thoroughly prior to conducting the survey.

MEASUREMENT SCALES

Attributes can be measured on nominal, ordinal, interval, and ratio scales:

- Nominal numbers are simply identifiers, with the only permissible mathematical use being for counting. *Example*: social security numbers.

- Ordinal scales are used for ranking. The interval between the numbers conveys no meaning. Median and mode calculations can be performed on ordinal numbers.
  Example: class ranking
- Interval scales maintain an equal interval between numbers. These scales can be used for ranking and for measuring the interval between two numbers. Since the zero point is arbitrary, ratios cannot be taken between numbers on an interval scale; however, mean, median, and mode are all valid.
  Example: temperature scale
- Ratio scales are referenced to an absolute zero values, so ratios between numbers on the scale are meaningful. In addition to mean, median, and mode, geometric averages also are valid.
  Example: weight

VALIDITY AND RELIABILITY

The validity of a test is the extent to which differences in scores reflect differences in the measured characteristic. Predictive validity is a measure of the usefulness of a measuring instrument as a predictor.

Proof of predictive validity is determined by the correlation between results and actual behaviour. Construct validity is the extent to which a measuring instrument measures what it intends to measure.

Reliability is the extent to which a measurement is repeatable with the same results. A measurement may be reliable and not valid. However, if a measurement is valid, then it also is reliable and if it is not reliable, then it cannot be valid. One way to show reliability is to show stability by repeating the test with the same results.

ATTITUDE MEASUREMENT

Many of the questions in a marketing research survey are designed to measure attitudes. Attitudes are a person's general evaluation of something.

Customer attitude is an important factor for the following reasons:

- Attitude helps to explain how ready one is to do something.
- Attitudes do not change much over time.
- Attitudes produce consistency in behaviour.
- Attitudes can be related to preferences.

Attitudes can be measured using the following procedures:

- *Self-reporting*: Subjects are asked directly about their attitudes. Self-reporting is the most common technique used to measure attitude.
- *Observation of behaviour*: Assuming that one's behaviour is a result of one's attitudes, attitudes can be inferred by observing behaviour. For example, one's attitude about an issue can be inferred by whether he/she signs a petition related to it.
- *Indirect techniques*: Use unstructured stimuli such as word association tests.
- *Performance of objective tasks*: Assumes that one's performance depends on attitude. For example, the subject can be asked to memorize the arguments of both sides of an issue. He/she is more likely to do a better job on the arguments that favour his/her stance.
- *Physiological reactions*: Subject's response to a stimuli is measured using electronic or mechanical means. While the intensity can be measured, it is difficult to know if the attitude is positive or negative.
- *Multiple measures*: A mixture of techniques can be used to validate the findings, especially worthwhile when self-reporting is used.

There are several types of attitude rating scales:

- *Equal-appearing interval scaling*: A set of statements are assembled. These statements are selected just as to their position on an interval scale of favourableness. Statements are chosen that has a small degree of dispersion. Respondents then are asked to indicate with which statements they agree.
- *Likert method of summated ratings*: A statement is made

and the respondents indicate their degree of agreement or disagreement on a five point scale.

- *Semantic differential scale*: A scale is constructed using phrases describing attributes of the product to anchor each end. For example, the left end may state, "Hours are inconvenient" and the right end may state, "Hours are convenient". The respondent then marks one of the seven blanks between the statements to indicate his/her opinion about the attribute.
- *Stapel Scale*: Similar to the semantic differential scale except that
  - Points on the scale are identified by numbers,
  - Only one statement is used and if the respondent disagrees a negative number should marked, and
  - There are 10 positions instead of seven.

  This scale does not require that bipolar adjectives be developed and it can be administered by telephone.
- *Q-sort technique*: The respondent if forced to construct a normal distribution by placing a specified number of cards in one of 11 stacks just as to how desirable he/she finds the characteristics written on the cards.

SAMPLING PLAN

The sampling frame is the pool from which the interviewees are chosen. The telephone book often is used as a sampling frame, but have some shortcomings. Telephone books exclude those households that do not have telephones and those households with unlisted numbers. Since a certain percentage of the numbers listed in a phone book are out of service, there are many people who have just moved who are not sampled. Such sampling biases can be overcome by using random digit dialing. Mall intercepts represent another sampling frame, though there are many people who do not shop at malls and those who shop more often will be over-represented unless their answers are weighted in inverse proportion to their frequency of mall shopping.

In designing the research study, one should consider the potential errors. Two sources of errors are random sampling error and non-sampling error. Sampling errors are those due to the fact that there is a non-zero confidence interval of the results because of the sample size being less than the population being studied. Non-sampling errors are those caused by faulty coding, untruthful responses, respondent fatigue, etc.

There is a tradeoff between sample size and cost. The larger the sample size, the smaller the sampling error but the higher the cost. After a certain point the smaller sampling error cannot be justified by the additional cost.

While a larger sample size may reduce sampling error, it actually may increase the total error. There are two reasons for this effect. First, a larger sample size may reduce the ability to follow up on non-responses. Second, even if there is a sufficient number of interviewers for follow-ups, a larger number of interviewers may result in a less uniform interview process.

DATA COLLECTION

In addition to the intrinsic sampling error, the actual data collection process will introduce additional errors. These errors are called non-sampling errors. Some non-sampling errors may be intentional on the part of the interviewer, who may introduce a bias by leading the respondent to provide a certain response. The interviewer also may introduce unintentional errors, for example, due to not having a clear understanding of the interview process or due to fatigue.

Respondents also may introduce errors. A respondent may introduce intentional errors by lying or simply by not responding to a question. A respondent may introduce unintentional errors by not understanding the question, guessing, not paying close attention, and being fatigued or distracted.

Such non-sampling errors can be reduced through quality control techniques.

DATA ANALYSIS-PRELIMINARY STEPS

Before analysis can be performed, raw data must be

transformed into the right format. First, it must be edited so that errors can be corrected or omitted. The data must then be coded; this procedure converts the edited raw data into numbers or symbols. A codebook is created to document how the data was coded. Finally, the data is tabulated to count the number of samples falling into various categories. Simple tabulations count the occurrences of each variable independently of the other variables.

Cross tabulations, also known as cross tabs, treats two or more variables simultaneously. However, since the variables are in a two-dimensional table, cross tabbing more than two variables is difficult to visualize since more than two dimensions would be required.

Cross tabulation can be performed for nominal and ordinal variables. Cross tabulation is the most commonly utilized data analysis method in marketing research. Many studies take the analysis no further than cross tabulation. This technique divides the sample into sub-groups to show how the dependent variable varies from one subgroup to another. A third variable can be introduced to uncover a relationship that initially was not evident.

CONJOINT ANALYSIS

The conjoint analysis is a powerful technique for determining consumer preferences for product attributes.

HYPOTHESIS TESTING

A basic fact about testing hypotheses is that a hypothesis may be rejected but that the hypothesis never can be unconditionally accepted until all possible evidence is evaluated. In the case of sampled data, the information set cannot be complete.

So if a test using such data does not reject a hypothesis, the conclusion is not necessarily that the hypothesis should be accepted. The null hypothesis in an experiment is the hypothesis that the independent variable has no effect on the dependent variable. The null hypothesis is expressed as H0. This hypothesis is assumed to be true unless proven otherwise.

The alternative to the null hypothesis is the hypothesis that the independent variable does have an effect on the dependent variable. This hypothesis is known as the alternative, research, or experimental hypothesis and is expressed as H1. This alternative hypothesis states that the relationship observed between the variables cannot be explained by chance alone.

There are two types of errors in evaluating a hypotheses:

- *Type I error*: Occurs when one rejects the null hypothesis and accepts the alternative, when in fact the null hypothesis is true.
- *Type II error*: Occurs when one accepts the null hypothesis when in fact the null hypothesis is false.

Because their names are not very descriptive, these types of errors sometimes are confused. Some people jokingly define a Type III error to occur when one confuses Type I and Type II. To emphasise the difference, it is useful to consider a trial by jury in which the null hypothesis is that the defendant is innocent. If the jury convicts a truly innocent defendant, a Type I error has occurred. If, on the other hand, the jury declares a truly guilty defendant to be innocent, a Type II error has occurred.

Hypothesis testing involves the following steps:

- Formulate the null and alternative hypotheses.
- Choose the appropriate test.
- Choose a level of significance—determine the rejection region.
- Gather the data and calculate the test statistic.
- Determine the probability of the observed value of the test statistic under the null hypothesis given the sampling distribution that applies to the chosen test.
- Compare the value of the test statistic to the rejection threshold.
- Based on the comparison, reject or do not reject the null hypothesis.
- Make the marketing research conclusion.

In order to analyse whether research results are statistically significant or simply by chance, a test of statistical significance can be run.

TESTS OF STATISTICAL SIGNIFICANCE

The chi-square goodness-of-fit test is used to determine whether a set of proportions have specified numerical values. It often is used to analyse bivariate cross-tabulated data.

Some examples of situations that are well-suited for this test are:

- A manufacturer of packaged products test markets a new product and wants to know if sales of the new product will be in the same relative proportion of package sizes as sales of existing products.
- A company's sales revenue comes from Product A (50%), Product B (30%), and Product C (20%). The firm wants to know whether recent fluctuations in these proportions are random or whether they represent a real shift in sales.

ANOVA

Another test of significance is the Analysis of Variance (ANOVA) test. The primary purpose of ANOVA is to test for differences between multiple means. Whereas the t-test can be used to compare two means, ANOVA is needed to compare three or more means. If multiple t-tests were applied, the probability of a TYPE I error (rejecting a true null hypothesis) increases as the number of comparisons increases. One-way ANOVA examines whether multiple means differ. The test is called an F-test. ANOVA calculates the ratio of the variation between groups to the variation within groups (the F ratio). While ANOVA was designed for comparing several means, it also can be used to compare two means. Two-way ANOVA allows for a second independent variable and addresses interaction.

To run a one way ANOVA, use the following steps:

- Identify the independent and dependent variables.
- Describe the variation by breaking it into three parts - the total variation, the portion that is within groups, and the portion that is between groups (or among groups for more than two groups). The total variation is the sum of the squares of the differences between

each value and the grand mean of all the values in all the groups. The in-group variation is the sum of the squares of the differences in each element's value and the group mean. The variation between group means is the total variation minus the in-group variation.

- Measure the difference between each group's mean and the grand mean.
- Perform a significance test on the differences.
- Interpret the results.

This F-test assumes that the group variances are approximately equal and that the observations are independent. It also assumes normally distributed data; however, since this is a test on means the Central Limit Theorem holds as long as the sample size is not too small. ANOVA is efficient for analyzing data using relatively few observations and can be used with categorical variables. Note that regression can perform a similar analysis to that of ANOVA.

DISCRIMINANT ANALYSIS

Analysis of the difference in means between groups provides information about individual variables, it is not useful for determine their individual impacts when the variables are used in combination. Since some variables will not be independent from one another, one needs a test that can consider them simultaneously in order to take into account their interrelationship.

One such test is to construct a linear combination, essentially a weighted sum of the variables. To determine which variables discriminate between two or more naturally occurring groups, discriminant analysis is used. Discriminant analysis can determine which variables are the best predictors of group membership.

It determines which groups differ with respect to the mean of a variable, and then uses that variable to predict new cases of group membership. Essentially, the discriminant function problem is a one-way ANOVA problem in that one can determine whether multiple groups are significantly different from one another with respect to the mean of a particular variable.

A discriminant analysis consists of the following steps:

- Formulate the problem.
- Determine the discriminant function coefficients that result in the highest ratio of between-group variation to within-group variation.
- Test the significance of the discriminant function.
- Interpret the results.
- Determine the validity of the analysis.

Discriminant analysis analyses the dependency relationship, whereas factor analysis and cluster analysis address the interdependency among variables.

FACTOR ANALYSIS

Factor analysis is a very popular technique to analyse interdependence. Factor analysis studies the entire set of interrelationships without defining variables to be dependent or independent. Factor analysis combines variables to create a smaller set of factors. Mathematically, a factor is a linear combination of variables. A factor is not directly observable; it is inferred from the variables. The technique identifies underlying structure among the variables, reducing the number of variables to a more manageable set. Factor analysis groups variables just as to their correlation.

The factor loading can be defined as the correlations between the factors and their underlying variables. A factor loading matrix is a key output of the factor analysis. An example matrix is shown below.

	Factor 1	Factor 2	Factor 3
Variable 1			
Variable 2			
Variable 3			

Column's Sum of Squares: Each cell in the matrix represents correlation between the variable and the factor associated with that cell. The square of this correlation represents the proportion of the variation in the variable explained by the factor. The sum of the squares of the factor loadings in each column is called an eigenvalue. An eigenvalue represents the amount of variance in the original variables that is associated with that factor. The communality is the amount of the variable variance explained by common factors.

A rule of thumb for deciding on the number of factors is that each included factor must explain at least as much variance as does an average variable. In other words, only factors for which the eigenvalue is greater than one are used. Other criteria for determining the number of factors include the Scree plot criteria and the percentage of variance criteria. To facilitate interpretation, the axis can be rotated. Rotation of the axis is equivalent to forming linear combinations of the factors. A commonly used rotation strategy is the varimax rotation. Varimax attempts to force the column entries to be either close to zero or one.

CLUSTER ANALYSIS

Market segmentation usually is based not on one factor but on multiple factors. Initially, each variable represents its own cluster. The challenge is to find a way to combine variables so that relatively homogenous clusters can be formed. Such clusters should be internally homogenous and externally heterogeneous. Cluster analysis is one way to accomplish this goal. Rather than being a statistical test, it is more of a collection of algorithms for grouping objects, or in the case of marketing research, grouping people. Cluster analysis is useful in the exploratory phase of research when there are no a-priori hypotheses.

Cluster analysis steps:

- Formulate the problem, collecting data and choosing the variables to analyse.
- Choose a distance measure. The most common is the Euclidean distance. Other possibilities include the squared Euclidean distance, city-block distance, Chebychev distance, power distance, and per cent disagreement.

- Choose a clustering procedure.
- Determine the number of clusters. They should be well separated and ideally they should be distinct enough to give them descriptive names such as professionals, buffs, etc.
- Profile the clusters.
- Assess the validity of the clustering.

MARKETING RESEARCH REPORT

The format of the marketing research report varies with the needs of the organization.

The report often contains the following:

- Authorization letter for the research
- Table of Contents
- List of illustrations
- Executive summary
- Research objectives
- Methodology
- Results
- Limitations
- Conclusions and recommendations
- Appendices containing copies of the questionnaires, etc.

CONCLUDING THOUGHTS

Marketing research by itself does not arrive at marketing decisions, nor does it guarantee that the organization will be successful in marketing its products. However, when conducted in a systematic, analytical, and objective manner, marketing research can reduce the uncertainty in the decision-making process and increase the probability and magnitude of success.

MARKETING SYSTEM

Marketing System is a high-performance, versatile platform that you use to perform targeted personalized e-marketing through the Web or electronic mail. It assists e-commerce enterprises in effectively communicating relevant messages to shoppers in order to improve sales either directly or indirectly.

The Marketing System includes support for the following functions:

- Content targeting, up-sell and cross-sell capabilities, advertisements and testing, e-mail campaigns, discounts, and coupons.
- Combining and prioritizing campaign items. *Campaign methods include the following:*
  - *Discounts*: Create and edit discounts, combine discounts, set discount interactions, apply order-level discounts, shipping and leveraged discounts. An example of a discount is buy one product, get a second product at a 20% discount.
  - *Awareness advertisement*: Create and edit ads. For example, showcase a newly introduced product on the homepage of the Web site.
  - *Suggestive selling*: Create expressions that you can use to target ads or discounts. For example, if a shopping cart contains Product A, show banner ad B.
  - *Direct mail*: Create and send direct mail to lists of users. For example, send a newsletter or promotional mail piece to all active customers each month.
- Managing campaigns for customers who compete in the same industry so that the competitor's ads never appear on the same page.
- Enabling customers on the Web site to see ads and apply discounts by using coupons or entering promotion codes.
- Enabling business managers to create and manage campaign items such as discounts, ads, and direct mail that they use as marketing tools to increase sales.
- Publishing campaigns into production so that campaigns only become visible to the run-time system on activation and approval.
- Generating reports to measure key metrics.

MARKETING SYSTEM INTEGRATION AND FEATURE AREAS

The Marketing System integrates with the Catalog, Orders, and Profiles Systems, and the Data Warehouse.

It includes these five main feature areas:

1. *Campaigns*: Manages the campaigns, customers, advertisements, and discounts which form marketing prigrammes. The Campaigns module is integrated with both the Profiles System and the Catalog System through expressions. Expressions enable you to target advertisements to users and to apply discounts to products.
2. *Content Selection Framework*: A platform-level framework for building targeted content delivery applications on the Internet and making customization and extension of the advertising and discount delivery systems easier. The CSF allows for multiple pieces of content to be retrieved as a record set with only one call, which creates a significant timesaving.
3. *Expression Evaluator Engine*: Provides the logic to evaluate expression objects. An expression is a condition that Commerce Server evaluates against profiles to determine whether to deliver content, or perform another action. For example, an expression might be user total visit > 100. If this expression evaluates to True.
4. *Mailing List Management*: Manages lists of users created for a direct mail campaign. Create, import, and export multiple lists focusing on different user profiles. Maintain opt-out lists and references as part of a direct mail campaign. The mailing list management database maintains direct mail lists, per job opt-out lists and global opt-out lists.
5. *Direct Mailer Service*: A fast, scalable service that use to send personalized e-mail messages from a Web page, or non-personalized mailings from a flat text file, to large groups of recipients. Direct Mailer tracks

e-mail and records which messages are sent and which are clicked. This enables to analyse the success of a direct mail campaign. The Direct Mailer service is designed to send bulk personalized e-mail messages to millions of users.

MARKET INFORMATION SYSTEMS

Market Information Systems are information systems used in gathering, analyzing and disseminating information about prices and other information relevant to farmers, animal rearers, traders, processors and others involved in handling agricultural products. Market Information Systems play an important role in agro-industrialisation and food supply chains. With the advance of ICTs in developing countries, the income- generation opportunities offered by Market Information Systems have been sought by international development organisations, NGOs and businesses alike.

AGRICULTURAL MARKET INFORMATION SYSTEMS

There is a wide variety of market information systems or services. OECD countries have traditionally emphasised the importance of information provision for the agricultural sector, a notable example being the service provided by USDA. Such systems are widely used in order to increase the transparency and the volume of information flowing through the supply chains for different agricultural products. The ability of market information systems to provide a valuable service has been strengthened with the development of the Internet and the advance of electronic commerce. Industry structure, product complexity and the demanding nature of agricultural transactions are considered determining factors for the development of B2B electronic commerce in agriculture.

AGRICULTURAL MARKET INFORMATION IN DEVELOPING COUNTRIES

In developing countries, market information initiatives are often part of broader interventions and part of the agricultural marketing and agribusiness development strategy that many governments are actively engaged in. It's commonly understood that long transaction chains, lack of transparency, lack of standards, and insufficient access to markets for products has perpetuated low incomes in predominantly agrarian economies. FAO has a unit focussed on agricultural marketing support, including through development of market information. Donor organizations, such as the CTA, IICD, USAID, DFID, and the Bill and Melinda Gates Foundation are all focussed on improving the efficiencies within the supply chain through greater information provision.

The recent surge of mobile phone usage in developing countries has provided an opportunity for innovative projects to leverage this new distribution channel to get critical market data into the hands of farmers and traders. Several projects by Reuters, Nokia, Esoko/TradeNet, KACE, Manobi and others have demonstrated the impact that such information can have. Studies in Niger and India demonstrate the impact of cell phones in reducing price variations and creating equilibrium among markets. Introduction of internet kiosks and cafes that provide wholesale price information to farmers has been shown to enhance the functioning of rural markets by increasing the competitiveness of local traders in India.

SOCIAL RESPONSIBILITY IN MARKETING

ETHICAL RESPONSIBILITIES AND CONSTRAINTS

Businesses and people face some constraints on what can ethically be done to make money or to pursue other goals. Fraud and deception are not only morally wrong but also inhibit the efficient functioning of the economy. There are also behaviourss that, even if they are not strictly illegal in a given jurisdiction, cannot be undertaken with a good conscience. There are a number of areas where an individual must consider his or her conscience to decide if a venture is acceptable. Some"paycheck advance" loan operators charge very high interest rates on small loans made in anticipation of a consumer's next paycheck. Depending on state laws, effective interest rates may exceed 20% per month. In some cases, borrowers put up their automobiles as security, with many losing their only source of transportation through default. Although some consider this practice unconscionable, others assert that such loans may be the only way that a family can obtain cash to fill an immediate need. Because of costs of administration are high, these costs, when spread over a small amount, will amount to a large percentage. Further, because the customer groups in question tend to have poor credit ratings with high anticipated rates of default, rates must be high enough to cover this.

SUSTAINABILITY

Sustainability is a notion that proposes that socially responsible firms will somehow financially outperform other less responsible firms in the long run. This might result from customer loyalty, better employee morale, or public policy favouring ethical conduct. Empirical results testing this hypothesis are mixed, neither suggesting that more responsible firms, on the average, have a clear financial advantage nor a large burden.

Thus, a useful approach may be to determine:

- Specific circumstances under which a firm may actually find the more responsible approach to be more profitable,
- Under which circumstances responsible behaviour can be pursued without an overall significant downside, and
- The ethical responsibilities that a firm faces when a more responsible approach may be more costly.

INDIVIDUAL, FIRM, AND SOCIETY

Different individuals vary in their ethical convictions. Some are willing to work for the tobacco industry, for example, while others are not. Some are willing to mislead potential customers while others will normally not do this. There are, however, also broader societal and companywide values that may influence the individual business decision maker. Some religions, including Islam, disfavor the charging of interest. Although different groups differ somewhat in their interpretations of this issue, the Koran at the very least prohibits usury-charging excessive interest rates.

There is some disagreement as to whether more modest, fair interest rates are acceptable. In cultures where the stricter interpretation applies, a firm may be unwilling to set up an interest-based financing plan for customers who cannot pay cash. The firm might, instead, charge a higher price, with no additional charge for interest. Some firms also have their own ethical stands, either implicitly or explicitly. For example, Google has the motto"Do no evil." Other firms, on the other hand, may actively encourage lies, deception, and other reprehensible behaviour. Some firms elect to sell in less developed countries products that have been banned as unsafe in their own countries.

MAKING IT PROFITABLE FOR THE TOBACCO INDUSTRY TO"HARVEST"

Many see the tobacco industry as the"enemy" and may not want to do anything that can benefit the industry. However, in principle, it may actually be possible to make it profitable for the tobacco industry to"harvest"-to spend less money on brand building and gradually reduce the quantities sold. The tobacco industry is heavily concentrated, with three firms controlling most of the market. Some other industries are exempt from many antitrust law provisions. If the tobacco companies were allowed to collude and set prices, the equilibrium market price would probably go up, and the quantity of tobacco demanded would then go down. It is been found that among teenagers, smoking rates are especially likely to decrease when prices increase. The tobacco companies could also be given some immediate tax breaks in return for giving up their trademarks some thirty years in the future. This would reduce the incentive to advertise, again leading to decreased demand in the future. The tax benefits needed might have to be very high, thus making the idea infeasible unless the nation is willing to trade off better health for such large revenue losses.

"WIN-WIN" MARKETING

In some cases, it may actually be profitable for companies to do good deeds. This may be the case, for example, when a firm receives a large amount of favourable publicity for its contributions, resulting in customer goodwill and an enhanced brand value. A pharmacy chain, for example, might pay for charitable good to develop information about treating diabetes. The chain could then make this information on its web site, paying for bandwidth and other hosting expenses that may be considerably less than the value of the positive publicity received.

"SPONSORED FUNDRAISING"

Non-profit groups often spend a large proportion of the money they take in on fundraising. This is problematic both because of the inefficiency of the process and the loss of potential proceeds that result and because potential donors who learn about or suspect high fundraising expenses may be less likely to donor. This is an especially critical issue now that information on fundraising overhead for different organizations is readily available on the Internet.

An alternative approach to fundraising that does not currently appear to be much in use is the idea of"sponsored" fundraising. The idea here is that some firm might volunteer to send out fundraising appeals on behalf of the organization. For example, Microsoft might volunteer to send out letters asking people to donate to the American Red Cross. This may be a very cost effective method of promotion for the firm since the sponsor would benefit from both the positive publicity for its involvement and from the greater attention that would likely be given a fundraising appeal for a group of special interest than would be given to an ordinary advertisement or direct mail piece advertising the sponsor in a traditional way.

One issue that comes up is the potential match between

the sponsor and sponsee organization. This may or may not be a critical issue since respondents are selected for the solicitation based on their predicted interest in the organization. Microsoft-directly or indirectly through the Bill and Melinda Gates Foundation-has been credited with a large number of charitable ventures and has the Congressional Black Caucus as one of its greatest supporters. In many cases, firms might volunteer for this fundraising effort in large part because of the spear heading efforts of high level executives whose families are affected by autism.

COMMERCIAL COMEDY

Another win-win deal potential between industry and non-profit groups involves the idea of commercial comedy. Many non-profit groups are interested in finding low cost, high quality entertainment for fundraising events. After all, money spent on buying entertainment reduces the net proceeds available for the organization's prigramme. Firms, on the other hand, have difficulty getting current and potential customers to give attention to advertising in traditional media. If firms were able to create some high quality entertainment involving their mascotss-e.g., the Energizer Bunny, the Pillsbury Doughboy, and the AFLAC Duck-the audience at a fundraising event would give attention for an extended period of time. Good will would also be generated, and it is likely that the performance would receive considerable media coverage.

2

Strategic Planning

BASICS OF STRATEGIC PLANNING

STRATEGIC PLANNING DEFINITION AND PHILOSOPHY

Strategic planning is more than ensuring your association will remain financially sound and be able to maintain its reserves—it's projecting where your association expects to be in five, ten, or fifteen years—and how your association will get there. It is a systematic planning process involving a number of steps that identify the current status of the association, including its mission, vision for the future, operating values, needs (strengths, weaknesses, opportunities, and threats), goals, prioritized actions and strategies, action plans, and monitoring plans.

Strategic planning is the cornerstone of every common-interest community. Without strategic planning, the community will never know where it is going—much less know if it ever got there. An important concept of strategic planning is an understanding that in order for the community to flourish, everyone needs to work to ensure the team's goals are mct.

Team members include all association homeowners, the board of directors, professional management—whether onsite or through a management company— and various service professionals such as accountants and reserve professionals. This team needs to work as a collective body to be successful. Part of the team concept is the establishment of roles for the team players. Teams usually perform poorly if everyone or no one is trying to be the quarterback.

GOALS, OBJECTIVES AND TARGETS

Strategic planning is a very important business activity. It is also important in the public sector areas such as education. It is practiced widely informally and formally. Strategic planning and decision processes should end with objectives and a roadmap of ways to achieve those objectives.

One of the core goals when drafting a strategic plan is to develop it in a way that is easily translatable into action plans. Most strategic plans address high level initiatives and over-arching goals, but don't get articulated (translated) into day-to-day projects and tasks that will be required to achieve the plan. Terminology or word choice, as well as the level a plan is written, are both examples of easy ways to fail at translating your strategic plan in a way that makes sense and is executable to others. Often, plans are filled with conceptual terms which don't tie into day-to-day realities for the staff expected to carry out the plan.

The following terms have been used in strategic planning: desired end states, plans, policies, goals, objectives, strategies, tactics and actions. Definitions vary, overlap and fail to achieve clarity. The most common of these concepts are specific, time bound statements of intended future results and general and continuing statements of intended future results, which most models refer to as either goals or objectives (sometimes interchangeably). One model of organizing objectives uses hierarchies. The items may be organized in a hierarchy of means and ends and numbered as follows: Top Rank Objective (TRO), Second Rank Objective, Third Rank Objective, etc. From any rank, the objective in a lower rank answers to the question "How?" and the objective in a higher rank answers to the question "Why?" The exception is the Top Rank Objective (TRO): there is no answer to the "Why?" question. That is how the TRO is defined.

People typically have several goals at the same time. "Goal congruency" refers to how well the goals combine with each other. Does goal A appear compatible with goal B? Do they fit together to form a unified strategy? "Goal hierarchy" consists of the nesting of one or more goals within other goal(s).

One approach recommends having short-term goals, medium-term goals, and long-term goals. In this model, one can expect to attain short-term goals fairly easily: they stand just slightly above one's reach. At the other extreme, long-term goals appear very difficult, almost impossible to attain. Strategic management jargon sometimes refers to "Big Hairy Audacious Goals" (BHAGs) in this context. Using one goal as a stepping-stone to the next involves goal sequencing. A person or group starts by attaining the easy short-term goals, then steps up to the medium-term, then to the long-term goals. Goal sequencing can create a "goal stairway". In an organizational setting, the organization may co-ordinate goals so that they do not conflict with each other. The goals of one part of the organization should mesh compatibly with those of other parts of the organization.

STRATEGIC PLANNING MODELS

Strategic planning is a relatively new genre of planning, adapted from primarily two sources. Business schools have equipped leaders with institutional planning processes, which were developed from decision making and production control. Community planning schools have prepared planning staffs with models of social planning and physical land-use planning. The business model is more often tailored for a hierarchical organization with top-down control, although this has softened in the dot-com era. The community- planning model is more grass roots, bottom-up, consensus building and is better suited for non profit organizations and local governments. The former is market share and profit oriented, and the latter is empowerment and constituent needs oriented. In between, there is a range of blended approaches.

MODEL 1: NON-PROFIT ORGANIZATIONS (NPOS)

Brian W. Barry details strategic planning for NPOs in the

pamphlet and workbook *Strategic Planning Workbook for Nonprofit Organizations*. The workbook is oriented to organizations such as soup kitchens, nascent neighbourhood groups, and other human services groups. It outlines the strategic planning process, but is tailored to a small organiza tion with a narrow focus. It also assumes that all of the stakeholders are represented, that they speak with authority, and that the constituencies they represent are fairly homogeneous. In order to be applied to community associations, this model must be modified to accommodate multiple missions in more complex organizations, which offer many services to very heterogeneous constituencies. However, it lacks attention on soliciting feedback and developing consensus.

NPO Strategic Planning includes:

- Recruiting stakeholders, power brokers, and leadership.
- Reviewing the organization's history and current situation.
- Reviewing and revising (or developing) the organization's mission statement.
- Identifying the organization's opportunities and threats.
- Identifying organizational strengths and weaknesses.
- Identifying the most critical issues arising from any of the organization's opportunities, threats, strengths, and weaknesses.
- Setting goals to remove weaknesses, blunt threats, and seizing opportunities.
- Brainstorming, evaluating, and selecting strategies to empower leaders.
- Critiquing and reviewing the plan.
- Revising goals, and re-implementing goals, as appropriate.

MODEL 2: APPLIED STRATEGIC PLANNING

The Applied Strategic Planning approach is described in the pamphlet *Applied Strategic Planning, An Introduction* by

Leonard D. Goodstein, Timothy M. Nolan, and William J. Pfeiffer. Business and military executives tend to favour this model. It assumes a top-down hierarchy with a plans and operations department, that is responsible for running the models and recruiting and involving appropriate and key personnel. It also presumes the existence of a fair degree of quantifiable data and business modeling decision making where one finds targets and executes prigrammes. This method might be well suited for solving problems where constituents have an identifiable problem and are unified in the opinion that better service is needed. The process also incorporates scanning the environment, brainstorming solutions, establishing a future orientation, and looking at the behaviour of competitors and new products on the horizon.

Applied Strategic Planning includes:

- Identifying consultants and key internal players.
- Garnering CEO support, identifying stakeholders, and setting planning goals.
- Scanning organizational values, philosophy, and culture.
- (Re)defining the organization's mission statement.
- Identifying new futures and new venture opportunities.
- Auditing threats, opportunities, strengths, and weaknesses.
- Identifying critical gaps between where the organization is and its future.
- Selecting strategies to expand or retrench as a means to close performance gaps.
- Implementing the strategies to acquire or divest.
- Monitoring actions, updating conditions, and restarting the cycle.

MODEL 3: ICMA STRATEGIC DEVELOPMENT

This model is the least relevant to community planning as it focuses very narrowly on the special issue of economic development. It makes a strong case for inventorying existing capacities and capabilities. It also contains several good elements that would stimulate association planning groups' thinking on consensus building. ICMA Strategic Development is described in *Economic Development: A Strategic Approach for Local Governments*, a 68-page leaders guide and student workbook for an International City/County Management Association (ICMA) course on local economic development.

ICMA Strategic Development includes:

- Augmenting existing planning structure with stakeholders.
- Conducting an environmental scan of community conditions.
- Identifying and evaluating the community resources.
- Identifying and rating different community business activities.
- Identifying and rating different community development agencies and prigrammes.
- Conducting an inventory of congruent and divergent values and visions in the community.
- Imagining and describing multiple visions of different community economic sectors.
- Developing visions into goals and establishing objectives to reach the goals.
- Describing who, what, when, how, and where resources are needed.
- Monitoring, reporting, updating, and reallocating efforts as targets are hit.
- Restarting the process again by recruiting a new group and conducting scans.

COMPONENTS OF STRATEGIC PLANNING

Strategic planning's three main components are plan development, plan execution, and plan review. Many of the functional areas within these components are similar in that all three require a team concept that is based on: ensuring the member's roles are defined, educating team members about the process, and using quality communication when interacting.

PLAN DEVELOPMENT

Plan development is the first component of strategic planning.

During this stage, the following steps should be completed:

- *Assess the association's history and significant accomplishments*: Develop a history of the association. List important milestones that brought the association to where it is today. In order to help visualize how the association has changed over the years, include items where impact occurred in the association's operations, such as: hiring additional staff, upgrade computer hardware/software, changing processes significantly, raising dues, building additional facilities, rebuilding/renovating existing facilities, etc., by dates and quantities/dollars, as appropriate.
- *Assess the association's current status*: Determine the association's current status by looking at such things as the state of the facilities, infrastructure of the operations, the financial statements, the demographics of the population, and so forth.
- *Evaluate the association's current governance structure*: Review the operations to determine how responsibilities are assigned, defining communi-cations and authorities. Examine policies, procedures, and desk guides available to determine the chain of command within the association's staff, within the board, and for oversight and communications between the staff or property management company and the board of directors. Critical is the point of contact for the staff or management company and the board, to preclude misunderstandings, duplications of effort, things falling through the cracks, etc.
- Determine the board's responsibilities versus that of the staff or management company's responsibilities. An example of a delineation of responsibilities between the staff or management company and the board is covered in Policy Governance, which simply stated, assigns the board's function as that of policy

making, the "what is" of the subject/issue, while the staff's or management company's function is that of carrying out the policies, the "how to" of the subject/issue.

- *Develop mission and vision statements*: The vision statement is the image or state to which the association aspires. It emphasizes the dream of where the association will be at a specific time. The mission statement is the organization's purpose stated in a memorable phrase. In short, an association's mission statement describes the business it's in. It should be geared toward fulfilling the association's purpose and what it is intended to do with some specifics contained in the governing documents. Mission and vision statements should not be a list of goals.
- *Determine operating values*: Also called guiding principles, these values state the association's intentions and expectations. They are used to judge the association's policies and actions, as well as individual conduct. Associations should include values such as: the importance of customers and customer service; commitment to quality and innovation; importance of honesty; integrity and ethical behaviour; corporate citizenship; respect for the employee and duty the association has to its employees; and importance of safety and protecting the environment, etc.
- *Perform a needs assessment*: Determine the needs of the association by analyzing the present state of the community, addressing any critical issues, and identifying the association's strengths, weaknesses, opportunities, and threats.
  - *Determination of key result areas*: Define five to ten areas in which the association must be successful in order to accomplish its mission, based on customer expectations.
    a. *Determine customer expectations*: Determine the customer [members, suppliers, and

employees] expectations of the association as stakeholders. Group the expectations into five to ten key results areas.

- *Determine critical issues*: List the critical issues faced by the association that must be addressed for the association to achieve its mission and vision, based on an assessment of its strengths, weaknesses, opportunities, and threats.
  - Assessment of strengths, weaknesses, opportunities, and threats (SWOT)
    a. *Strengths*: List the organizational attributes that promote the association's ability to meet its mission and vision.
    b. *Weaknesses*: List those organizational attributes that hamper the association's ability to meet its mission and vision. Some examples include inadequate technology or use of technology, lack core competency training, poor service, and so forth.
    c. *Opportunities*: List those factors, internal and external, that would enable the association to meet its mission and vision. Some examples include technological advances in needed areas, consolidating functions, etc.
    d. *Threats*: List those factors, internal or external, that would hamper the association from meeting its mission and vision. Some examples include high rate of foreclosures, drawn out worker strike, change in developer focus, etc.
- *Define the roles of key players*: Who will be the key people responsible for each aspect of the strategic plan? Answer questions such as: What level of control will the board have? Is the manager going to be a proactive leader or an administrator? Are the homeowners going to be active as committee members or are they going to be less involved? Role definition is extremely important so that efforts are

not duplicated-or neglected overall. One way to establish a team and define specific roles is to adopt a model similar to a city council and city manager form of government. The city council (board of directors) sets policies, votes on contracts and bids, and is the on-site eyes and ears (oversight) of the community. The city manager (management) should be the professionally educated, proactive, paid leader who manages the day-to-day operations and then implements the board's decisions. The citizens (homeowners) should attend meetings, serve on committees, and elect competent individuals to the board of directors. This concept of team roles goes much deeper than this discussion allows, especially in the areas of compliance, budgeting, and homeowner interaction.

- *Educate and communicate the plan*:Without education and communication, team members can neither perform their roles nor effectively interact with each other. Make sure that every player has the necessary documents and basic knowledge to perform effectively. Further ensure that each of the players communicate with each other-provide updates as necessary and always ask for others' input. Better to catch a potential problem earlier rather than later. In the event that there is a change in management, association boards should also be sure to communicate their strategic plans to the new manager, and revise it, if necessary. Also, if the Strategic Plan calls for specific management participation, make sure it is spelled out in the management contract.
- *Listen and take notes*: During the strategic planning process it is important for all parties to actively listen and take notes. Many type-A personalities, who may be involved with the association at any level, will want to solve the community's issues quickly and efficiently. If they do this without listening to the board of

directors, homeowners, and vendors, they may be executing a plan, but not a quality strategic plan.

- *Develop and prioritize long-range goals*: Develop long-range goals to address the critical issues identified through the needs assessment; then prioritize those goals.
- *Develop short-term goals and action plans*: Establish short-term goals and specific action plans along with scheduled completion dates.
- *Monitor the progress*: Establish a monitoring process to assess the progress made on both short-term and long-range goals.

PLAN EXECUTION

Plan execution is the second phase of strategic planning. In this step, an association puts its plan into action through the allocation of resources.

This step has three components:

1. *Prigrammes*: Association prigrammes serve as blueprints for converting objectives into realities.
2. *Procedures*: Procedures are the specific sequence of tasks required to complete the prigrammes.
3. *Budgets*: An association should prepare budgets to fund prigrammes. Instead, many develop prigrammes based on their budgets. Simply put, an association should be strategy-driven, not budget-driven.

If the plan development phase was put together well, then the plan execution phase is much easier. Items such as teamwork, roles, communication, and education are important and apply to the plan execution phase. Hold periodic meetings to review progress on short-term goals and plans. Without periodic meetings and reviews, the community will not move forward and achieve its goals. Lastly, adaptability is crucial to the plan execution phase since all plans will have flaws. If the team members are not adaptable, there may be simple issues that will not be resolved in a reasonable manner and the community will suffer.

PLAN REVIEW

Plan review is required constantly to improve the plan and ensure its execution. Part of the plan review occurs naturally when there's board turnover, a new homeowner, or changes in the law.

In addition, plan review needs to be scheduled to ensure the plan is meeting the community's goals. This can be achieved through surveys, management review conferences, or discussions at meetings. If the community fails to update the plan, the plan will eventually fail the community. Industry experts suggest that associations and their managers review their strategic plans annually and completely overhaul their strategic plans every three to five years.

USE OF A CONSULTANT

An outside consultant or professional facilitator brings impartiality, pointed questions, and the facilitation skills needed to balance differences of opinion. Associations should be aware that consultants will take different approaches to strategic planning as no one, right way exists. While hiring a consultant can be expensive, he or she will greatly accelerate the association's learning curve and help to ensure that the strategic planning process will complete a full cycle. If budgetary restraints do not allow for such assistance, associations may want to consider using a consultant for the initial sessions, where an objective assessment of the association's current position is necessary.

ASPECTS OF STRATEGIC PLANNING

BENEFITS OF THE LONG-RANGE PLAN

- Stimulates thinking to make better use of the association's resources.
- Assigns responsibility and schedules work.
- Coordinates and unifies efforts.
- Facilitates control and evaluation of the association's activities (accountability).
- Creates awareness of obstacles to overcome.

- Identifies opportunities.
- Avoids the trap of linear thinking.
- Facilitates progressive advancement of the association's goals.

CHARACTERISTICS OF A USEFUL STRATEGIC PLAN

A useful strategic plan many characteristics. Specifically, it should be:

- *A set of priorities*: Setting priorities allows for the plan to be adjusted just as to changing needs or resources.
- *Achievable, measurable, and time sensitive*: Remember, it's better to do a few things well than many things poorly. The plan should contain goals that are measurable and have deadlines.
- *Flexible and responsive to changing conditions*: The plan is a road map that may contain unforeseen detours such as unexpected crises, new opportunities, or changes in resources.
- *Short and simple*: Plans that are more like a book will sit on a shelf. Keep it focused on the most important things to accomplish.
- *A unit, not a menu*: A useful plan is not a wish book. Everything in the plan needs to be accomplished.
- *The means to an end, not an end in itself*: The plan is the process by which it reaches its destination; it is not the destination.
- *Based on a three- to five-year period*: The strategic plan should be a living document that has a one-year drop off and a new year added so that it always covers the same time period.

SAMPLE AGENDA FOR A STRATEGIC PLANNING SESSION

- Introduction and review of the process.
- History of the association and its significant milestones.
- Overview of the community today.

- Review of current governance structure.
- Development of association mission and vision statements.
- Challenges and threats to the association.
- Opportunities for improvement.
- Classification and prioritization.
- Implementation: timeline and responsibility assignments.
- Summary and conclusion.

PITFALLS TO BE AVOIDED IN THE LONG-RANGE PLANNING PROCESS

- Becoming so engrossed in current problems that insufficient time is spent on long-range planning, and the process becomes discredited.
- Failing to assume the necessary involvement in the planning process by other association committees.
- Failing to use plans as standards for measuring performance.
- Consistently rejecting the formal planning mechanism by making intuitive decisions which conflict with the formal long-range plan.
- Failing to develop association goals suitable as a basis for formulating long-range plans.

3

Marketing Environment

INTRODUCTION

The market environment is a marketing term and refers to all of the forces outside of marketing that affect marketing management's ability to build and maintain successful relationships with target customers. The market environment consists of both the macroenvironment and the microenvironment.

The microenvironment refers to the forces that are close to the company and affect its ability to serve its customers. It includes the company itself, its suppliers, marketing intermediaries, customer markets, competitors, and publics.

The company aspect of microenvironment refers to the internal environment of the company. This includes all departments, such as management, finance, research and development, purchasing, operations and accounting. Each of these departments has an impact on marketing decisions. For example, research and development have input as to the features a product can perform and accounting approves the financial side of marketing plans and budgets.

The suppliers of a company are also an important aspect of the microenvironment because even the slightest delay in receiving supplies can result in customer dissatisfaction. Marketing managers must watch supply availability and other trends dealing with suppliers to ensure that product will be delivered to customers in the time frame required in order to maintain a strong customer relationship. Marketing intermediaries refers to resellers, physical distribution firms, marketing services agencies, and financial intermediaries. These are the people that help the company promote, sell, and distribute its products to final buyers. Resellers are those that hold and sell the company's product. They match the distribution to the customers and include places such as Wal-Mart, Target, and Best Buy. Physical distribution firms are places such as warehouses that store and transport the company's product from its origin to its destination. Marketing services agencies are companies that offer services such as conducting marketing research, advertising, and consulting. Financial intermediaries are institutions such as banks, credit companies and insurance companies.

Another aspect of microenvironment is the customers. There are different types of customer markets including consumer markets, business markets, government markets, international markets, and reseller markets. The consumer market is made up of individuals who buy goods and services for their own personal use or use in their household. Business markets include those that buy goods and services for use in producing their own products to sell. This is different from the reseller market which includes businesses that purchase goods to resell as is for a profit. These are the same companies mentioned as market intermediaries. The government market consists of government agencies that buy goods to produce public services or transfer goods to others who need them. International markets include buyers in other countries and includes customers from the previous categories.

Competitors are also a factor in the microenvironment and include companies with similar offerings for goods and services. To remain competitive a company must consider who their biggest competitors are while considering its own size and position in the industry. The company should develop a strategic advantage over their competitors.

The final aspect of the microenvironment is publics, which is any group that has an interest in or impact on the organization's ability to meet its goals. For example, financial publics can hinder a company's ability to obtain funds affecting the level of credit a company has. Media publics include newspapers and magazines that can publish substances of interest regarding the company and editorials that may influence customers' opinions.

Government publics can affect the company by passing legislation and laws that put restrictions on the company's actions. Citizen-action publics include environmental groups and minority groups and can question the actions of a company and put them in the public spotlight. Local publics are neighbourhood and community organizations and will also question a company's impact on the local area and the level of responsibility of their actions.

The general public can greatly affect the company as any change in their attitude, whether positive or negative, can cause sales to go up or down because the general public is often the company's customer base. And finally, the internal publics include all those who are employed within the company and deal with the organization and construction of the company's product.

The macroenvironment refers to all forces that are part of the larger society and affect the microenvironment. It includes concepts such as demography, economy, natural forces, technology, politics, and culture.

Studying human populations in terms of size, density, location, age, gender, race, and occupation. This is a very important factor to study for marketers and helps to divide the population into market segments and target markets. An example of demography is classifying groups of people just as to the year they were born. These classifications can be referred to as baby boomers, who are born between 1946 and 1964, generation X, who are born between 1965 and 1976, and generation Y, who are born between 1977 and 1994. Each classification has different characteristics and causes they find important. This can be beneficial to a marketer as they can decide who their product would benefit most and tailor their marketing plan to attract that segment. Demography covers many aspects that are important to marketers including family dynamics, geographic shifts, work force changes, and levels of diversity in any given area.

Another aspect of the macroenvironment is the economic environment. This refers to the purchasing power of potential customers and the ways in which people spend their money. Within this area are two different economies, subsistence and industrialized. Subsistence economies are based more in agriculture and consume their own industrial output. Industrial economies have markets that are diverse and carry many different types of goods. Each is important to the marketer because each has a highly different spending pattern as well as different distribution of wealth.

The natural environment is another important factor of the macroenvironment. This includes the natural resources that a company uses as inputs and affects their marketing activities. The concern in this area is the increased pollution, shortages of raw materials and increased governmental intervention. As raw materials become increasingly scarcer, the ability to create a company's product gets much harder. Also, pollution can go as far as negatively affecting a company's reputation if they are known for damaging the environment. The last concern, government intervention can make it increasingly harder for a company to fulfill their goals as requirements get more stringent.

The technological environment is perhaps one of the fastest changing factors in the macroenvironment. This includes all developments from antibiotics and surgery to nuclear missiles and chemical weapons to automobiles and credit cards. As these markets develop it can create new markets and new uses for products. It also requires a company to stay ahead of others and update their own technology as it becomes outdated. They must stay informed of trends so they can be part of the next big thing, rather than becoming outdated and suffering the consequences financially.

The political environment includes all laws, government agencies, and groups that influence or limit other organizations and individuals within a society. It is important for marketers to be aware of these restrictions as they can be complex. Some products are regulated by both state and federal laws. There are even restrictions for some products as to who the target market may be, for example, cigarettes should not be marketed to younger children. There are also many restrictions on subliminal messages and monopolies. As laws and regulations change often, this is a very important aspect for a marketer to monitor.

The final aspect of the macroenvironment is the cultural environment, which consists of institutions and basic values and beliefs of a group of people. The values can also be further categorized into core beliefs, which passed on from generation to generation and very difficult to change, and secondary beliefs, which tend to be easier to influence. As a marketer, it is important to know the difference between the two and to focus your marketing campaign to reflect the values of a target audience.

When dealing with the marketing environment it is important for a company to become proactive. By doing so, they can create the kind of environment that they will prosper in and can become more efficient by marketing in areas with the greatest customer potential. It is important to place equal emphasis on both the macro and microenvironment and to react accordingly to changes within them.

SWOT ANALYSIS

SWOT analysis is a simple framework for generating strategic alternatives from a situation analysis. It is applicable to either the corporate level or the business unit level and frequently appears in marketing plans. SWOT stands for Strengths, Weaknesses, Opportunities, and Threats. The SWOT framework was described in the late 1960's by Edmund P. Learned, C. Roland Christiansen, Kenneth Andrews, and William D. Guth in Business Policy, Text and Cases. The General Electric Growth Council used this form of analysis in the 1980's. Because it concentrates on the issues that potentially have the most impact, the SWOT analysis is useful when a very limited amount of time is available to address a complex strategic situation.

The diagram shows how a SWOT analysis fits into a strategic situation analysis.

Situation Analysis:	
/	\
Internal Analysis	External Analysis
/ \	/ \
Strengths Weaknesses	Opportunities Threats
I	
SWOT Profile	

The internal and external situation analysis can produce a large amount of information, much of which may not be highly relevant. The SWOT analysis can serve as an interpretative filter to reduce the information to a manageable quantity of key issues. The SWOT analysis classifies the internal aspects of the company as strengths or weaknesses and the external situational factors as opportunities or threats. Strengths can serve as a foundation for building a competitive advantage, and weaknesses may hinder it. By understanding these four aspects of its situation, a firm can better leverage its strengths, correct its weaknesses, capitalize on golden opportunities, and deter potentially devastating threats.

INTERNAL ANALYSIS

The internal analysis is a comprehensive evaluation of the internal environment's potential strengths and weaknesses. *Factors should be evaluated across the organization in areas such as*:

- Company culture
- Company image
- Organizational structure
- Key staff
- Access to natural resources
- Position on the experience curve
- Operational efficiency
- Operational capacity
- Brand awareness
- Market share
- Financial resources
- Exclusive contracts
- Patents and trade secrets

The SWOT analysis summarizes the internal factors of the firm as a list of strengths and weaknesses.

EXTERNAL ANALYSIS

An opportunity is the chance to introduce a new product or service that can generate superior returns. Opportunities can arise when changes occur in the external environment. Many of these changes can be perceived as threats to the market position of existing products and may necessitate a change in product specifications or the development of new products in order for the firm to remain competitive.

Changes in the external environment may be related to:

- Customers
- Competitors
- Market trends
- Suppliers
- Partners
- Social changes
- New technology
- Economic environment
- Political and regulatory environment

The last four items in the list are macro-environmental variables, and are addressed in a PEST analysis.

The SWOT analysis summarizes the external environmental factors as a list of opportunities and threats.

SWOT PROFILE

When the analysis has been completed, a SWOT profile can be generated and used as the basis of goal setting, strategy formulation, and implementation. The completed SWOT profile sometimes is arranged as follows:

Table. SWOT Analysis Framework

Environmental Scan	
/	\
Internal Analysis	External Analysis
/ \	/ \
Strengths Weaknesses	Opportunities Threats
|	
SWOT Matrix	

When formulating strategy, the interaction of the

quadrants in the SWOT profile becomes important. For example, the strengths can be leveraged to pursue opportunities and to avoid threats, and managers can be alerted to weaknesses that might need to be overcome in order to successfully pursue opportunities.

MULTIPLE PERSPECTIVES NEEDED

The method used to acquire the inputs to the SWOT matrix will affect the quality of the analysis. If the information is obtained hastily during a quick interview with the CEO, even though this one person may have a broad view of the company and industry, the information would represent a single viewpoint. The quality of the analysis will be improved greatly if interviews are held with a spectrum of stakeholders such as employees, suppliers, customers, strategic partners, etc.

SWOT ANALYSIS LIMITATIONS

While useful for reducing a large quantity of situational factors into a more manageable profile, the SWOT framework has a tendency to oversimplify the situation by classifying the firm's environmental factors into categories in which they may not always fit.

The classification of some factors as strengths or weaknesses, or as opportunities or threats is somewhat arbitrary. For example, a particular company culture can be either a strength or a weakness.

A technological change can be a either a threat or an opportunity. Perhaps what is more important than the superficial classification of these factors is the firm's awareness of them and its development of a strategic plan to use them to its advantage.

PEST ANALYSIS

It is very important that an organization considers its environment before beginning the marketing process. In fact, environmental analysis should be continuous and feed all aspects of planning.

The organization's marketing environment is made up of:

- The internal environment e.g. staff, office technology, wages and finance, etc.
- The micro-environment e.g. our external customers, agents and distributors, suppliers, our competitors, etc.
- The macro-environment e.g. Political forces, Economic forces, Sociocultural forces, and Technological forces. These are known as PEST factors.

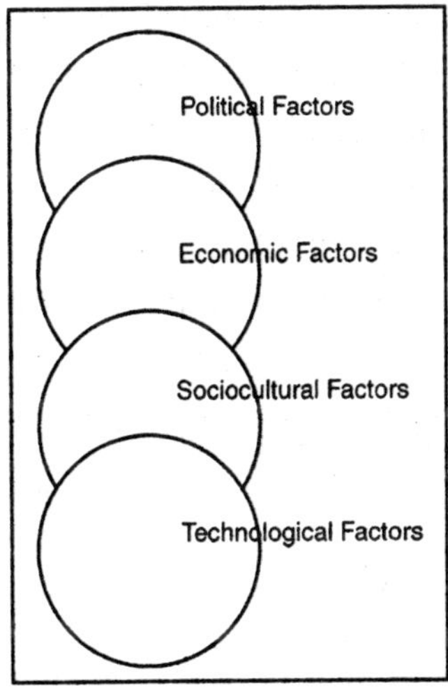

POLITICAL FACTORS

The political arena has a huge influence upon the regulation of businesses, and the spending power of consumers and other businesses.

You must consider issues such as:

- How stable is the political environment?
- Will government policy influence laws that regulate or tax your business?
- What is the government's position on marketing ethics?
- What is the government's policy on the economy?
- Does the government have a view on culture and religion?

- Is the government involved in trading agreements such as EU, NAFTA, ASEAN, or others?

ECONOMIC FACTORS

Marketers need to consider the state of a trading economy in the short and long-terms.

This is especially true when planning for international marketing:

- Interest rates.
- The level of inflation Employment level per capita.
- Long-term prospects for the economy Gross Domestic Product per capita, and so on.

SOCIOCULTURAL FACTORS

The social and cultural influences on business vary from country to country. It is very important that such factors are considered.

Factors include:

- What is the dominant religion?
- What are attitudes to foreign products and services?
- Does language impact upon the diffusion of products onto markets?
- How much time do consumers have for leisure?
- What are the roles of men and women within society?
- How long are the population living? Are the older generations wealthy?
- Do the population have a strong/weak opinion on green issues?

TECHNOLOGICAL FACTORS

Technology is vital for competitive advantage, and is a major driver of globalization.

Consider the following points:

- Does technology allow for products and services to be made more cheaply and to a better standard of quality?
- Do the technologies offer consumers and businesses more innovative products and services such as

Internet banking, new generation mobile telephones, etc?

- How is distribution changed by new technologies e.g. books via the Internet, flight tickets, auctions, etc?
- Does technology offer companies a new way to communicate with consumers e.g. banners, Customer Relationship Management, etc?

THE FIVE-FACTOR MODEL

MODEL

One of the long held goals of psychology has been to establish a model that can conveniently describe human personality, and disorders therein, with the intent to use this model in the remedying of personality disorders and improving general understanding of personality. Currently, a handful of models have risen to prominence, and have thus far stood the test of time. Some models are more generally accepted than others. Support for some models seems to come and go in cycles.

One of the more prominent models in contemporary psychology is what is known as the five-factor model of personality. This theory incorporates five different variables into a conceptual model for describing personality. These five different factors are often referred to as the "Big 5". The five-factor theory is among the newest models developed for the description of personality, and this model shows promise to be among the most practical and applicable models available in the field of personality psychology. Thorough critical attention is given to the proposal that the five-factor model is in fact a great theory.

Five Factors

As it became evident to many psychologists that, mathematically, combinations of five factors were useful in describing personality, there was a need to clearly define what these factors were. Indeed, this process led to some dissent in the ranks. One dissenter from the five-factor theorists was renowned psychologist H. J. Eysenck. Eysenck felt that, due to overlaps in the five factors and their correlates, in fact a three-factor model was more appropriate and accurate. His theory is called the PEN model or sometimes is even shortened to the two factor E-IN model. "Factor analysis has improved the situation...but the problem of naming factors is of course still with us".

Many psychologists support Eysenck's PEN model. However, of the major "factor-analytic models...the Big Five dominates the landscape of current psychological research". Through extensive debating and experimenting, there is currently a general consensus in the realms of scholarly psychology as to the identity of the five factors, and their basic interpretations and values to analysis of personality. The five factors are extroversion-introversion, neuroticism, agreeableness, conscientiousness, and openness.

Extroversion has long been one of the traits that has appeared in factor-analytic models, and is one of the two traits to appear in both the five-factor model and Eysenck's PEN and E-IN models. Extroversion also is sometimes referred to as social adaptability, though the popularity of this term seems to be waning. Extroversion is defined as "a trait characterized by a keen interest in other people and external events, and venturing forth with confidence into the unknown".

Neuroticism is the other trait to play a role in most of the contemporary factor models for personality. In some studies, adjustment is examined as a factor, instead of neuroticism. In this case, higher scores will indicate a positive result, consistent with the other four factors. This is because the term neuroticism has an inherent negative denotation. The bases of neuroticism are levels of anxiety and volatility. Within these bounds, neuroticism is "a dimension of personality defined by stability and low anxiety at one end as opposed to instability and high anxiety at the other end".

Openness, agreeableness, and conscientiousness are all terms with which most people outside the realm of psychology are familiar. In general, openness refers to how willing people are to make adjustments in notions and activities in accordance with new ideas or situations. Agreeableness measures how compatible people are with other people, or basically how able they are to get along with others. Conscientiousness refers to how much a person considers others when making decisions.

As with the two factors in the big five from Eysenck's E-IN, these three are also placed on sliding scales. These three scales, like neuroticism and extroversion, slide between their limits to give a clear picture of personality. The limits of these scales give a clear idea of their applications and are defined as "trusting and helpful versus suspicious and uncooperative, hard working and reliable versus lazy and careless, and nonconformist and creative versus conventional and down-to-earth.

Clinical Use of the Five Factors

With the five factors themselves more or less firmly established, the model is of little importance to psychology if it can not somehow be applied. Clinically, the five-factor model works much like Freud's psychoanalysis. People who have a certain characteristic that falls at an extreme on the chart of one or more of the five variables are likely to have some sort of psychological abnormality associated with that trait. People are likely to select their environment in such a way that this trait is perpetuated. To keep this cycle from iterating, psychologists make their patients come to terms with the flawed trait, allowing the patient to break the cycle. The five-factor model is perhaps even more useful in research and learning than it currently is for psychological patients. To this end, supporters of the five-factor model point to the fact that factor analysis"serves as a useful bridge between the more clinical theories...and the learning, behavioural theories".

Determining the Greatness of the Theory

To determine the greatness of a psychological theory, it is necessary to examine several key factors. First, to truly be labeled a great theory, it should be established that the theory does not contradict currently held or accepted theories. Also, once this is established, a great theory would include some kind of taxonomy. In addition, a truly great theory would be applicable. In other words, the theory would have some sort of clinical uses and would be able to predict experimental results without contradiction and with a relatively high level of consistency. Also, a great theory requires a ring of originality. It is not a great deed by anyone's standards to simply restate a long existing belief, or to remold it slightly and call it new. Finally, a great personality theory also needs to be universal. Cultural or situationally dependent models, although certainly of some relevance, are not worthy of being called great.

Compatibility

To establish the five-factor model's compatibility with other models, it is necessary to examine other popular or long held psychological theories. First and foremost, it is easy to see that the five-factor model is consistent with other factor-analytical models. Eysenck developed his PEN model from Cattell's sixteen-factor model. In this same vein of factor-analytic models, it is now proposed that"the structure of personality is best conceptualized as consisting of five major traits, rather than Eysenck's three types". Still, it seems natural that any factor analytic model should not directly contradict other factor analytic models.

It has been established in recent years that the five-factor model is quite compatible with other popular psychological theories as well, not just those concerned with factor analysis. It has been a recent endeavor of some psychologists to build bridges between the five-factor model and Freud's theories of psychoanalysis. For example, recent experiments have shown correlates between Freud's concept of the ego and the five variables in the five-factor model. As stated in the report of one such experiment conducted by Huey and Weisz, focusing on ego resiliency and ego control in adolescent boys,"Ego resiliency seems to reflect, in part, the well adjusted pole of each FFM dimension, whereas Ego undercontrol...reflects high extroversion, low agreeableness, and low conscientiousness". The correlation between elements of Freud's theory of psychoanalysis and elements of the five-factor model helps demonstrate the compatibility of the five-factor model.

Taxonomy

With the five factors placed on sliding scales, it becomes only an exercise in persistence to associate various human characteristics with one or more of the five factors. Strong correlates quickly become evident, and as trends develop it becomes possible to assign very accurate descriptions about people via their placement on the sliding scales associated with the five factors. Certainly, it seems plausible that these results can be used to extrapolate many behavioural characteristics, including such dependent traits as financial success and depth of religious faith.

Psychologists are currently working towards this end, attempting to empirically establish what Langston and Sykes called"a taxonomy of personality". Naturally, this taxonomy has long been the goal of personality psychologists, though it seems that, of late, somewhat of a snag has developed in trying to extrapolate past the very broadest of personality traits. This problem with the five-factor model is that, although often very categorical and taxonomic, it does not delve deeply into the causation of certain correlates. In fact, some relationships are even somewhat counterintuitive, making extrapolation by common sense difficult. For example, one recent study found that type A behaviour, which is characterized by general optimism and ambitiousness, had a low correlation to conscientiousness

Application

In accordance with the aforesaid flaw in the second criterion for greatness, the five-factor model runs into the most trouble when approached through the standards set forth by the third criterion. This criterion calls for a great theory to be applicable. McAdams states,"Personality theories do more than specify traits". In essence, what he is getting at is that the five-factor model falls short of attaining or ever having a chance to attain the title of the unified psychological theory.

As stated, the five-factor model is used effectively in application. Because of this, it can be said that it is applicable, even though this does not address McAdams' claim that the five-factor theory should not really be considered a theory, but more appropriately just a list of five variables that are useful when attempting to identify and classify personality traits. In general, though, most of the applications of the five-factor model as it now exists seem to come in the academic and experimental forum. In reference to the model's usefulness in academics, Digman, "At a minimum, research on the five-factor model has given us a useful set of very broad dimensions that characterize individual differences. These dimensions can be measured with high reliability and impressive validity". In summary, Digman states that the five variables that compose the five-factor model "provide a good answer to the question of personality structure".

Originality

It would be possible to argue that the five-factor model does not meet the criterion of originality. Indeed, when Fiske first derived a model for predicting behaviour that consisted of five factors, Cattell's sixteen-factor system was already nearly five years old. Despite this, the five-factor model could arguably be considered distant enough from Cattell's model to warrant the label of originality. Perhaps instead, though, it is more useful to think of the factor models together, as a single set of theories that, although very different individually, all fit into one family. This family of models, starting with Cattell's sixteen-factor system, and including Eysenck's model and the five-factor model, grew from a study of language initiated by German psychologists Allport and Odbert, who were inspired for their studies by two other German psychologists, Baumgarten and Klages. Through this family history of the factor models, it is easy to see that they came to exist more or less independently of any other major psychological theories.

Universality

The fulfillment of the fourth criterion listed for a great

theory in personality is that the theory should be nearly universally true. In a non-physical science, like psychology, it is naturally too much to ask that a theory always hold true. The basic premise, though, is that the theory should transcend culture and situation. As the premise is in two parts, so too shall be the response.

It appears that the five-factor model holds very well across cultural and linguistic lines. Digman gives three examples of other cultures in which the five-factor theory has held up nicely. His three studies took place in Japan, the Philippines, and Germany, and in all three cases, a five-factor solution was clearly evident at the end of testing. On the subject of the ability of the five-factor model to cross cultural and linguistic barriers, Digman writes, "something quite fundamental is involved here. Is this the way people everywhere construe personality, regardless of language or culture?".

A current fault of the five-factor model seems to be that it fails to anticipate behaviour in many situations. The same virtue that allows the five-factor model to hold true across cultural boundaries is its fault in specific situations: The five variables are too broad. McAdams accurately sums up this problem by saying, "Because the Big Five operate at such a general level of analysis, trait scores...may not be especially useful in the prediction of specific behaviour in particular situations".

ISSUES DESCRIPTIVE AND EVALUATIVE

In"The Five-Factor Model: Emergence of a Taxonomic Model for Personality Psychology," Popkins summarizes and evaluates a factor analytic description of personality that has risen to prominence in the last decade. However, there are problems with both Popkins' summary and his evaluation that this commentary will bring to light.

Perhaps Popkins is well within the scope of mainstream psychology when he discusses the five-factor model as a single, unitary development. However, proponents of the five-factor model prefer to make more fine-grained distinctions. Two related, yet distinct, five-factor models can be distinguished:

the OCEAN model of Costa and McCrae, and the big five of Goldberg and colleagues. Costa and McCrae's OCEAN model is known by its acronym for the five factors: openness, conscientiousness, extraversion, agreeableness, and neuroticism. This naming of factors has the advantage of making them memorable to newcomers, but the disadvantage that the order is not meaningful, and the further disadvantage that the factors are not all named just as to the positive pole of each axis. In the big five variant, Goldberg prefers to name the factors just as to their positive poles, and in the order derived from the amount of variance each explains, as follows: surgency, agreeablenss, conscientiousness, emotional stability, and intellect. Currently, debates rage over whether the fifth factor is a'60's style openness to experience construct, or whether it represents a general intellect factor--and if the latter, then how intellect differs from general intelligence.

A further difference between the OCEAN and big five models is that the former is hierarchical whereas the latter is circular. The big five are circular because many variables have large loadings on two factors as opposed to only one, or three or more. Because the big five are circular, they have swallowed up both the interpersonal circumplex and the affective circumplex, incorporating these into a broader taxonomy

Another important difference between the OCEAN model and the big five is the theoretical basis that exists for the latter, but not for the former--namely, the lexical hypothesis. This hypothesis contends that those individual differences that are most salient and socially relevant will come to be encoded as terms in the natural language. This conjecture makes into a meaningful activity the culling of all personality-relevant terms from an unabridged dictionary, and the subjecting of self- and peer-ratings on these terms to factor analysis.

Having now discussed the descriptive errors of omission in Popkins' paper, One will go on to point out some evaluative errors of commission. Popkins concludes that the five-factor model is not a great theory because it is not a theory, but only a taxonomy. In corroboration of Popkins' thesis, two leading big five researchers go so far as to state,"we would ban the use of the term'theoretical'...in favour of more exact terms such as'premises,''assumptions,' and'hypotheses,' as well as more meaningful distinctions such as'broad versus narrow' and'phenotypic versus genotypic' attributes".

Popkins to specify what is the difference between a theory and a taxonomy. The difference is not so obvious as it might appear at first blush. Prefer the more neutral term"research prigramme", because research can be done to challenge and improve both theories and taxonomies. Popkins' metatheory dictates that theories should be compatible. This idea, however, is incompatible with the history of science. Instead, scientific progress tends to come about when rival theories clash, and when there are many critics on every side.

Take the example of the Copernican revolution. Galileo insisted that Copernicus' heliocentric theory of the solar system be taken as literally true, rather than as merely a possible alternative to Ptolemy's geocentric theory. His insistence won him the retribution of the Church of that time, but the veneration of generations of scientists ever since. Moreover, this change from one contradictory theory to another is generally thought of as a paradigmatic case of scientific progress. Back when Copernicus was insisting that his theory and Ptolemy's were mutually consistent, progress languished. Similarly, one believe that the science of personality will progress most when various theories are found to be mutually contradictory, and the results of scientific tests are used to determine which is superior.

This idea of progress through contradiction can be applied to models of personality. Perhaps the OCEAN and big five models are not all that compatible after all. Certainly one substantive area on which they disagree is the interpretation of the fifth factor--is it intellect or openness? If these models contradict each other, then they almost surely contradict such alternative models as Eysenck and company's psychoticism-extraversion-neuroticism model and Ainsworth and company's attachment styles. Theoretical elaboration on the reasons for these divergences would likely engender progress in the science of personality, just as in other sciences.

FIVE FACTORS, BUT FACTORS OF WHAT

Popkins', five-factor theories of personality is a relatively good introduction to the basic idea, but falls short of being a good survey and analysis of the related literature. He describes one popular set of five factors, the"OCEAN" model, and also discusses some common criticisms of this and factor theories in general. He then"evaluates the theory's greatness" including addressing the issue of its status as a theory or as only a taxonomy.

First"Clinically, the five-factor model works much like Freud's psychoanalysis...." This is a huge error. To make this claim simply on the grounds that both find a problem and then help the patient to deal with it is a logical leap that one cannot make. Psychoanalysis involves many things that are wholly neglected by any factor model, and recognizes the infinite complexity of human character rather than trying to analyse it along a finite number of dimensions. Psychoanalysis looks for the root and exposes it, whereas five-factor treatment could only involve the five surface traits described in the model. In any case, the two are by no means clinically similar. As for the question of theory versus taxonomy, there is no battle to be fought. A taxonomy is simply a specific genre of theory. Psychoanalysis even involves an element of taxonomy in its unconscious-preconscious-conscious model, among other places." As to the question of whether or not a taxonomy in and of itself could ever be considered a great theory of personality, that is a separate issue. Also, the PEN model, considered to be the biological model nor is the issue of the numerous different five-factor models.

Beyond the simple factual errors and elements of related literature that are neglected. Primarily, feel that the aspect of the underlying research is important in evaluating this theory, and this has been almost completely neglected. Only tangentially and with no real explanation in the devoted to the universality of the theory. This is a huge error for a paper intended as an introduction to this theory. The theory was linguistically derived by factor analysis of personality-descriptive terms in natural language, using unabridged dictionaries. The study was done in English, then replicated in other languages, sometimes successfully and sometimes not. This is probably the single most interesting aspect of the five-factor model, and is very helpful in putting this particular theory in the context of other theories.

First of all, the method of research on the five-factor model is subjective. This in itself makes the theory scientifically at least a bit questionable.

Who is to say what words mean? Dictionary definitions say very little of what a word means in context, and nobody, including psychology researchers, or even linguists for that matter, can provide a complete, objective definition of each of these words that takes connotation into account. Even if such a monstrous task were to be mistakenly undertaken, the data set would become impossibly complicated. Describing words with words is hard enough; quantifying them with numbers is kidding oneself.

Beyond the questionable basis of the research, what do the findings really describe? The fact that the study has not been perfectly reproducible in foreign tongues proves what think should have been a predictable outcome from the start: the theory is a cultural one, not a natural one. It is very interesting in itself to study the nature of how we speak about personality in this culture, and think it could reveal some things directly and indirectly about our personalities. It would be even more interesting to study the similarities and differences that the research would show in doing many cross-cultural cross-linguistic studies.

So what does the theory say as it is? It says what we as a culture think it is important and appropriate to talk about in regards to personality. What does this give us? It gives us a way to see how we analyse and discuss each other, and how we might be discussed. It points out characteristics that we see as important. It is, however, very possible that we are not good judges of what is important. It is possible that we know what is important, but that we do not speak of it. For these reasons, the theory fails to say definitively what characteristics are important.

THE BIG FIVE: TAXONOMY OF TRAIT THEORY

Advocates of the"big five" often field criticisms that accuse the taxonomy as not living up to the standards of a"true" theory. Popkins points this out in his paper; still, he continues to assess its validity as a"great theory" in personality, and repeatedly uses the words"theory" and"model" as if they were interchangeable. However, the purpose of a model is to emphasise clearly the concepts that underlie a theory. Although the differing opinions in this matter, support the idea that the big five taxonomy is indeed a model of a much broader theory that continues to be an important influence in personality research: trait theory.

Personality theorists can be classified within two different schools of thought: situational theorists and trait theorists. There are those who, along with social psychologists and behaviourists, believe that environmental factors are key determinants of personality. These"situationists" declare that specific environments reinforce and influence behaviour, ultimately shaping one's personality. Individual differences are explained away by attributing them to"error variance" and responses to a given situation are sometimes explained as species-typical reflexes.

However, it can be seen both in and out of the laboratory that not everyone reacts the same in similar situations. Trait theorists sharply contradict situational theorists by offering an explanation for the "error variance" found between subjects experiencing the same situation. In fact, these individual differences are supported by the existence of traits, which remain stable across numerous situations, and which influence individuals to performance differently when experiencing similar situations. However, individual differences can be quite messy to deal with during an experimental situation. Questions of parsimony arise: How many traits are there? How big are the differences between people? How can one ever classify them all?

Answers to these questions are addressed nicely by Popkins, in a brief history of the development of the big five.

Apparently, these questions were quite relevant, and numerous theorists set off to find their answers. In order to get around the problem of semantics and duplicate meanings, factor analyses and meta-analyses were employed to shave down and coagulate the mess. After much consideration, the big five model was pieced together from existing theories, and offered a concise description of five traits that attempted to encompass the vast realms of the human personality. Indeed, it emphasised trait theory quite nicely, as it suggested very simply that different combinations and gradations of these traits among individuals could influence the way individuals performance in any given situation.

One problem with the big five lies in the fact that it is merely a descriptive taxonomy, lumping together similar behaviours under a common label. Other trait theorists take another route, and attempt to link genetic or anatomical structures to traits, offering putative explanations for why people have differing traits, how they develop, and how they actually influence behaviour. Given that the big five lacks this, its usefulness in a clinical situation is not always trusted. Perhaps linking the big five traits to biological substrates may lend more insight into the treatment of disorders. However, assigning traits and behaviours to specific biological causes is more difficult than it appears, and much of the data resulting from these attempts appear to be more correlative than causal.

Despite problems, descriptive trait taxonomies can be useful in other situations, such as assessing potential employees. The descriptive nature of the big five offers exactly what employers need to choose between similar applications and resumes. Given that the purpose of the big five is to provide correlational evidence between traits and specific behaviours, it may aid an employer to predict which of her applicants is most likely to behave favourably in a given situation. In this way, the big five model serves trait theory quite well.

The big five model is an attempt to organize and to quantify traits, which make up the foundation of trait theory. As a descriptive taxonomy, it helps to support trait theory as a "great idea in personality." However, on its own it lacks the causal explanations that it needs in order for it to be considered a theory in its own right. Nevertheless, it provides a foundation for present and future trait theorists to build on, so that these "great ideas" can be formulated into one great theory.

SEMANTIC AND THEORETICAL CLARIFICATIONS

Most of the responders to this paper had similar questions or qualms. Generally, many of the complaints arose from the use of the terms "theory," "taxonomy," and "model" somewhat interchangeably, as pointed out by both Tasker and Trzop. First of all, the terms "taxonomy" and "model" are both applicable to the big five, and are therefore correctly used as synonyms throughout this paper. The distinction between these two terms and the word "theory," within the context of this paper, is the following: The term "theory" is used at times referring to the evaluation of the big five as a great theory in psychology, whereas the other two terms can be used to describe the big five in any context.

This brings me to another very important semantic point. In the first of these, he questions the two phrases, "[The theory] falls somewhat short of being a great theory in personality because it is not truly a theory," and, "Thorough critical attention is given to the proposal that the five-factor model is in fact a great theory." The first statement is an evaluative conclusion. The second is a proposal, much like a hypothesis, that is eventually debunked.

The second semantic error Tasker points out concerns the statement, " Eysenck developed his PEN model from Cattell's sixteen-factor model." " In reference to Eysenck's PEN model, not to the entire statement, though upon rereading this, the statement clearly makes no sense as it stands. "

Two of the other major problems responders seem to have with the paper revolved around the discussion of compatibility. First of all, Acton disagrees with me on the point that a good theory should be compatible with existing theories. He uses the classic example of the two theories of Ptolemy and

Copernicus to emphasise his point. Unfortunately, argument is based around a dated example that is too archaic to still be valid. The story of Copernicus, Ptolemy, and Galileo unfolded at a time when science was young, and there was much dissent as to the nature of even the most basic facts of science. Although one will not dispute the fact that psychology is a relatively young science, we are no longer at the point at which we believe the heart controls emotions or any such things. That no longer will there be the grand, romantic, Newtonesque epiphanies of Galileo's time; science has come too far for that.

The five-factor model is used similarly to psychoanalysis. Although one will stick to this statement, it requires more explanation. In psychoanalysis, a psychologist uses psychoanalytic theory to find and remedy the problem. The five-factor model is good at locating the problem, but still leaves much of the cure up to the psychologist.

ECONOMIC FACTORS

The economic factors involved in any fisheries management measure will always require their own detailed analysis using tools specifically designed for economic analysis. However, sociological analysis also has to look at the influence and interaction of economic and sociological issues as there are many ways in which these areas are closely linked and sometimes difficult to separate.

ECONOMIC IMPACTS ON SPECIFIC STAKEHOLDER GROUPS

Gender Issues

As women are often involved in very small-scale fisheries, the economic contribution these make can be easily underestimated. In some areas, women have special skills which have developed into important money-earning fisheries. In coastal areas of Bangladesh, for example, women are among the most important producers in the very extensive fishery for shrimp fry which is vital for the expanding shrimp culture industry.

The economic contributions to the fishery made by women may not always be obvious or may be difficult to analyse in the same way as more formal "commercial" enterprises operated by men. Some apparently very unproductive fisheries with little "economic" importance in comparison to other fisheries may be relatively far more important for those actually involved in them. For very poor or vulnerable households, which are often female-headed households, the small amounts of fish they obtain from pushnetting in nearby swamps may play a far more important role in providing them with a livelihood than a much more commercially oriented fishery carried out by other households as one among a range of enterprises and not necessarily the most important.

Sociologists need to assist in first identifying the range of activities carried out by women which contribute to the fisheries economy and in measuring their importance.

Gender-specific Impacts of Fisheries Interventions

Some fisheries interventions can have direct impacts on women's access to the fisheries in which they are active. The effects of interventions or changes can also be more subtle. Involvement of formal fisheries agencies in attempting to develop or regulate the fisheries in which women are engaged may improve the status and productivity of those fisheries and lead to their being taken over by men, at the expense of women's ability to contribute to the household economy.

Where women are displaced from a fishery, for whatever reason, their social status, cultural norms regarding their behaviour and their reproductive roles within the household are likely to affect their mobility and their ability to take up alternative forms of income-generating or income-substituting activities.

Age Issues

Potentially significant economic contributions by young and old people involved in fisheries also need to be considered.

Like women, older people in fishing communities may depend on open access fishing for a relatively important part of their diet even though the amount of fish they catch may be small.

Also, old people sometimes play significant roles in activities servicing the fisheries sector such as the repair of fishing gear and in fish processing. This may be one of the only ways in which older people in fishing communities can contribute to the family's livelihood and be important in maintaining their status within the household. Clearly such contributions can be affected by changes in the types of gear promoted by fisheries development programmes or by the introduction of new fish-processing technology.

INTERACTIONS IN THE LOCAL AND REGIONAL ECONOMY

Sociological analysis of fishing activity at the community level needs to consider a variety of economic factors which are likely to influence the structure of the fishing community, patterns of dependency and patronage and the flows of benefits within the community.

Interdependence of Fisheries and other Economic Activities

In some areas, particularly remote coastal communities, fisheries may be the "motor" of the community which effectively drives all other activities by providing income and employment. In such circumstances, changes which might affect the contribution of the sector to the local economy, or threaten the sustainability of the sector, need to be carefully studied with a full awareness of possible "ripple effects".

The degree to which other activities in the community and surrounding area depend on particular types of fishing activity has to be clearly understood before interventions are recommended which might change the productivity or locations of fishing activity. Apparently minor shifts in the types of fisheries being targeted may result in changes in patterns of handling of catches which can radically change local economies.

For example, a change in the fishery from targeting fish

primarily for processing to targeting fish for fresh sale may lead to a change in landing-place or change in handling procedures which could negatively affect a whole range of sideline activities which may have depended on fish landings - servicing of fishing operations, informal sales of food, cigarettes and other goods, provision of fuelwood for smoking, scavenging of fish discards, and any number of local services could suddenly be deprived of their customers by an "improvement" in fisheries production.

Support Networks for Fisheries

Small-scale fisheries operations are often dependent on flows of resources, notably credit, which are linked to fish marketing channels. The relationships between fishers and credit providers are extremely complex. On the one hand, bonds of obligation and dependence may bind fishers to particular buyers/moneylenders in a way which effectively prevents them from obtaining economic independence. Interest rates, measured by normal financial tools, are often usurious and exploitative.

But frequently these links between primary producers and various middlemen responsible for channelling fish back to the consumer are essential for the support of risky, small-scale operations.

Middlemen/moneylenders are often the only source of easily available credit in remote rural and coastal communities and they often provide flexible terms and a range of other services and assistance which it is difficult for formal credit institutions to imitate. Perhaps most importantly, they may be related to fishers themselves or at least come from the same community, speak the same language and be familiar with the needs and problems of local fishers.

Economic Diversification

The degree of diversification of the economy in areas where fisheries interventions are planned will affect both people's motivations to enter fisheries, in the case of fisheries development programmes, and their ability to find alternative sources of livelihood, in the case of fisheries management programmes.

Sociologists have to take into account the extent to which the economies of fishing communities or particular areas may be linked and integrated with other communities and centres of trade and consumption through such channels. This will enable managers to understand how impacts at different points of the production chain may affect groups and individuals at other points.

Fisheries, particularly coastal marine fisheries, tends to be an activity which "catches" people falling out of other sectors. Therefore fishing pressure is often sensitive to shifts in other sectors which result in people looking for alternative employment. The perception is often that fishing is open to anyone who can afford a net.

Therefore developments in other adjacent sectors need to be carefully looked at in order to understand what is happening in fisheries. Box describes a case from Melanesia where the links between fisheries and other sectors were of considerable importance in determining intensity of exploitation of the fisheries resource and therefore very significant for fisheries managers.

INDEBTEDNESS

Particularly in small-scale fisheries, levels of indebtedness among fishing households can be an important economic factor which managers need to be aware of before considering recommendations which might require further investment of resources among fishers or fish-processors.

Problems can arise where debts are"informal", as is often the case where loans from fish traders or middlemen are concerned. These debts may be difficult to quantify as they are"paid back" through regular sale at preferential prices rather than by any fixed repayment at a set interest rate. However, such debts may still constitute a set of obligations which will be extremely important for fishers as they are also linked with more complex sets of social exchange mechanisms and obligations.

CRITERIA FOR MEASURING BENEFITS AND NEGATIVE IMPACTS

Most introduced changes will generate benefits and negative impacts which need to be measured in order to assess the effects of those interventions. Measurement of these positive and negative impacts in economic terms is clearly important but sociologists also have to assist in identifying benefits and disbenefits as they are perceived by local people. In some cases there may be important benefits which cannot be readily measured in economic terms but which can be very important for local communities.

In some cultures, assumptions that wealth maximisation is a key criteria for engagement in a particular occupation are invalid. In many rural communities greater importance is attached to networks of reciprocal obligations and efforts to raise social status than to accumulating personal wealth and"developing" fishing enterprises through reinvestment. Understanding how people express value and and measure benefits or success is critical if interventions are to be designed which effectively respond to real needs and priorities among local people.

Perceptions of Advantages and Disadvantages of Management

Understanding people's perceptions of what is important is likely to be particularly crucial in fisheries management programmes where fishers and those dependent on fisheries may be asked to renounce immediate benefits with a view to ensuring that the exploitation of the resource as a whole performs better in economic terms and is sustainable into the future.

While the argument in favour of management may seem extremely clear to fisheries scientists and fisheries economists, other forms of argument may be given far higher priority by resource users.

Communities living at a minimum level of subsistence and generating little or no surplus may simply not be able to afford any kind of renunciation of the exploitation of whatever resources are at their disposal, including fish. In such circumstances, fisheries managers' arguments for ensuring the sustainability of resources for the future are unlikely to carry much weight unless supported by tangible alternatives and concrete forms of compensation.

Arguments regarding future economic benefits resulting from current management will also be strongly affected by the extent to which specific groups or communities can control access to the resource being managed.

Compensation—Evaluating the Impacts of Management

Efforts to mitigate the impacts of management measures often rely on monetary compensation as a means of softening the impact on people's livelihoods. In most "developed" economies, such an approach is more likely to be acceptable as the notion of putting a monetary value on people's means of livelihood is more familiar and fairly precise data on earnings can be obtained to help in the evaluation of people's livelihoods. Debate tends to centre around the relative levels of compensation.

However, even in a relatively developed economic context, problems can arise where management measures force people to abandon fisheries altogether. Besides forcing people to change their livelihood, this may also require changes in life-style and place of residence. In these conditions, compensation packages may need to include measures to facilitate the movement of people affected into other occupations and all assistance to overcome the problems which may arise from such a move.

This in turn may require specific programmes of retraining and access to credit facilities. Generally, in more developed economies, there should be more opportunity for fish workers who lose their livelihood as a result of management to invest their compensation package in other sectors and occupations. But support services and access to good advice regarding alternative activities and investment opportunities is likely to be very important.

Compensation—Non-quantifiable Impacts

While the social and cultural boundaries between fishing communities and non-fishing communities in "developed" countries may be less marked than in some "traditional" societies, fishing communities the world over tend to have a distinct identity linked to the nature of the profession. Changes in profession will lead to a loss of social identity which can be very disorienting for the individuals and families involved. In addition, such communities often have cultural practices and sets of beliefs and customs which may risk being lost when shifts are made out of fishing.

The extent to which the customs peculiar to fishing communities represent a part of the nation's cultural heritage, and the value which is attached to such a heritage will depend very much on national priorities. But, in any case, the extent to which such a heritage might be threatened by changes in fisheries, whether through management or development, needs to be assessed as part of the sociological analysis.

In artisanal fisheries, compensation may represent a more complex proposition. Compensation for loss of livelihood is generally viewed as a means for assisting people to establish themselves in alternative occupations. In poor rural areas where alternative economic opportunities are extremely limited, compensation packages may end up being used up by their recipients for short-term survival without any opportunity arising for reinvestment in new, sustainable activities. Movement into alternative occupations may have very little to do with having access to the required capital and more to do with having ties of kinship or traditional associations with people within that occupation.

In some parts of South Asia, in particular, it can be socially and culturally impossible for a fisher to simply change professions, no matter what economic support they are given. It may take generations of gradual change for a shift in occupation to be accepted.

In many high-density rural areas there is often such intense pressure on any form of employment niche that movement at any point within the system is liable to cause considerable disruption all around - for example if fishers want to become agricultural labourers what happens to the people already working as agricultural labourers who they are likely to displace?

The social and cultural impacts and general viability of compensatory packages in "less developed" countries therefore need to be carefully considered. Interventions to limit or eliminate certain types of fishery or significantly change the structure of the sector may have to be inserted into quite complex, integrated programmes which train resource users in alternative occupations and, at the same time, look at the entire local economy to ensure that local livelihood strategies are not seriously compromised by changes in fisheries. Credit availability, small enterprise development and the acquisition of new marketing skills are liable to be key components in any such programme.

COSTS OF FISHERIES DEVELOPMENT AND MANAGEMENT

Most fisheries interventions, whether for development or for management will generally entail costs in terms of the time spent on activities and costs in terms of renounced benefits from other activities. External agencies encouraging communities to undertake management have a responsibility to call stakeholders' attention to these costs and help them to decide how they are likely to be covered.

It is frequently the case that the enthusiasm of a few community members who appreciate the value of management may be able to generate sufficient enthusiasm to initiate management measures on the simple grounds that"conserving natural resource for future generations is a"good thing". Equally frequently, this enthusiasm lasts until people realise that there are real costs involved and that they are expected to bear those costs, at which point management can easily collapse.

Prior discussion of costs and benefits of management, and a community analysis of how to deal with the costs and mitigate their impacts can ensure better sustainability.

DISPOSABLE INCOME

Disposable income is total personal income minus personal current taxes. In national accounts definitions, personal income, minus personal current taxes equals disposable personal income. Subtracting personal outlays yields personal savings.

Restated, consumption expenditure plus savings equals disposable income after accounting for transfers such as payments to children in school or elderly parents' living arrangements.

The marginal propensity to consume is the fraction of a change in disposable income that is consumed. For example, if disposable income rises by $100, and $65 of that $100 is consumed, the MPC is 65%. Restated, the marginal propensity to save is 35%. Discretionary income is income after subtracting taxes and normal expenses to maintain a certain standard of living. It is the amount of an individual's income available for spending after the essentials have been taken care of:

Discretionary income = Gross income–taxes–necessities

Despite the formal, disposable income is commonly used to denote Discretionary income. The meaning should therefore be interpreted from context.

Commonly, disposable income is the amount of"play money" left to spend or save. The Consumer Leverage Ratio is the expression of the ratio of Total Household Debt to Disposable Income.

BUSINESS CYCLE

The term business cycle refers to economy-wide fluctuations in production or economic activity over several months or years.

These fluctuations occur around a long-term growth trend, and typically involve shifts over time between periods of relatively rapid economic growth and periods of relative stagnation or decline.

These fluctuations are often measured using the growth rate of real gross domestic product. Despite being termed cycles, most of these fluctuations in economic activity do not follow a mechanical or predictable periodic pattern.

IDENTIFYING

In 1946, economists Arthur F. Burns and Wesley C. Mitchell provided the now standard definition of business cycles in their book Measuring Business Cycles:

Business cycles are a type of fluctuation found in the aggregate economic activity of nations that organize their work mainly in business enterprises: a cycle consists of expansions occurring at about the same time in many economic activities, followed by similarly general recessions, contractions, and revivals which merge into the expansion phase of the next cycle; in duration, business cycles vary from more than one year to ten or twelve years; they are not divisible into shorter cycles of similar characteristics with amplitudes approximating their own. Business cycles are not merely fluctuations in aggregate economic activity. The critical feature that distinguishes them from the commercial convulsions of earlier centuries or from the seasonal and other short term variations of our own age is that the fluctuations are widely diffused over the economy—its industry, its commercial dealings, and its tangles of finance. The economy of the western world is a system of closely interrelated parts.

He who would understand business cycles must master the workings of an economic system organized largely in a network of free enterprises searching for profit. The problem of how business cycles come about is therefore inseparable from the problem of how a capitalist economy functions.

In the United States, it is generally accepted that the National Bureau of Economic Research is the final arbiter of the dates of the peaks and troughs of the business cycle. An expansion is the period from a trough to a peak, and a recession as the period from a peak to a trough. The NBER identifies a recession as "a significant decline in economic activity spread across the economy, lasting more than a few months, normally visible in real GDP, real income, employment, industrial production".

Cycles or Fluctuations

In recent years economic theory has moved towards the study of economic fluctuation rather than a 'business cycle' —though some economists use the phrase 'business cycle' as a convenient shorthand. For Milton Friedman calling the business cycle a "cycle" is a misnomer, because of its non-cyclical nature. Friedman believed that for the most part, excluding very large supply shocks, business declines are more of a monetary phenomenon.

Rational expectations theory states that no deterministic cycle can persist because it would consistently create arbitrage opportunities. Much economic theory also holds that the economy is usually at or close to equilibrium. These views led to the formulation of the idea that observed economic fluctuations can be modeled as shocks to a system.

In the tradition of Slutsky, business cycles can be viewed as the result of stochastic shocks that on aggregate form a moving average series. However, the recent research employing spectral analysis has confirmed the presence of business cycles in the world GDP dynamics at an acceptable level of statictical significance.

EXPLAINING

The explanation of fluctuations in aggregate economic activity is one of the primary concerns of macroeconomics. The most commonly used framework for explaining such fluctuations is Keynesian economics. In the Keynesian view, business cycles reflect the possibility that the economy may reach short-run equilibrium at levels below or above full employment.

If the economy is operating with less than full employment, i.e., with high unemployment, Keynesian theory states that monetary policy and fiscal policy can have a positive role to play in smoothing the fluctuations of the business cycle.

There are a number of alternative heterodox economic theories of business cycles, largely associated with particular schools or theorists. There are also some divisions and alternative theories within mainstream economics, notably real business cycle theory and credit-based explanations such as debt deflation and the financial instability hypothesis.

Credit/Debt Cycle

One alternative theory is that the primary cause of economic cycles is due to the credit cycle: the net expansion of credit yields economic expansions, while the net contraction causes recessions, and if it persists, depressions. In particular, the bursting of speculative bubbles is seen as the proximate cause of depressions, and this theory places finance and banks at the centre of the business cycle.

A primary theory in this vein is the debt deflation theory of Irving Fisher, which he proposed to explain the Great Depression. A more recent complementary theory is the Financial Instability Hypothesis of Hyman Minsky, and the credit theory of economic cycles is often associated with Post-Keynesian economics such as Steve Keen.

Post-Keynesian economist Hyman Minsky has proposed a explanation of cycles founded on fluctuations in credit, interest rates and financial frailty, called the Financial Instability Hypothesis. In an expansion period, interest rates are low and companies easily borrow money from banks to invest. Banks are not reluctant to grant them loans, because expanding economic activity allows business increasing cash flows and therefore they will be able to easily pay back the loans. This process leads to firms becoming excessively indebted, so that they stop investing, and the economy goes into recession.

While credit causes have not been a primary theory of the economic cycle within the mainstream, they have gained occasional mention, such as cited approvingly by.

Real Business Cycle Theory

Within mainstream economics, Keynesian views have been challenged by real business cycle models in which fluctuations are due to technology shocks. This theory is most associated with Finn E. Kydland and Edward C. Prescott, and more generally the Chicago school of economics. They consider that economic crisis and fluctuations cannot stem from a monetary shock, only from an external shock, such as an innovation.

RBC theory has been categorically rejected by a number of mainstream economists in the Keynesian tradition, such as and Paul Krugman.

Alternative Hypothesis

The remaining explanations given here are generally not considered credible by mainstream economists.

Politically-based Business Cycle

Another set of models tries to derive the business cycle from political decisions. The partisan business cycle suggests that cycles result from the successive elections of administrations with different policy regimes. Regime A adopts expansionary policies, resulting in growth and inflation, but is voted out of office when inflation becomes unacceptably high. The replacement, Regime B, adopts contractionary policies reducing inflation and growth, and the downwards swing of the cycle. It is voted out of office when unemployment is too high, being replaced by Party A.

The political business cycle is an alternative theory stating that when an administration of any hue is elected, it initially adopts a contractionary policy to reduce inflation and gain a reputation for economic competence. It then adopts an expansionary policy in the lead up to the next election, hoping to achieve simultaneously low inflation and unemployment on election day.

The political business cycle theory is strongly linked to the name of Micha³ Kalecki who argued that no democratic government under capitalism would allow the persistence of full employment, so that recessions would be caused by political decisions. Persistent full employment would mean increasing workers' bargaining power to raise wages and to avoid doing unpaid labour, potentially hurting profitability. In recent years, proponents of the "electoral business cycle" theory have argued that incumbent politicians encourage prosperity before elections in order to ensure re-election—and make the citizens pay for it with recessions afterwards.

Marxist Economics

For Marx the economy based on production of commodities to be sold in the market is intrinsically prone to crisis. In the Marxian view profit is the major engine of the market economy, but business profitability has a tendency to fall that recurrently creates crises, in which mass unemployment occurs, businesses fail, remaining capital is centralized and concentrated and profitability is recovered. In the long run these crises tend to be more severe and the system will eventually fail. Some Marxist authors such as Rosa Luxemburg viewed the lack of purchasing power of workers as a cause of a tendency of supply to be larger than demand, creating crisis, in a model that has similarities with the Keynesian one. Indeed a number of modern authors have tried to combine Marx's and Keynes's views. Others have contrarily emphasized basic differences between the Marxian and the Keynesian perspective: while Keynes saw capitalism as a system worth maintaining and susceptible to efficient regulation, Marx viewed capitalism as a historically doomed system that cannot be put under societal control

Austrian School

Economists of the Austrian school argue that business cycles are caused by monetary expansion, which is often created by central banks and the practice of fractional reserve banking in modern economies. Austrian business cycle theory, following the work of Ludwig von Mises and Friedrich Hayek, points to the role of interest rates as the price of investment capital, guiding investment decisions. They argue that in a free-market economy where interest rates are determined by market actors rather than a central bank, interest rates reflect the time preference of lenders and borrowers. Knut Wicksell called this the "natural" interest rate. Adherents to Austrian business cycle theory argue that a central bank is incapable of determining the proper, natural interest rate due to the Local

Knowledge Problem, and the mismatch between the natural rate and the central bank rate distorts the natural equilibrium. If the interest rate is held artificially low by the government or central bank, then the demand for loans will exceed the supply of willing lenders, and if the interest rate is artificially high, the opposite will occur. This pricing misinformation leads investors to misallocate capital, borrowing and investing either too much when interest rates are too low, or too little when the rates are too high.

One of the primary critiques of Austrian business cycle theory is the observation that the United States suffered recurrent economic crises in the 19th century, most notably the Long Depression following the Panic of 1873, prior to the establishment of a U.S. central bank in 1907. Adherents, such as the historian Thomas Woods, rebut this criticism by pointing out that these earlier financial crises were prompted by government and bankers' efforts to expand credit despite restraints imposed by the prevailing gold standard, and are thus consistent with Austrian Business Cycle Theory.

MITIGATING

Most social indicators worsen during economic recessions. As periods of economic stagnation are painful for the many who lose their jobs, there is often political pressure for governments to mitigate recessions. Since the 1940s, following the Keynesian revolution, most governments of developed nations have seen the mitigation of the business cycle as part of the responsibility of government, under the rubric of stabilization policy.

Since in the Keynesian view, recessions are caused by inadequate aggregate demand, when a recession occurs the government should increase the amount of aggregate demand and bring the economy back into equilibrium. This the government can do in two ways, firstly by increasing the money supply and secondly by increasing government spending or cutting taxes.

By contrast, some economists, notably New classical economist Robert Lucas, argue that the welfare cost of business cycles are very small to negligible, and that governments should focus on long-term growth instead of stabilization.

However, Keynesian theory, managing economic policy to smooth out the cycle is a difficult task in a society with a complex economy. Some theorists, notably those who believe in Marxian economics, believe that this difficulty is insurmountable. Karl Marx claimed that recurrent business cycle crises were an inevitable result of the operations of the capitalistic system. In this view, all that the government can do is to change the timing of economic crises. The crisis could also show up in a different form, for example as severe inflation or a steadily increasing government deficit. Worse, by delaying a crisis, government policy is seen as making it more dramatic and thus more painful.

Additionally, since the 1960s neoclassical economists have played down the ability of Keynesian policies to manage an economy. Since the 1960s, economists like Nobel Laureates Milton Friedman and Edmund Phelps have made ground in their arguments that inflationary expectations negate the Phillips curve in the long run. The stagflation of the 1970s provided striking support for their theories, defying the simple Keynesian prediction that recessions and inflation cannot occur together. Friedman has gone so far as to argue that all the central bank of a country should do is to avoid making large mistakes, as he believes they did by contracting the money supply very rapidly in the face of the Wall Street Crash of 1929, in which they made what would have been a recession into the Great Depression.

4

Marketing Planning and Strategy

INTRODUCTION

The Principles of Marketing Tutorials we take all that has been discussed to this point and see how marketers use this information to manage business decisions. In particular, we focus attention on the importance of marketing planning with special attention given to the role marketing strategy plays in the planning process.

For marketers planning is an essential task that must be continually undertaken. Shifting market conditions, including changing customer needs and competitive threats, almost always insure that what worked in the past will not work in the future, thus requiring revisions in how a product is marketed. Marketing planning is also important since it is often a prerequisite for obtaining funding whether one is a marketer in a large corporation seeking additional money for his or her department or is part of a small startup company looking for initial funding.

To aid in our understanding of planning we introduce a key concept in marketing: the Product Life Cycle. As suggested, see the Product Life Cycle offers valuable insight and guidance for marketing decisions. In this tutorial we also discuss different types of marketing strategy that can be followed to meet marketing objectives. Additionally, we look at how innovative products are adopted within a market and how this impacts marketing planning.

IMPORTANCE OF PLANNING

The Principles of Marketing Tutorials, marketers consider many factors when making decisions. Of course the main factors are those directly associated with how customers respond to an organization's marketing efforts, such as how they may react to changes in a product, new advertisements, special pricing promotions, etc.

But when making decisions marketers face other concerns that are not directly customer related.

For instance, we have discussed how marketing decisions may place pressure on other areas of the organization Other examples include:

- As we noted in our definition of marketing back in the What is Marketing? tutorial, decisions must be made with an understanding of the value these provide not only to customers but to the marketing organization. Consequently, marketers must be well aware of how their decisions fit with the overall objectives of the company. For example, a company whose goal is to be the low-price leader may have concerns if the company's marketing department wants to market a very high-end product, since this would go against the reputation and core strengths of the company.
- In the Managing External Forces tutorial, we showed that marketers' decisions may affect peripheral stakeholders who are not directly connected to the marketing organization but have the potential to impact the organization if issues arise that draw their attention.
- Marketing decisions also directly affect an organization's financial condition. Marketers' efforts generate the funds needed for the company to survive, but do so while using company resources, in particular, expenditure of funds. Controls must be put in place to insure the results of what the organization spends through marketing meet expectations.

Because marketing decisions have both internal and external impact, marketers are wise to make their decisions only after engaging in a careful, disciplined planning process. Marketers who make hasty, off-the-cuff decisions without regard to the implications are taking risks that may lead to problems.

Instead, marketing decisions should be made with consideration of how these affect others and the resources required to carry out the plan.

MARKETING PLAN

The central point in planning for marketing decisions is the Marketing Plan.

As we note in the highly detailed How to Write a Marketing Plan tutorial, the plan serves several functions including:

- Forcing marketing personnel to look internally in order to fully understand the results of past marketing decisions.
- Forcing marketing personnel to look externally in order to fully understand the market in which they operate.
- Setting future goals and providing direction for future marketing efforts that everyone within the organization should understand and support.
- Serving as a key component in obtaining funding to pursue new initiatives.

The scope of the Marketing Plan depends on the company and industry. A small technology startup company may, for instance, have a less elaborate plan that is highly flexible to meet the needs of a rapidly changing market.

A more established marketing organization, such a large consumer products firm, may create a very structured plan that clearly identifies all activities that take place over a 12-month period.

Whether the marketer is creating a short plan intended to cover a narrow timeframe or a full-blown document laying out plans for a year or more, any plan requires undertaking significant market research to better understand the market.

COMPONENTS OF THE MARKETING PLAN

The Marketing Plan is often a complex and diverse document that examines many areas.

For most plans the key components found in the document include:

- *Organizational Mission*: Represents the guiding force of an organization by identifying the long-run vision for what the organization hopes to achieve. The mission comes from the top leaders of the organization and often remains unchanged for many years.
- *Objectives*: Reflects what the organization expects to achieve with its marketing efforts. As with the mission, objectives also flow from the top of the organization down to the marketing department. Objectives can be in the form of financial goals or marketing goals.
- *Marketing Strategy*: Achieving objectives requires the marketer engage in marketing decision-making which indicates where resources will be directed. However, before spending begins on individual marketing decisions the marketer needs to establish a general plan of action that summarizes what will be done to reach the stated objectives.
- *Tactical Prigrammes*: Marketing strategy sets the stage for specific actions that will take place. Marketing tactics are the day-to-day actions that marketers undertake and involve the major marketing decision areas. As would be expected, this is the key area of the Marketing Plan since it explains exactly what will be done to reach the organization's objectives.
- *Marketing Budget*: Carrying out marketing tactics almost always means that money must be spent. The marketing budget lays out the spending requirements needed to carry out marketing tactics. While the marketing department may request a certain level of funding they feel is required, in the end it is upper-

management that will have final say on how much financial support will be offered.

MARKETING STRATEGY

The marketing concept of building an organization around the profitable satisfaction of customer needs has helped firms to achieve success in high-growth, moderately competitive markets. However, to be successful in markets in which economic growth has leveled and in which there exist many competitors who follow the marketing concept, a well-developed marketing strategy is required. Such a strategy considers a portfolio of products and takes into account the anticipated moves of competitors in the market.

MARKETING RESEARCH FOR STRATEGIC DECISION-MAKING

The two most common uses of marketing research are for diagnostic analysis to understand the market and the firm's current performance, and opportunity analysis to define any unexploited opportunities for growth. Marketing research studies include consumer studies, distribution studies, semantic scaling, multidimensional scaling, intelligence studies, projections, and conjoint analysis.

A few of these are outlined below:

- *Semantic scaling*: A very simple rating of how consumers perceive the physical attributes of a product, and what the ideal values of those attributes would be. Semantic scaling is not very accurate since the consumers are polled just as to an ordinal ranking so mathematical averaging is not possible. For example, 8 is not necessarily twice as much as 4 in an ordinal ranking system. Furthermore, each person uses the scale differently.
- Multidimensional scaling addresses the problems associated with semantic scaling by polling the consumer for pair-wise comparisons between products or between one product and the ideal. The assumption is that while people cannot report

reliably which attributes drive their choices, they can report perceptions of similarities between brands. However, MDS analyses do not indicate the relative importance between attributes.

- Conjoint analysis infers the relative importance of attributes by presenting consumers with a set of features of two hypothetical products and asking them which product they prefer. This question is repeated over several sets of attribute values. The results allow one to predict which attributes are the more important, the combination of attribute values that is the most preferred. From this information, the expected market share of a given design can be estimated.

MULTI-PRODUCT RESOURCE ALLOCATION

The most common resource allocation methods are:

- Percentage of sales
- Executive judgement
- All-you-can-afford
- Match competitors
- Last year based

Another method is called decision calculus.Managers are asked four questions.

What would sales be with:

- No sales force
- half the current effort
- 50% greater effort
- A saturation level of effort.

From these answers, one can determine the parametres of the S-curve response function and use linear programming techniques to determine resource allocations.

Decision algorithms that result in extreme solutions, such as allocating most of the sales force to one product while neglecting another product often do not yield practical solutions.

For mature products, sales increase very little as a function of advertising expenditures. For newer products however, there is a very positive correlation. Portfolio models may be used to allocate resources among major product lines or business units. The BCG growth-share matrix is one such model.

NEW PRODUCT DIFFUSION CURVE

As a new product diffuses into the market, some types of consumers such as innovators and early adopters buy the product before other consumers. The product adoption follows a trajectory that is shaped like a bell curve and is known as the product diffusion curve. The marketing strategy should take this adoption curve into account and address factors that influence the rate of adoption by the different types of consumers.

DYNAMIC PRODUCT MANAGEMENT STRATEGIES

Two fundamental issues of product management are whether to pioneer or follow, and how to manage the product over its life cycle.

Order of market entry is very important. In fact, the forecasted market share relative to the pioneering brand is the pioneering brand's share divided by the square root of the order of entry. For example, the brand that entered third is forecasted to have 1/"3 times the market share of the first entrant This rule was determined empirically.

The pioneering advantage is obtained from both the supply and demand side. From the supply side, there are raw material advantages, better experience effects to provide a cost advantage, and channel preemption. On the demand side, there is the advantage of familiarity, the chance to set a standard, and the choice of perceptual position. Once a firm gains a pioneering advantage, it can maintain it by improving the product, creating a standard, advertise that it was the first, and introduce a new product in the market that may cannibalize the first but deter other firms from entering.

There also are disadvantages to being the pioneer. Being first allows a competitor to leapfrog the early technology. The incumbent develops inertia in its R&D and may not be a flexible as newcomers. Developing an industry has costs that the pioneer must bear alone, and the way the industry develops and its potential size are not deterministic.

There are four classic price/selling effort strategies:

	Price	
Selling Effort	**Low**	**High**
Low	Necessity Goods	Classic Skim Strategy Vulnerable to new entrants
High	Classic Penetration Strategy	Luxury Goods

In general, products are clustered in the low-low or high-high categories. If a product is in a mixed category, after introduction it will tend to move to the low-low or high-high one. Increasing the breadth of the product line as several advantages.

A firm can better serve multiple segments, it can occupy more of the distributors' shelf space, it offers customers a more complete selection, and it preempts competition. While a wider range of products will cause a firm to cannibalize some of its own sales, it is better to do so oneself rather than let the competition do so.

The drawbacks of broad product lines are reduced volume for each brand, greater manufacturing complexity, increased inventory, more management resources required, more advertising, clutter and confusion in advertising for both customers and distributors.

To increase profits from existing brands, a firm can improve its production efficiency, increase the demand through more users, more uses, and more usage. A firm also can defend its existing base through line extensions, flanker brands, and brand extensions.

TYPES OF MARKETING STRATEGY

One of the most important concepts of the marketing

planning process is the need to develop a cohesive marketing strategy that guides tactical prigrammes for the marketing decision areas.

In marketing there are two levels to strategy formulation:

- General Marketing Strategies
- Decision Area Strategies

GENERAL STRATEGIES

Status Quo

This strategy looks to maintain the marketer's current position in the market, such as maintaining the same level of market share.

Market Exit

This strategy looks to remove the product from the organization's product mix.

This can be accomplished by:

- Selling the product to another organization
- Eliminating the product the company's product offerings

DECISION AREA STRATEGIES

These are used to achieve the General Marketing Strategies by guiding the decisions within important marketing areas.

For example, a General Marketing Strategy that centres on entering a new market with new products may be supported by Decision Area Strategies that include:

- *Target Market Strategy*: Employ segmenting techniques
- *Product Strategy*: Develop new product line
- *Pricing Strategy*: Create price prigrammes that offer lower pricing versus competitors
- *Distribution Strategy*: Use methods to gain access to important distribution partners that service the target market
- *Promotion Strategy*: Create a plan that can quickly build awareness of the product

Achieving the Decision Area Strategies is accomplished through the development of detailed Tactical Prigrammes for each area. For instance, to meet the Pricing Strategy that lowers cost versus competitors' products, the marketer may employ such tactics as: quantity discounts, trade-in allowances or sales volume incentives to distributors.

5

Marketing Information Systems

AN OVERVIEW

The Internet is rapidly changing the way business views marketing information systems. New business models present challenges and opportunities as organizations seek to adopt "ebusiness" methodologies in the search for competitive advantage. Organizations of all sizes are feeling the "ripple effect" of Internet-enabled customers, supply chains and competitors. This pressure is particularly acute in the marketing function where information technology touches the customer and is increasingly becoming the key to creating superior customer value.

The importance of marketing information is particularly apparent as the economy continues to emphasize services as a primary source of value. Services are heavily information dependent. Information is rapidly becoming a service in its own right. Even in industries that are primarily manufacturing in nature, the information content of the final product is rapidly increasing. Mass customization, often described as "one-to-one" marketing or the customizing of products and services for individual customers, is heavily dependent on comprehensive and timely customer information.

Modern marketing organizations, with their focus on the Internet. They create and manage the customer interface where interactions are more virtual than face-toface. They leverage IT technology to integrate and coordinate with customers and business partners to rapidly achieve measurable business results. The emphasis in on the rapid conversion of knowledge into customer value which depends on the ability to develop, deploy, and manage powerful new marketing information systems (MkIS). The key to competitive advantage depends on the firm's ability to convert knowledge into customer relationships, reduced time to market and lower costs

To survive in highly competitive markets, companies need to be able to develop the marketing function and scale it up on "Internet time" with best-of-class decision support solutions for customer relationship management, sales force automation, market research, marketing communications, logistics, and product development.

DEFINITION

'Simply put, a MkIS is a computerized system that is designed to provide an organized flow of information to enable and support the marketing activities of an organization. The MkIS serves collaborative, analytical and operational needs. In the collaborative mode, the MkIS enables managers to share information and work together virtually. In addition, the MkIS can enable marketers to collaborate with customers on product designs and customer requirements. The analytical function is addressed by decision support applications that enable marketers to analyse market data on customers, competitors, technology and general market conditions. These insights are becoming the foundation for the development of marketing strategies and plans. The MkIS addresses operational needs through customer management systems that focus on the day-to-day processing of customer transactions from the initial sale through customer service. MkIS systems are designed to be comprehensive and flexible in nature and to integrate with each other functionally. They are formal, forward looking and essential to the organization's ability to create competitive advantage. The MkIS is the firm's"window on the world" and, increasingly, it is the primary customer interface.

STRATEGIC ROLE OF THE MARKETING INFORMATION SYSTEMS

Historically, the role of the marketing function has been

to support"make and sell" business strategies that emphasized increases in market share over the creation of long-term customer value. This view started to change after World War II with the recognition that satisfying the customer's needs and wants should be the focus of a firm's business activities.

The emphasis on the customer elevated the importance of marketing as a core business function on a par with research and development and production. The marketing function has become the firm's window to the world in the sense that it must monitor the marketing environment for changes in buyer behaviour, competition, technology, economic conditions, and government policies. Marketing is a"strategic" function in that marketing activities enable organizations to identify and adapt to changes in the market environment.

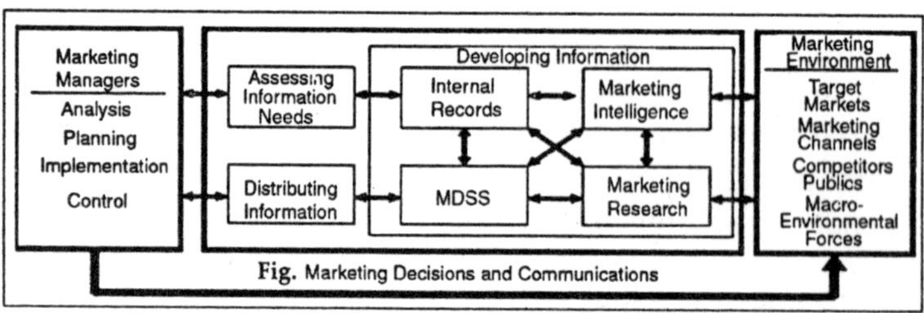

Fig. Marketing Decisions and Communications

The strategic function of marketing is further emphasized as Internet-based technologies have enabled radically new approaches to selling where information technology for th e first time touches customers and provides new means for collecting marketing information. In a knowledge-intensive economy, the ability to collect, analyse and performance upon marketing information more rapidly than the competition is the core competency from which competitive advantage flows. Marketing information systems provide the information technology backbone for the marketing organization's strategic operations.

In a broader sense, the MkIS creates an organized and timely flow of information required by marketing decision makers. It involves the equipment, software, databases, and also the procedures, methodologies and people necessary for the system to meet its organizational objectives. MkIS encompasses a broad spectrum of activities from simple transaction processing complex marketing strategy decision making.

ROLE OF THE INTERNET

Information technology has transformed how firms conduct business. For example, financial service providers such as banks, stockbrokers and insurance companies could not do business today without their client-server-based information technology. This technology has long supported marketing activities. However, it is the recent advent of the Internet, and especially the browserbased World Wide Web, which has ignited a revolution in MkISs.

The term "cybermarketing" is often used to describe the Internet's convergence of computers, information systems, telecommunications and the customer with the marketing process. Internet marketing is characterized by interactivity, graphical user interfaces, multimedia content, and one-to-one connectivity.

Internet technologies are not only providing new ways to reach the customer, but also to enable the reengineering of the entire marketing process and, indeed, the entire enterprise. It is no longer acceptable to view marketing as a standalone activity with lengthy time lapses between product concept, marketing strategy and commercialization. Marketing has become interactive and real time.

The rapidly growing field of marketing automation encompasses customer management functions to support e-commerce. As depicted in Figure, customer management applications include marketing decision support systems, customer relationship management, sales force automation, customer service and e-commerce activities.

These activities are often described as "front office" customer-oriented activities. "Back office" enterprise resource planning (ERP) activities include manufacturing, finance and human resources. "Supply chain management" (SCM) activities encompass electronic procurement, inventory management, quality management and logistics systems to link an organization with its suppliers. These three elements comprise the enterprise information system.

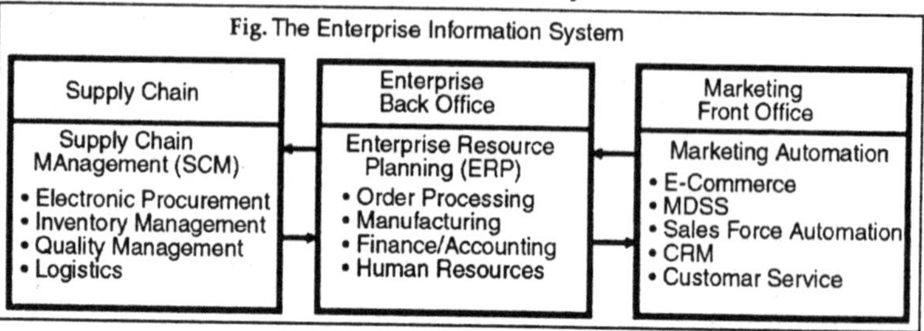

Large integrated enterprise software companies such as Oracle, SAP, PeopleSoft, and IBM address all three major applications and they are beginning to use Web-based technologies to redesign business processes throughout the organization.

The result is leaner organizations, faster response times, and lower costs. Decisionmakers are able to integrate information from customers, suppliers, and the internal organization to obtain an enterprise-wide view of their ability to develop and execute marketing strategy.

Until truly integrated browser-based systems are widely in use, the principal challenge for marketers is to tie e-commerce generated data with legacy information systems in order to create a unified view of each customer. Marketers will need to understand all the various ways that customers are touching the business through existing interfaces and e-commerce.

Many of the older interfaces, such as telemarketing centres, point of sale (POS) systems, and the sales force are likely to be supported by legacy client-server technology. Marketers need to consolidate data from those systems with that from the Web-based ecommerce sources into a holistic view of the customer and make it available to decisionmakers.

BENEFITS OF THE MARKETING INFORMATION SYSTEM

The MkIS increases the number of options available to

decision-makers and supports every element of marketing strategy.

MkIS affects marketing's interfaces with customers, suppliers and other partners. The primary benefits of the MkIS impact in the areas of functional integration, market monitoring, strategy development, and strategy implementation.

- *Market Monitoring*: Through the use of market research and marketing intelligence activities the MkIS can enable the identification of emerging market segments, and the monitoring of the market environment for changes in consumer behaviour, competitor activities, new technologies, economic conditions and governmental policies. Market research is situational in nature and focuses on specific strategic or tactical marketing initiatives. Marketing intelligence is continuous in nature and involves monitoring and analyzing a broad range of market-based activities and information sources. There are three major sources of market information. The first is syndicated data published by market research companies and industry associations. Company-sponsored primary research is another option. It is much more focused ask specific questions of respondents within your markets. But, it is considerably more expensive and time consuming. Perhaps the best data available are your own customer's behaviour captured from web site viewing, point of sale (POS) transactions, and systematic feed back from the sales force.
- *Strategy Development*: The MkIS provides the information necessary to develop marketing strategy. It supports strategy development for new products, product positioning, marketing communications (advertising, public relations, and sales promotion), pricing, personal selling, distribution, customer service and partnerships and alliances. The MkIS provides the foundation for the development

information system-dependent e-commerce strategies.

- *Strategy Implementation*: The MkIS provides support for product launches, enables the coordination of marketing strategies, and is an integral part of sales force automation (SFA), customer relationship management (CRM), and customer service systems implementations. The MkIS enables decisionmakers to more effectively manage the sales force as well as customer relationships. Some customer management software companies are extending their CRM applications to include partner relationship management (PRM) capabilities. This has become increasingly important as many marketers are choosing to outsource important marketing functions and form strategic alliances to address new markets.
- *Functional integration*: The MkIS enables the coordination of activities within the marketing department and between marketing and other organizational functions such as engineering, production, product management, finance, manufacturing, logistics, and customer service.

MARKETING INFORMATION SYSTEM FUNCTIONAL COMPONENTS

As shown in Figure, a MkIS consists of four major components:

1.	User interfaces,	2.	Applications software,
3.	databases,	4.	Systems support.

1. *User Interfaces*: The essential element of the MkIS is the managers who will use the system and the interfaces they need to effectively analyse and use marketing information.

   The design of the system will depend on what type of decisions managers need to make. The interface includes the type of hardware that will be used, the way information is analysed, formatted and displayed, and how reports are to be compiled and distributed. Issues to resolve are ease of use, security, cost, and access.

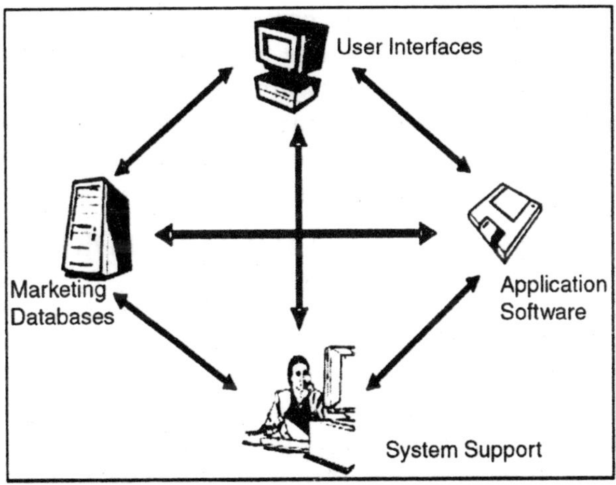

Fig. MIS Functional Components

2. *Applications Software*: These are the prigrammes that marketing decision makers use to collect, analyse, and manage data for the purpose of developing the information necessary for marketing decisions. Examples include the marketing decisions support software (MDSS) and customer management software for on-line sales and customer service
3. *Marketing Databases*: A marketing database is a system in which marketing data files are organized d stored. Data may be collected from internal and external sources. Internal sources largely result from transactions. They provide data from e-commerce sites, sales results, shipping data, inventories, and product profitability. External sources include market research, competitor intelligence, credit bureaus, and financial institutions. Data can be organized in a *flat file* (Text file with one data record per line) or a *relational database* (Data is stored in tabular form where each row represents one entity and each column represents one characteristic of that entity). For instance, each row could represent a customer

with the columns providing name, identification number, and purchase information.

4. *System Support*: This component consists of system managers who manage and maintain the systems assets including software and hardware network, monitor its activities and ensure compliance with organizational policies. This function may also include a help desk for system users.

MARKETING DECISION SUPPORT SYSTEM

Marketing decision support systems (MDSS) constitute a set of core applications of the MkIS. The MDSS provides computer-based tools, models, and techniques to support the marketing manager's decision process. In the general case, MDSS is optimized for queries of historical data. MDSS data typically are derived from both internal and external market sources.

The MDSS features inquiry and report generation functions where the manager can access marketing data, analyse it statistically, and use the results to determine an optimal course of action.

FUNCTIONS

The MDSS can provide analytical models for forecasting, simulation, and optimization. MDSS tools include simple spreadsheets such as Excel, statistical analysis packages such as SPSS and SAS, on-line analytical processing (OLAP) tools, data mining applications, and neural networks. The MDSS provides the user with the ability to explore multiple options.

Typical MDSS functions include models and tools for:

- *Sensitivity analysis*: Decision-makers can explore changes in a strategic variable such as price and model its impact on demand or competitive behaviour.
- *What-if analysis*: Can be easily accomplished with a spreadsheet. Revenues and costs can be manipulated to show the impact of each variable on profits and cash flows.

- *Goal setting*: Analysis focuses on the desired result and builds the resource base necessary to accomplish the goal.
- *Exception reporting*: Analysis looks for results that exceed or fall short of stated goals or benchmarks. Which products or segments exceeded sales forecasts? Sometimes called gap analysis.
- *Pareto analysis*: Analysis looks for activities that generate disproportionate results. For instance, the top 20 per cent of customers may account for 80 per cent of sales revenues.
- *Forecasting models*: Econometric models are used to analyse time series data for the purpose of predicting future sales and market share levels.
- *Simulation models*: Monte Carlo simulations address marketing decision making under conditions of uncertainty. Variables such as the market price, unit variable cost, and quantity sold are not known ahead of the product investment decision. Simulation models allow the marketer to analyse risk and assess the probabilities of likely outcomes of their decisions.
- *Scorecards and dashboards*: Scorecard systems can present a consistent framework for tracking the effectiveness of marketing activities. They often have different modules for senior executives, marketing managers, product managers, and customer service managers. Scorecard systems allow the user to "drill down" on an analytic and workflow basis to determine the status of any strategic initiative. Dashboards allow frontline managers to monitor their critical performance indicators. These systems are often used in conjunction with "best practice" standards for call-centre-based customer support.

MDSS ANALYSES

Marketers typically use MDSS models and tools to analyse markets, customers, competitors, and internal operations.

The following list presents some of the most common types of issues targeted by MDSS analyses:

- *Market segment analysis*: Use of modeling techniques to identify segments and analyse economic trends, demographics and behaviour.
- *Market share analysis*: Analyse trends and determinants of market share.
- *Competitor analysis*: Analysis of competitors' market positions, economics customer base, and marketing strategies.
- *Pricing analysis*: Identifies and analyses the factors that influence a firm's ability to set prices including price elasticity and demand analysis. Includes internal economics and market related factors.
- *Cost analysis:* Studies a firm's overall cost structure and its impact on product cost. Margin analysis combines cost analysis with pricing analysis. Variance analysis looks for explanations of costs overages and underages.
- *Sales analysis*: Studies the distribution of a firm's sales by region, product, brand, sales territory, etc.
- *Sales forecasting:* Develops estimates of sales potential by product, region, sales territory, brand, etc.
- *Sales force productivity*: Studies sales force effectiveness and efficiency and contributing factors.
- *Advertising analysis*: Analyses advertising effectiveness, media choices and brand awareness.
- *Distribution*: Analyses channel decisions from economic and strategic perspectives.
- *Simulation:* Simulates decision making under various strategic scenarios.
- *Customer satisfaction*: Analyses issues concerning the customer's expectations and outcomes with the product.

DATA WAREHOUSING

IBM defines a data warehouse as a place that stores enterprise data designed to facilitate management decisions.

In essence, a data warehouse provides the basis for an analytical system where periodic data points are collected and stored at specified times for future analysis. Data warehousing enables marketers to capture, organize, and store potentially useful data about customers and markets for decision-making purposes.

Every record of a transaction or interaction with a customer, supplier, channel member, or sales person is an opportunity to create knowledge. Firms collect data from these day-today business operations. In order for this data to be useful, it is often organized and stored in a data warehouse. Simply put, a marketing data warehouse is a repository for data that has been collected from internal and external data sources. Each customer generates a stream of transaction records over time. Data sources may include scanner data, billing records, applications, registration forms, warranty forms, call reports, customer service inquiries, and web site data. Data warehousing enables the firm to organize and store this data for analysis purposes. By careful analysis of this and other data, firms can design more effective and efficient ways to serve their customers. Data warehouses exist to support the decision-making process by providing ready access to market and customer data.

The Internet has shifted power away from marketers to customers by lowering search costs and providing greater choice. Competitors are only a "click" away. Consequently, marketers need to work smarter to create and manage the one-to-one relationships that customers desire. This goal requires increased knowledge about customer preferences, behaviours, and value expectations in order to create better products and services. Conversely, marketers need to understand which customers are the most valuable to them over time. They need to regularly monitor and evaluate the "lifetime value" of each customer in order to determine which customers to continue investing in and which ones to drop.

Data Warehouse Processes

Data warehouses can provide narrow or broad strategic

views of key marketing activities for the purpose of generating higher customer value and business returns. Data warehousing activities commonly support customer relationship management, product development, and customer service delivery.

Data warehouse architectures are based on the following three processes:

1. *Data collection*: Processes need to be developed for capturing data from the appropriate internal and external sources and then organizing, verifying, integrating and otherwise preparing it for loading into the database.
2. *Data management*: This step involves formatting and storing that data for easy access by data warehouse users.
3. *Data access*: This process involves specialized tools to query the data, analyse it and create and distribute useful business reports.

Data warehouses are an integral part of the MDSS. They provide the ability to access data for creating marketing operations reports, analyse sales results over time, identifying and mapping patterns, trends, that may be emerging in the market, and enabling the development of new products, pricing, market segmentation strategies, marketing communications campaigns, and distribution channels.

DATA MARTS

A data mart is a scaled-down version of a data warehouse. It is more focused, less complex, and holds a subset of the entire data, often in summary form. It is usually designed for a smaller number of users. They provide fast, specialized access and applications. They are sometimes calld epartmental data warehouses.

Data marts are useful when it is not feasible for a data warehouse to meets the needs of all potential users. Data marts enable a more limited number of users to exert greater control over the data they need. Data marts enable increased data access speed and minimize preemption of user queries. They also minimize performance sacrifices inherent in large data warehouses by enabling small groups to get the data they most need when they need it. They may also include specialized data sets that can be analysed with statistical or data mining tools. Not all the data in the data mart need come from the data warehouse. A marketing researcher may overlay customer purchase histories from the data warehouse with Geographic information system (GIS) data from a commercial service and store it in the data mart.

DATA MINING

Internet-based marketing strategies generate extremely large data sets from customer interactions. Purchase histories, financial records, customer service records, and web site usage are just some of the data that reside in customer databases. In order to transform this mountain of diverse data into operationally useful information, marketers are increasingly using *data mining* procedures. Data mining is the computer-based exploration and analysis of large quantities of data in order to discover meaningful patterns and rules for the purpose of improving marketing, sales, and customer support operations. The combination of data mining procedures with data warehousing enables the MDSS to move beyond just support for the operational processes in the marketing organization and to focus on actual customer behaviour. Data mining and data warehousing provide the means and the infrastructure for extracting strategic opportunity from knowledge of the customer.

Data Mining Process

Large multinational organizations produce much more marketing data per day than its managers can assimilate. The Internet facilitates the rapid growth of data on a worldwide basis. But, exponential growth of data can, paradoxically, lead to a situation where more data leads to less information as managers become swamped by the flood of data that defies ready interpretation. Marketers need to develop procedures for processing, filtering and interpreting this data for strategic marketing purposes. Data mining is essentially the engine for a knowledge-based marketing strategy. It provides the ability to collect, process, disseminate, and performance upon information more rapidly than the competition that is essential to for the creation of first-mover advantage.

The first step in the process is to collect data on what the customer does. On-line transaction processing (OLTP) systems do precisely that. Virtually everything a customer does when purchasing a product or service generates a string of transaction records. If the customer calls an "800" number to order a product, the phone company will capture data on the time of the call, the number dialed and the duration of the call. The marketing company will generate similar data in addition to that on products and services purchased, catalogue referenced, special offers, credit card number, order size, and time since last purchase. Further transactions are generated by the order entry, billing, and shipping systems. The bank and the shipping company will log further transactions. The customer may need to call customer service to solve post-purchase problems. Internet transactions can generate even more data as the customer's purchase behaviour can be linked to web-browsing behaviour within a site and throughout the web. This data can then be linked to purchase histories, financial history and other personal-identity information.

DATA MINING TASKS

After the data have been collected and reside in the data warehouse, approaches to analyzing the data are considered. Data mining methodologies may encompass a range of approaches from rigorous scientific methodologies and hypothesis testing to qualitative sifting through massive amounts of data in search of relationships. The type of analysis typically is a function of the task the researcher wants the data mining exercise to accomplish.

Typical data mining tasks include:

- *Classification*: A predetermined classification code is assigned to a database record. Decision tree analysis techniques are commonly associated with this task.

- *Estimation:* Input data are used to estimate continuous variables such as age, income, and likely behaviours. Neural networks are often used for estimation.
- *Affinity Grouping*: Rules of association are developed from the data and used to group variables that seem to go together. Market basket analysis is a preferred technique that analyses the linkages between items consumers buy in a basket of items.
- *Description*: Summary observations are made about the data that serve to increase the understanding of the phenomena that generated the data. Description often motivates further research and data analysis. Market basket analysis, query tools, and visualization (mapping) techniques are commonly used.
- *Clustering*: Used to segment a large heterogeneous population into homogeneous clusters based on measures of similarity. The researcher must determine the meaning of each cluster. Clustering algorithms are used to analyse the data.
- *Prediction*: Records are classified based on predicted future values or behaviours. Neural networks, market basket analysis, and decision trees are common techniques.

Data Mining Techniques

Researchers looking for behavioural insights in large customer databases commonly use the following data mining techniques:

- *Market Basket Analysis*: Searches for associations in the data such as professional women who drive 5-Series BMWs also use web-enabled mobile phones. The weakness of the technique is there are an infinite number of possible rules in any given database and only a few have marketing importance. The problem is to find them. Techniques works best when the researcher has an idea of what to look for.
- *Cluster Analysis*: Based on the hypothesis that customers of the same type will similar behaviours. K-means cluster analysis is the most common

method. The purpose is to assign objects to groups that are relatively homogeneous within and heterogeneous between.

- *Decision Trees*: Decision trees enable classification for directed data mining. Simple rules are often used to divide the data into subsets in which key attributes can be more readily evaluated. Decision trees can facilitate prediction by linking customer characteristics with purchase behaviours.
- *Query Tools:* Structured Query Language (SQL) is often used for conducting a preliminary analysis of a data set. Data summaries such as simple averages, frequencies, and cross-tabulations are useful for looking for patterns and rules that may form the basis for more structured analyses.
- *Neural Networks:* Neural networks are a class of tools that are used for classification, clustering and prediction. These networks are computer models that simulate the neural connections in the human brain. There are two critical stages for using neural networks—the encoding stage where the network is trained to perform a task and the decoding stage where network executes the assigned task. In practice, these machine learning tools are used to identify loyal customer clusters, find fraudulent credit card transactions, diagnose medical conditions, and predict the failure rate of aircraft engines.

ON-LINE ANALYTICAL PROCESSING (OLAP)

OLAP is a family of analysis and reportgenerating tools that are used to access large databases. It enables partially aggregated data or full reports to be stored in a multidimensional format for fast, convenient access and analysis. OLAP methods are based on databases that allow multidimensional views of business data. OLAP is useful for visualization of relationships between pre-designated variables. OLAP applications are used achieve a higher view of the data such as total sales or profitability by product line, sales territory, or market segment. The OLAP database is usually updated in batch mode from multiple sources. OLAP is optimized for analysis and reporting. In contrast, users of on-line transaction processing (OLTP) applications are involved with creating, updating, or retrieving individual customer records. OLTP databases are optimized for updating transactions.

An OLAP system essentially stores answers to predefined business questions for report generation needs. The user can choose from a predetermined set of options for types of data and display formats. Output is typically in the form of charts, graphs, tables or maps. OLAP solves the problem of distributing information to large numbers of users with diverse reporting needs. OLAP relieves the long response times that can be encountered when many users need to repeatedly query large databases for extended periods of time.

Time series data are probably the most common dimensionality in an OLAP database. Marketers want to look at trends in all aspects of the business—sales trends, market trends, pricing trends, profitability trends, etc. OLAP can compare current results with prior periods, calculate year-to-date results, and present other comparative historical data. OLAP can also present multiple hierarchies and classes within given dimensions. For instance, data may be "drilled down" by "state-county-city-customer" or "sales region-sales district-sales personcustomer."

OLAP may be used in conjunction with data mining, but it is not a substitute. OLAP tools are powerful and fast tools for generating reports on data, whereas data mining tools find patterns in the data. OLAP users are constrained in the questions they can ask since OLAP and only answer the questions that the data formats were designed to address. They cannot go back to the original data and search for new solutions. Therefore, data mining is more powerful than OLAP.

GEOGRAPHICAL INFORMATION SYSTEMS

GIS systems enable marketers to geographically map their customers, competitors, suppliers, sales concentrations, prospects, suppliers and partners. Site selection, trade-area analysis, environmental analysis, territory design, network planning, risk analysis are common applications. Newer (GPS) capability for location reports from resources in motion such as mapping transportation fleet movements, sales representative reporting, and locating and managing key assets in real time. GIS data provide powerful new visualization opportunities for customer data that can link consumer behaviour to a fixed location at a specified time.

Geographical Information System Marketing Applications

- *Customer location*: Links behavioural data from customer master files, subscription lists, support and warranty claims, transaction history and identity with time and location information. This is very powerful information for mapping and predicting consumer behaviour. The advent of mobile ecommerce will enable marketers to identify and map consumers at the actual point of purchase. The wireless carriers will be able to provide this data.
- *Geographic market information*: Links marketing data to physical maps. Data may be classified by county, city, ZIP code, Census tract, etc.
- *Marketing activity location*: Links POS transactions, distribution patterns, direct response results, sales forecasts, advertising expense, etc. to geographic location.
- *Business location:* Labels business facilities on a map that can display retail density, population density, buying power, media coverage, etc.
- *Marketing resource location*: Links assets in motion to physical location through GPS from trucks, autos, aircraft and wireless devices.

CUSTOMER MANAGEMENT SYSTEMS

Companies need a method for viewing all customer and marketing-related information in an integrated way. Often marketing organizations maintain multiple databases for each business and marketing activity with data that is not easily integrated for strategic or operational purposes. A new generation of software that is Internet based gathers information from customer service, Web sites, direct mail operations, telemarketing, field sales, customer service, distributors, retailers and suppliers for the purpose of managing marketing, sales and customer service activities.

The major applications families are commonly referred to as sales force automation (SFA) and customer relationship management (CRM) systems. Some CRM systems are fully integrated with SFA applications and some are standalone. The worldwide market for such systems is projected to grow five times faster than the overall software market, from $5 billion in 1999 to more than $22 billion in 2003.

SALES FORCE AUTOMATION

The fastest growing elements of the MkIS. SFA applications are often integrated with the CRM system. SFA involves the application of information technology to the sales function or, more appropriately, to the activities leading to a sale. These activities include acquiring sales leads, managing the sales opportunity, closing the sale and managing the customer relationship.

The historic role of personal selling has been to move the product—to generate transactions. As selling has become increasingly more professional, sales people emphasize building relationships with customers that will generate loyalty-based repeat transactions over time. Relationship building often necessitates that the sales person has consultative and advisory skills in addition to product knowledge and sales abilities. Team-based selling places emphasis on role specialization, collaboration and coordination. Customers have become more sophisticated as well. Requirements for customised solutions, rapid response times and the need for concurrent and post-sale service have greatly increased the need for information technology in the sales process.

The goals of SFA are to increase the effectiveness of the sales organization, improve its efficiency and to create superior value for the customer. *Sales effectiveness* focuses on getting the sale by improving lead generation, qualifying prospects, coordinating sales efforts, and tracking commitments. Effectiveness is a function of improving the sales process. *Sales efficiency* is evaluated by measuring the return on sales efforts. SFA can improve sales efficiency by reducing sales cycle time, by managing workflow, and tracking the current status of critical activities related to the sale. Proposal generation, opportunity management, fulfillment, and follow up are facilitated by SFA. *Superior customer value* is achieved when the customer expectations are exceeded. It is a primary determinant of customer satisfaction. SFA enables better understanding of customer expectations and management of the customer account.

CUSTOMER RELATIONSHIP MANAGEMENT

The Internet has facilitated a fundamental shift in market power from sellers to buyers. Customers, newly endowed with the power of market information, have much different expectations than before.

Customers can easily move their business to another vendor with the click of a mouse. They have access to the same cost data as their suppliers and they demand 24x7 customer service. Customers now have almost unlimited ability for interactions with organizations through the Web in addition to the traditional phone and mail methods. Company web sites facilitate information search, shopping and customer support. E-mail communication can target specific offers on a one-to-one basis. Understanding and meeting demanding expectations has placed a renewed emphasis on managing customer relationships.

The primary goal of CRM systems is to increase the return on marketing expenditures by enabling the understanding of the complete history of a firm's interactions with its customers. CRM applications can deliver targeted solutions that promote customer loyalty as measured by increased response to promotions, purchase frequencies and volume, and minimizes the time between orders. CRM systems are able to target marketing communications to likely buyers, facilitate sales efforts and deliver customer service. CRM systems increase revenue, lower costs and optimize customer lifetime value.

Design Principles

The CRM field is rapidly evolving into an integrated discipline that manages all of a company's touches with the customer.

Accordingly, several design principles have evolved as the foundation for CRM development:

- The CRM system should offer the customer multiple channels for communication such as the telephone, e-mail, fax, on-line or some combination. Each channel should lead to an interaction that satisfies customer expectations. Customers must be able to choose the method that best meets their needs on each occasion.
- Each CRM interaction should deliver value to the customer. The CRM system must be able to determine what value is required and deliver it quickly whether it is a product or service transaction or a customer service request.
- The CRM system integrates the customer throughout the firm's value chain. Customers should be able to reach into all necessary functions of the organization not just to the sales organization, or customer service, but to manufacturing and even the CEO. Better integration of the customer into the process can lead to higher levels of trust, loyalty and repeat purchases. The cost of acquiring a new customer often far exceeds that of retaining existing ones.
- Knowledge is captured during each CRM interaction. The CRM system should capture knowledge about the customer and the customer's relationship with the company over time. Sales and customer support histories should be analysed for indications of how

well the vendor is doing in meeting customers' needs and how valuable the customer is to the marketer.

Functions

CRM applications provide the customer-related information that is necessary to drive a firm's ebusiness activities. Better customer information enables more effective demand forecasting, product launches and marketing campaigns. CRM functions are sometimes referred to as the company's "front office."

CRM functionality includes:

- E-commerce support
- Sales force automation
- Telesales and call centre automation
- Direct mail and catalog sales
- Email and e-newsletter response
- Web sales and personalization
- Analysis of Web generated data
- Traditional customer support and service
- On-line support and customer service
- Mobile support through laptops, handheld devices.
- Training

Modern CRM systems are fully integrated with the "back office" elements of the enterprise resource planning (ERP) system such as accounting, manufacturing, project management, and human resources. This integration enables the sharing of customer information that can impact the operations of the enterprise and vice versa. Common customer definitions, price lists, employee definitions, service requests, call histories, order histories, contracts, service level agreements are accessible by all who need them. Correspondingly, marketing can access information on items such as new product development, product costs, order status, delivery dates and backorders.

PRIVACY AND THE MARKETING INFORMATION SYSTEM

Privacy in the Internet Age has become a major concern

for customers and marketers alike. Webenabled marketing information systems have the potential to collect highly sensitive and voluminous information on customers, competitors, suppliers and channel members. The speed in which this information can be collected, analysed and acted upon can provide real competitive advantage to the user. This information can be used to better serve customers, streamline a company's operations, and develop better strategy. Some marketers use the data to better target advertising and marketing plans. Others sell or trade the data with other Web sites. Unfortunately, guidelines for how this information is collected, how it may be used, and how it is to be protected are not widely accepted.

Since most non-IS people use privacy, confidentiality and security interchangeable, it is important to clarify some definitions before moving on. Privacy, as marketers define it, is the right not to be contacted or marketed to unless the customer has granted specific permission or "opted in." Security means keeping unauthorized persons from gaining access by breaking into the information system.

Confidentiality is defined as maintaining appropriate controls on information so that only those authorized can access or use it. A marketer may respect a customer's privacy and only contact her after gaining permission, but they may have an insecure system that allows hackers to access credit card transaction data. Alternatively, a marketer may respect privacy rights and have a very secure system, but inadvertently releases a patient's health care record to the news media. In order to avoid these and other pitfalls, marketers must performance to increase system security, establish confidentiality procedures and training, and implement privacy policies.

TRACKING INTERNET USERS

It is axiomatic that no one is anonymous on the Web. At the current state of technology, marketers are able to develop customer profiles and track their behaviour over the Web. Soon marketers will be able to track the locations and behaviours of Web-enabled cell phone and other wireless device users. The public uproar over such capabilities has caused several Web advertising networks to abandon efforts to link Web-use profiles to personal information. In order to track consumers on the Web, enabling IS infrastructure has been developed that links a surfer's Web-behaviour to his Internet Protocol (IP) address. Once that occurs the information gathering begins.

The following infrastructure elements are essential to the information model of the Internet:

- *Advertising networks*: Web-based advertising agencies such as DoubleClick, Engage, and 24/7 create profiles of Web surfers by tracking their on-line behaviours. Ads are customised and presented on-line to those most likely to buy when they visit supported Web sites.
- *Cookies:* A tiny text file that is placed on a consumer's hard drive when they first visit a site. It allows the site to track the user's behaviour on the site. Most Web users are not knowledgeable about cookies. If a consumer removes the cookies from the browser most membership-based sites will prompt for user names and passwords and install another cookie.
- *IP Address*: A number used to identify a consumer's personal computer so that Web data can be sent. These addresses enable profiling and ad targeting. IP addresses can be associated with behavioural and personal information.
- *On-line Profiling*: Web sites build consumer profiles of page viewing, time spent and shopping behaviour by combining cookies with other information. This sounds ominous, but the ostensible reason is to provide better automated service.
- *Personal Information*: This includes the consumer's name, address, credit card number, driver's license number, social security number, and consumer behaviour that is linked to customers personal identity. Most consumers are still reticent about e-commerce because they fear for the safety of their

personal information. Identity theft is a rising problem.

- *Referers*: This is information that a Web browser passes along as a surfer moves from site to site. Referers are commonly collected and used to target advertising.
- *Registrations*: This is personal information that is collected when a consumers fills out a sign-up form on a web site. Data can be sold or shared. Many firms do not closely follow their stated privacy policies with regard to selling customer data.

DEVELOPING A PRIVACY POLICY

Forward-looking Web marketers are at the forefront of the consumer privacy movement. Advertising network firms, such as DoubleClick, were caught on the wrong side of this issue and have suffered greatly in terms of company image and market capitalization. There is a growing realization that Web marketers should post disclosure notices on what information a company collects and how it is used or shared. At present privacy policies vary widely from marketer to marketer and there is no monitoring of their effectiveness. Concerned marketers are reacting to privacy concerns in an attempt to ameliorate consumer fears and to head off potential government regulation.

The major actions marketers are taking include:

- *Disclosure of privacy practices*: Smart marketers should clearly and prominently explain what information is collected, how it is tracked, how it is used, and under what conditions it is disclosed to partners. New technology may help solve the privacy problem. Soon the P3P software standard will allow consumers to set privacy preferences in their browsers that will alert them when a site's privacy policy differs from their desires.
- *Ask permission*: Web users should be able to opt in, especially if the data to be collected is sensitive. Sensitive data include medical information, financial

information, insurance claims, and consumer behaviour that can be traced to the individual by name. Opt-In means the site cannot collect personal information unless the user gives permission. Opt-Out is a default situation where the site collects personal data and is free to use or sell it unless the consumer specifically denies permission

- *Allow access:* Consumers should be allowed access to the personal data each site has collected on them in a manner similar to the access they have to their credit report. Perhaps this can be accomplished by enabling consumers to obtain the aggregated profiles the advertising network firms have constructed. Consumers should be allowed to correct or delete inaccurate data.
- *Establish industry-wide privacy rules:* The On-line Privacy Alliance is an association of leading global companies and trade associations dedicated to the protection of privacy on-line. They are working to educate on-line businesses on the need for a standardized privacy policy to inform customers about what information is being collected, how it is used, how it is protected, and how people can access the information to prevent errors and how to opt-out.

6

Consumer Behaviour

AN OVERVIEW

The study of consumers helps firms and organizations improve their marketing strategies by understanding issues such as how.

- The psychology of how consumers think, feel, reason, and select between different alternatives;
- The psychology of how the consumer is influenced by his or her environment;
- The behaviour of consumers while shopping or making other marketing decisions;
- Limitations in consumer knowledge or information processing abilities influence decisions and marketing outcome;
- How consumer motivation and decision strategies differ between products that differ in their level of importance or interest that they entail for the consumer; and
- How marketers can adapt and improve their marketing campaigns and marketing strategies to more effectively reach the consumer.

One "official" definition of consumer behaviour is "The study of individuals, groups, or organizations and the processes they use to select, secure, use, and dispose of products, services, experiences, or ideas to satisfy needs and the impacts that these processes have on the consumer and society."

Although it is not necessary to memorize this definition, it brings up some useful points:

- Behaviour occurs either for the individual, or in the context of a group or an organization.
- Consumer behaviour involves the use and disposal of products as well as the study of how they are purchased. Product use is often of great interest to the marketer, because this may influence how a product is best positioned or how we can encourage increased consumption. Since many environmental problems result from product disposal this is also an area of interest.
- Consumer behaviour involves services and ideas as well as tangible products.
- The impact of consumer behaviour on society is also of relevance. For example, aggressive marketing of high fat foods, or aggressive marketing of easy credit, may have serious repercussions for the national health and economy.

There are four main applications of consumer behaviour:

- The most obvious is for *marketing strategy*—i.e., for making better marketing campaigns. For example, by understanding that consumers are more receptive to food advertising when they are hungry, we learn to schedule snack advertisements late in the afternoon. By understanding that new products are usually initially adopted by a few consumers and only spread later, and then only gradually, to the rest of the population, we learn that
  - Companies that introduce new products must be well financed so that they can stay afloat until their products become a commercial success and
  - It is important to please initial customers, since they will in turn influence many subsequent customers' brand choices.
- A second application is *public policy*. In the 1980s, Accutane, a near miracle cure for acne, was introduced. Unfortunately, Accutane resulted in

severe birth defects if taken by pregnant women. Although physicians were instructed to warn their female patients of this, a number still became pregnant while taking the drug. To get consumers' attention, the Federal Drug Administration took the step of requiring that very graphic pictures of deformed babies be shown on the medicine containers.

- *Social marketing* involves getting ideas across to consumers rather than selling something. Marty Fishbein went on sabbatical to work for the Centres for Disease Control trying to reduce the incidence of transmission of diseases through illegal drug use. The best solution, obviously, would be if we could get illegal drug users to stop. This, however, was deemed to be infeasible. It was also determined that the practice of sharing needles was too ingrained in the drug culture to be stopped. As a result, using knowledge of consumer attitudes, Dr. Fishbein created a campaign that encouraged the cleaning of needles in bleach before sharing them, a goal that was believed to be more realistic.
- As a final benefit, studying consumer behaviour should make us better consumers. Common sense suggests, for example, that if you buy a 64 liquid ounce bottle of laundry detergent, you should pay less per ounce than if you bought two 32 ounce bottles. In practice, however, you often pay a size *premium* by buying the larger quantity. In other words, in this case, knowing this fact will sensitize you to the need to check the unit cost labels to determine if you are *really* getting a bargain.

There are several units in the market that can be analysed. Our main thrust in this course is the *consumer*. However, as suggested, also need to analyse our own firm's strengths and weaknesses and those of *competing firms*. Suppose, for example, that we make a product aimed at older consumers, a growing segment. A competing firm that targets babies, a shrinking market, is likely to consider repositioning toward our market. To assess a competing firm's potential threat, we need to examine its assets against pressures it faces from the market. Finally, we need to assess conditions. For example, although we may have developed a product that offers great appeal for consumers, a recession may cut demand dramatically.

CONSUMER RESEARCH METHODS

Market research is often needed to ensure that we produce what customers really want and not what we *think* they want.

Primary vs. secondary research methods. There are two main approaches to marketing. *Secondary* research involves using information that others have already put together. For example, if you are thinking about starting a business making clothes for tall people. *Primary* research, in contrast, is research that you design and conduct yourself. For example, you may need to find out whether consumers would prefer that your soft drinks be sweater or tarter.

Research will often help us *reduce risks* associated with a new product, but it *cannot take the risk away entirely*. It is also important to ascertain whether the research has been complete. For example, Coca Cola did a great deal of research prior to releasing the New Coke, and consumers seemed to prefer the taste. However, consumers were *not* prepared to have this drink replace traditional Coke. Sources of influence on the consumer. The consumer faces numerous sources of influence.

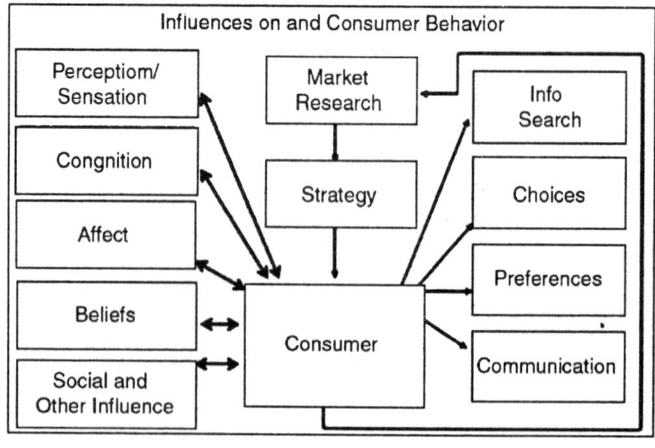

Often, we take cultural influences for granted, but they are significant. An American will usually not bargain with a store owner. This, however, is a common practice in much of the World. Physical factors also influence our behaviour. We are more likely to buy a soft drink when we are thirsty, for example, and food manufacturers have found that it is more effective to advertise their products on the radio in the late afternoon when people are getting hungry.

A person's self-image will also tend to influence what he or she will buy-an upwardly mobile manager may buy a flashy car to project an image of success. Social factors also influence what the consumers buy-often, consumers seek to imitate others whom they admire, and may buy the same brands. The social environment can include both the mainstream culture and a subculture. Thus, sneaker manufacturers are eager to have their products worn by admired athletes. Finally, consumer behaviour is influenced by learning-you try a hamburger and learn that it satisfies your hunger and tastes good, and the next time you are hungry, you may consider another hamburger.

CONSUMER CHOICE AND DECISION-MAKING: PROBLEM

One model of consumer decision making involves several steps. The first one is problem recognition-you realise that something is not as it should be. Perhaps, for example, your car is getting more difficult to start and is not accelerating well. The second step is information search-what are some alternative ways of solving the problem? You might buy a new car, buy a used car, take your car in for repair, ride the bus, ride a taxi, or ride a skateboard to work. The third step involves evaluation of alternatives. A skateboard is inexpensive, but may be ill-suited for long distances and for rainy days. Finally, we have the purchase stage, and sometimes a post-purchase stage. In reality, people may go back and forth between the stages. For example, a person may resume alternative identification during while evaluating already known alternatives.

Consumer involvement will tend to vary dramatically depending on the type of product. In general, consumer involvement will be higher for products that are very expensive or are highly significant in the consumer's life in some other way.

It is important to consider the consumer's motivation for buying products. To achieve this goal, we can use the Means-End chain, wherein we consider a logical progression of consequences of product use that eventually lead to desired end benefit. Thus, for example, a consumer may see that a car has a large engine, leading to fast acceleration, leading to a feeling of performance, leading to a feeling of power, which ultimately improves the consumer's self-esteem. A handgun may aim bullets with precision, which enables the user to kill an intruder, which means that the intruder will not be able to harm the consumer's family, which achieves the desired end-state of security. In advertising, it is important to portray the desired end-states. Focusing on the large motor will do less good than portraying a successful person driving the car.

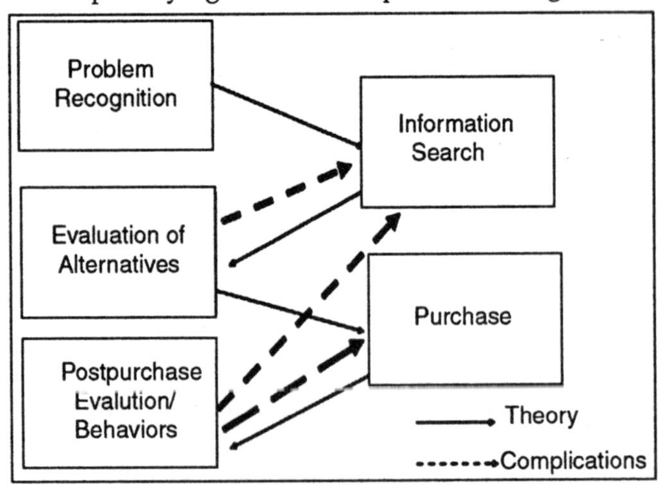

INFORMATION SEARCH AND DECISION-MAKING

Consumers engage in both internal and external information search. Internal search involves the consumer identifying alternatives from his or her memory. For certain low involvement products, it is very important that marketing prigrammes achieve"top of mind" awareness. For example, few people will search the Yellow Pages for fast food restaurants; thus, the consumer must be able to retrieve one's restaurant from memory before it will be considered. For high involvement products, consumers are more likely to use an external search. Before buying a car, for example, the consumer may ask friends' opinions, read reviews in Consumer Reports, consult several web sites, and visit several dealerships. Thus, firms that make products that are selected predominantly through external search must invest in having information available to the consumer in need-e.g., through brochures, web sites, or news coverage.

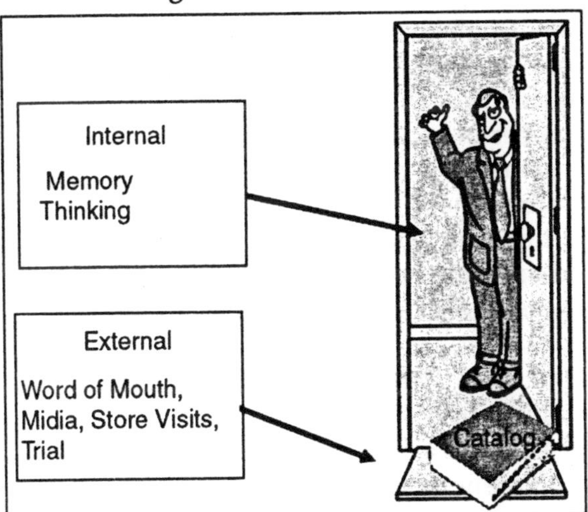

A compensatory decision involves the consumer"trading off" good and bad attributes of a product. For example, a car may have a low price and good gas mileage but slow acceleration. If the price is sufficiently inexpensive and gas efficient, the consumer may then select it over a car with better acceleration that costs more and uses more gas. Occasionally, a decision will involve a non-compensatory strategy. For example, a parent may reject all soft drinks that contain artificial sweeteners. Here, other good features such as taste and low calories cannot overcome this one"non-negotiable" attribute.

The amount of effort a consumer puts into searching depends on a number of factors such as the market, product characteristics, consumer characteristics, and situational characteristics.

Two interesting issues in decisions are:

- *Variety seeking* where consumers seek to try new brands not because these brands are expected to be "better" in any way, but rather because the consumer wants a "change of pace," and
- *"Impulse" purchases*—unplanned buys. This represents a somewhat "fuzzy" group. For example, a shopper may plan to buy vegetables but only decide in the store to actually buy broccoli and corn. Alternatively, a person may buy an item which is currently on sale, or one that he or she remembers that is needed only once inside the store.

A number of factors involve consumer choices. In some cases, consumers will be more *motivated*. For example, one may be more careful choosing a gift for an in-law than when buying the same thing for one self. Some consumers are also more motivated to *comparison shop* for the best prices, while others are more *convenience* oriented. *Personality* impacts decisions. Some like variety more than others, and some are more receptive to stimulation and excitement in trying new stores. *Perception* influences decisions.

Some people, for example, can taste the difference between generic and name brand foods while many cannot. *Selective* perception occurs when a person is paying attention only to information of interest. For example, when looking for a new car, the consumer may pay more attention to car ads than when this is not in the horizon. Some consumers are put off by perceived *risk*.

Thus, many marketers offer a money back guarantee. Consumers will tend to change their behaviour through *learning*—e.g., they will avoid restaurants they have found to be crowded and will settle on brands that best meet their tastes.

Consumers differ in the *values* they hold. As suggested, consider the issue of lifestyle under segmentation.

ORGANIZATIONAL BUYERS

A large portion of the market for goods and services is attributable to *organizational,* as opposed to individual, buyers. In general, organizational buyers, who make buying decisions for their companies for a living, tend to be somewhat more sophisticated than ordinary consumers. However, these organizational buyers are also often more risk averse. There is a risk in going with a new, possibly better supplier whose product is unproven and may turn out to be problematic. Often the fear of running this risk is greater than the potential rewards for getting a better deal. In the old days, it used to be said that "You can't get fired for buying IBM." This attitude is beginning to soften a bit today as firms face increasing pressures to cut costs.

Organizational buyers come in several forms. *Resellers* involve either wholesalers or retailers that buy from one organization and resell to some other entity. For example, large grocery chains sometimes buy products directly from the manufacturer and resell them to end-consumers. Wholesalers may sell to retailers who in turn sell to consumers. *Producers* also buy products from sub-manufacturers to create a finished product. For example, rather than manufacturing the parts themselves, computer manufacturers often buy hard drives, motherboards, cases, monitors, keyboards, and other components from manufacturers and put them together to create a finished product. *Governments* buy a great deal of things. For example, the military needs an incredible amount of supplies to feed and equip troops. Finally, large *institutions* buy products in huge quantities. For example, UCR probably buys thousands of reams of paper every month.

Organizational buying usually involves more people than individual buying.

Often, many people are involved in making decisions as to:

- Whether to buy,
- What to buy,

- At what quantity, and
- From whom.

An engineer may make a specification as to what is needed, which may be approved by a manager, with the final purchase being made by a purchase specialist who spends all his or her time finding the best deal on the goods that the organization needs.

Often, such long purchase processes can cause long delays. In the government, rules are often especially stringent—e.g., vendors of fruit cake have to meet fourteen pages of specifications put out by the General Services Administration. In many cases, government buyers are also heavily bound to go with the lowest price. Even if it is obvious that a higher priced vendor will offer a superior product, it may be difficult to accept that bid.

CUSTOMER VALUE AND SATISFACTION

CUSTOMER VALUE

As it is used in the business world, customer value is the amount of benefit that a customer will get from a service or product relative to its cost. Some businesspeople explain customer value as "realization" compared to "sacrifice." Realization is a formal term for what customers get out of their purchases. Sacrifice is what they pay for the product or service.

Businesses of all sizes use customer value as part of a greater analysis to determine how well they are supplying their customer base. Detailed research might include what customers generally do with the products they receive, or how they use services to increase the value of assets like real estate. Businesses also look at the prices of their products in order to price them competitively.

Businesses that identify the value of their wares to customers might go a step further and consider other similar ideas. In order to generate more thought about customer value, and to reach out to a customer base, a business might promote a customer value proposition. The customer value proposition is basically a promise of benefits from a vendor to customers.

We see examples of customer value propositions all the time in advertising. Companies pinpoint the benefits that they believe a customer will realise, and display them in advertising to attract more customers. The question is whether these propositions are made in good faith, or whether they may not be entirely true. When business leaders and others are talking about customer value, it is important that everyone at the table understands that customer value does not relate to the value of customers, but to the value that customers receive from the business. Those who are talking about how valuable customers are to a business might use terms like customer retention, or refer to the customer base as "valued customers," or VIPs. Since customer service is also a critical element for many businesses, it's possible that these two ideas might sometimes get confused.

Along with the basic idea of customer value, other terms help further define that value precisely. Relative performance identifies how the product or service gives customer value relative to what competitors offer. Access cost is something that business analysts add into the mix as an estimated cost of the effort involved in purchase. Value propositions often include these levels of detail to help leaders look at how well a business is serving its intended audience.

SATISFACTION

Customer satisfaction, a business term, is a measure of how products and services supplied by a company meet or surpass customer expectation. It is seen as a key performance indicator within business and is part of the four of a Balanced Scorecard. In a competitive marketplace where businesses compete for customers, customer satisfaction is seen as a key differentiator and increasingly has become a key element of business strategy. There is a substantial body of empirical literature that establishes the benefits of customer satisfaction for firms.

Measuring Customer Satisfaction

Organizations need to retain existing customers while

targeting non-customers;. Measuring customer satisfaction provides an indication of how successful the organization is at providing products and/or services to the marketplace.

Customer satisfaction is an abstract concept and the actual manifestation of the state of satisfaction will vary from person to person and product/service to product/service. The state of satisfaction depends on a number of both psychological and physical variables which correlate with satisfaction behaviours such as return and recommend rate. The level of satisfaction can also vary depending on other factors the customer, such as other products against which the customer can compare the organization's products.

Work done by Parasuraman, Zeithaml and Berry between 1985 and 1988 delivered SERVQUAL which provides the basis for the measurement of customer satisfaction with a service by using the gap between the customer's expectation of performance and their perceived experience of performance. This provides the researcher with a satisfaction "gap" which is semi-quantitative in nature. Cronin and Taylor extended the disconfirmation theory by combining the "gap" described by Parasuraman, Zeithaml and Berry as two different measures into a single measurement of performance relative to expectation.

The usual measures of customer satisfaction involve a survey with a set of statements using a Likert Technique or scale. The customer is asked to evaluate each statement in terms of their perception and expectation of performance of the service being measured.

Improving Customer Satisfaction

Published standards exist to help organizations develop their current levels of customer satisfaction. The International Customer Service Institute has released The International Customer Service Standard. TICSS enables organizations to focus their attention on delivering excellence in the management of customer service, whilst at the same time providing recognition of success through a 3rd Party registration plan. TICSS focuses an organization's attention on delivering increased customer satisfaction by helping the organization through a Service Quality Model.

TICSS Service Quality Model uses the 5 P's - Policy, Processes, People, Premises, Product/Services, as well as performance measurement. The implementation of a customer service standard should lead to higher levels of customer satisfaction, which in turn influences customer retention and customer loyalty.

CONSUMERISM

Consumerism is a social and economic order that is based on the systematic creation and fostering of a desire to purchase goods or services in ever greater amounts. The term is often associated with criticisms of consumption starting with Thorstein Veblen or, more recently by a movement called Enoughism. Veblen's subject of examination, the newly emergent middle class arising at the turn of the twentieth century, comes to full fruition by the end of the twentieth century through the process of globalization.

In economics, consumerism refers to economic policies placing emphasis on consumption. In an abstract sense, it is the belief that the free choice of consumers should dictate the economic structure of a society.

FACTORS INFLUENCING CONSUMER BEHAVIOUR

Consumer purchases are influenced strongly by or there are four factors.

1.	Cultural Factor	2.	Social Factor
3.	Personal Factor	4.	Psychological Factor.

CULTURAL FACTOR

Cultural factor divided into three sub factors:

1. Culture
2. Sub Culture
3. Social Class

- *Culture:*

  - The set of basic values perceptions, wants, and behaviours learned by a member of society from family and other important institutions. Culture is the most basic cause of a person's wants and behaviour. Every group or society has a culture, and cultural influences on buying behaviour may vary greatly from country to country.
- *Sub Culture*:
  - A group of people with shared value systems based on common life experiences and situations.
  - Each culture contains smaller sub cultures a group of people with shared value system based on common life experiences and situations. Sub culture includes nationalities, religions, racial group and geographic regions. Many sub culture make up important market segments and marketers often design products.
- *Social Class*:
  - Almost every society has some form of social structure, social classes are society's relatively permanent and ordered divisions whose members share similar values, interests and behaviour.

SOCIAL FACTORS

A consumer's behaviour also is influenced by social factors, such as the:

1. Groups
2. Family
3. Roles and status

- *Groups*:
  - Two or more people who interact to accomplish individual or mutual goals.
  - A person's behavious is influenced by many small groups. Groups that have a direct influence and to which a person belongs are called membership groups.
  - Some are primary groups includes family,

friends, neighbours and coworkers. Some are secondary groups, which are more formal and have less regular interaction. These includes organizations like religious groups, professional association and trade unions.

- *Family*:

  Family members can strongly influence buyer behaviour. The family is the most important consumer buying organization society and it has been researched extensively. Marketers are interested in the roles, and influence of the husband, wife and children on the purchase of different products and services.

- *Roles and Status*:
  - A person belongs to many groups, family, clubs, organizations.
  - The person's position in each group can be defined in terms of both role and status.
  - For example. M & "X" plays the role of father, in his family he plays the role of husband, in his company, he plays the role of manager, etc. A Role consists of the activities people are expected to perform just as to the persons around them.

PERSONAL FACTORS

- *It includes*:

  (i) Age and life cycle stage

  (ii) Occupation

  (iii) Economic situation

  (iv) Life Style

  (v) Personality and self concept.

  - *Age and Life cycle Stage*:
    a. People changes the goods and services they buy over their lifetimes. Tastes in food, clothes, furniture, and recreation are often age related. Buying is also shaped by the stage of the family life cycle.
  - *Occupation*:

a. A person's occupation affects the goods and services bought. Blue collar workers tend to buy more rugged work clothes, whereas white-collar workers buy more business suits. A Co. can even specialize in making products needed by a given occupational group. Thus, computer software companies will design different products for brand managers, accountants, engineers, lawyers, and doctors.

- *Economic situation:*
  a. A person's economic situation will affect product choice
- *Life Style:*
  a. Life Style is a person's Pattern of living, understanding these forces involves measuring consumer's major AIO dimensions.
  b. i.e. activities interest and opinions
- *Personality and Self concept*:
  a. Each person's distinct personality influence his or her buying behaviour. Personality refers to the unique psychological characteristics that lead to relatively consistent and lasting responses to one's own environment.

PSYCHOLOGICAL FACTORS

- It includes these Factors.
  (i) Motivation
  (ii) Perception
  (iii) Learning
  (iv) Beliefs and attitudes
- *Motivation*:
  - Motive a need that is sufficiently pressing to direct the person to seek satisfaction of the need
- *Perception*:
  - The process by which people select, Organize, and interpret information to form a meaningful picture of the world.
- *Learning*:

  - Changes in an individuals behaviour arising from experience.
- *Beliefs and attitudes:*
  - Belief is a descriptive thought that a person holds about something
  - Attitude, a Person's consistently favourable or unfavourable evaluations, feelings, and tendencies towards an object or idea

CONSUMER BUYING BEHAVIOUR

Consumer Buying Behaviour the decision processes and acts of final household consumers associated with evaluating, buying, consuming, and discarding products for personal consumption.

Consider the purchase an automobile. You generally will not consider different options until some event triggers a need, such as a problem needing potentially expensive repair. Once this need has put you "on the market", you begin to ask your friends for recommendations regarding dealerships and car models.

After visiting several dealerships, you test drive several models and finally decide on a particular model. After picking up your new car, you have doubts on the way home, wondering if you can afford the monthly payments, but then begin to wonder if instead you should have purchased a more expensive but potentially more reliable model.

Over the next five years, the car has several unexpected breakdowns that lead you to want to purchase a different brand, but you have been very happy with the services of the local dealership and decide to again purchase your next car there.

In this particular case, the following generic model of consumer decision making appears to hold:

- Need recognition
- Information search
- Evaluation of alternatives
- Purchase decision
- Postpurchase behaviour

Now consider the purchase of a quart of orange juice. This product when you do your grocery shopping once per week. You have a favourite brand of orange juice and usually do your grocery shopping at the same store. When you buy orange juice, you always go to the same place in the store to pick it up, and never notice what other brands are on the shelf or what are the prices of other brands. How is it that the generic model works differently in this second scenario? Why does it work differently? Why would we generally need the ministrations of a sales person in the sale of a car, but we generally do not need the help of a salesperson in the purchase of orange juice?

How can the marketer of orange juice get a consumer like you to exert more effort into information search or to consider alternative products? How is it that the marketer of your brand got you to ignore alternative competing brands? What is the involvement of salespeople in *sales promotions* that might be associated with products such as orange juice? Consumer behaviour researchers are not so interested in studying the validity of the above generic model, but are more interested in various factors that influence how such a model might work.

GROUP INFLUENCES ON CONSUMER BEHAVIOUR

Culture

Culture the set of basic values, beliefs, norms, and associated behaviours that are learned by a member of society

Note that culture is something that is *learned* and that it has a relatively long lasting effect on the behaviours of an individual. As an example of cultural influences, consider how the salesperson in an appliance store in the U.S. must react to different couples who are considering the purchase of a refrigerator. In some subcultures, the husband will play a dominant role in the purchase decision; in others, the wife will play a more dominant role.

Social Class

Social Class a group of individuals with similar social rank, based on such factors as *occupation, education,* and *wealth*

Reference Groups

Reference groups, often temporary, that affect a person's values, attitude, or behaviours:

- E.g., your behaviours around colleagues at work or friends at school are probably different from your behaviours around your parents, no matter your age or stage in the family life cycle. If you were a used car salesperson, how might you respond differently to a nineteen year old prospect accompanied by her boyfriend from one accompanied by two girlfriends?
- Opinion leadera person within a reference group who exerts influence on others because of special skills, knowledge, personality, etc.
  - You might ask the webmaster at work for an opinion about a particular software application. Software manufacturers often give away free beta copies of software to potential opinion leaders with the hope that they will in turn influence many others to purchase the product.

Family

Family a group of people related by blood, marraige, or other socially approved relationship

INTERNAL INFLUENCES ON CONSUMER BEHAVIOUR

Personality

Personality a person's distinguishing psychological characteristics that lead to relatively consistent and lasting responses to stimuli in the environment

We are each unique as individuals, and we each respond differently as consumers. For example, some people are "optimizers" who will keep shopping until they are certain that they have found the best price for a particular item, while other people are "satisficers" who will stop shopping when they believe that they have found something that is "good enough." If you are a salesperson in a retail shoe store, how might you work differently with these two personalities?

Lifestyle and Psychographics

- Lifestyle is a pattern of living expressed through a person's activities, interests, and opinions
- Psychographics is a technique for measuring personality and lifestyles to developing lifestyle classifications

Motivation: Multiple Motives

Consumers usually have multiple motives for particular behaviours. These can be a combination of:

- Manifest known to the person and freely admitted
- Latent unknown to the person or the person is very reluctant to admit

Note: different motives can lead to the same behaviour; observing behaviour is not sufficient to determine motives.

Involvement

Involvement has to do with an individual's:

- *Intensity of interest* in a product and the
- *Importance* of the product for that person

The purchase of a car is much more risky than the purchase of a quart of orange juice, and therefore presents a higher involvement situation. This modifies the way that the generic model works.

As involvement increases, consumers have greater motivation to comprehend and elaborate on information salient to the purchase. A life insurance agent, for example, would typically be more interested in contacting a young couple who just had a baby than an eighteen year old college student - even though the new parents might be struggling to make ends meet while the student is living more comfortably. Although the annual investment into a policy is much lower if started at a younger age, most young college students are not open to thinking about long term estate planning. A young couple with a new child, however, is much more open to thinking about issues associated with planning for the child's future education, saving to buy a house, or even saving to take an extended vacation upon retirement.

TYPES OF CONSUMER PROBLEM-SOLVING PROCESSES

Routenized

- Used when buying frequently purchased, low cost items
- Used when little search/decision effort is needed
- E.g., buying a quart of orange juice once per week

Limited Problem Solving

- Used when products are occasionally purchased
- Used when information is needed about an unfamiliar product in a familiar product category

Extended Problem Solving

- Used when product is unfamiliar, expensive, or infrequently purchased
- E.g., buying a new car once every five years

POST-PURCHASE CONSUMER BEHAVIOUR

Satisfaction

After the sale, the buyer will likely feel either satisfied or dissatisfied. If the buyer beleives that s/he received more in the exchange than what was paid, s/he might feel satisfied. If s/he believes that s/he received less in the exchange than what was paid, then s/he might feel dissatisfied. Dissatisfied buyers are not likely to return as customers and are not likely to send friends, relatives, and acquaintences. They are also more likely to be unhappy or even abusive when the product requires post-sale servicing, as when an automobile needs warranty maintenance.

The idea can be modeled as Homans' basic exchange equation:

Profit = Rewards–Costs

Unfortunately, even a buyer who "got a good deal" with respect to price and other terms of the sale might feel dissatisfied under the perception that the salesperson made out even better.

This idea is called equity theory, where we are concerned with:

Outcomes of A Inputs of A

vs.

Outcomes of B Inputs of B

Consider value is listed at $16,000. You are probably delighted with the purchase until you accidentally meet the prior owner who had received a trade-in of $10,000 on the car just a few days before. That the dealer appears to have received substantially greater benefit than you could lead to extreme dissatisfaction, even though you received good value for the money spent.

An issue related to this is attribution theory. Attribution theory, people tend to assign cause to the behaviour of others. Mary's life insurance agent advises her to purchase a whole life policy, while her accountant advises her, "buy term insurance and invest the difference.". The reason, explains the accountant, "is that insurance agents receive substantially higher commission payments on sales of whole life policies."

If Mary believes that the insurance agent is recommending a product merely because he receives a higher commission, she will likely be displeased with the relationship and will not take his recommendation. If the agent is able to show Mary that the recommended product is the best solution for her situation, then she will likely attribute his recommendation to having her best interests in mind and will not be concerned about how it is that he is compensated for his services.

Cognitive Dissonance

cognitive dissonance has to do with the doubt that a person has about the wisdom of a recent purchase.

It is very common for people to experience some anxiety after the purchase of a product that is very expensive or that will require a long term commitment. Jane and Fred, for example, signed a one year lease on an apartment, committing themselves to payments of $1500 per month. A week later, they are wondering if they should have instead leased a smaller $900 apartment in a more rough part of town; they are not sure if they really can afford this much of a monthly obligation. Dick and Sally, on the other hand, ultimately rented the $900 apartment, and now are wondering if the savings in rent will be offset by noisy and sometimes unsafe conditions in this neighbourhood.

Perhaps neither couple would be experiencing this anxiety if their landlords had given them just the smallest of assurances that they had made a good decision. After a close on products that are expensive or that require a long term commitment, the salesperson should provide the prospect with some reasons to be happy with the decision. Allow the car buyer to reinforce her own positive feelings by calling her a week after the purchase to ask how things are going. Call the new life insurance policy holder after two months to see if there are any questions; a lack of questions can only help the buyer to convince himself that he did the right thing.

BUYING DECISION PROCESS

Whenever folks make a buying decision, that decision represents the culmination of a process. It may take place almost instantaneously or stretch out over a long period of time–but it's a process, not an event.

No matter how long the process takes, the buying decision always begins when folks become aware of a need. Once they have identified that need, they begin to search for and explore possible avenues for meeting it. While gathering information, they refine and evaluate all the buying criteria that will affect the decision to purchase and narrow the field of choice to the "best few" alternatives.

Once they reach a decision and choose, they take action by making a purchase. The final step in the process involves a reevaluation of the decision and its results.

To summarize, the steps of the buying decision process are:

- Identify
- Search
- Evaluate
- Decide
- Purchase
- Reevaluate

NATURE OF THE BUY

The way folks make buying decisions depends on the complexity of the problem they are trying to solve and the complexity of each step in the decision process. This will affect how you manage the sale.

If their needs and the decision-making process are simple, all you need to do is make your visitors aware of you, build confidence, differentiate yourself, demonstrate value and guide them through a very simple shopping and buying process. This is why lower-end, branded products sell so well.

If the needs and the decision-making process are highly complex, then you need to make people aware of you, build relationships, educate them show sensitivity to the different decision-makers, influencers and groups, and resolve conflicting needs, so you can custom-tailor your solutions and make the buying process as painless and positive as possible. Think of purchasing a multi-million dollar piece of equipment that needs five departments to sign off to close the deal.

It also helps if you understand and incorporate how folks think about buying what you offer. Are they going to compare similar models in different brands? Are they looking for the range offered by one manufacturer? Do they think of the purchase in terms of a hierarchy of benefits, with some more important than others? Is the best way to showcase your product or service to compare it with someone else's stuff?

PROPENSITY TO BUY

You get four types of traffic, and each group is primed with a different level of motivation and preparedness - the classic"propensity to buy." First, you've got the to-die-for perfect visitors; they are the ones who know exactly what they want and come to you looking for features, brands, and model numbers.

Then you've got the visitors who sort of know what they want. These are folks who have identified a strongly felt need, but they're still in the process of narrowing down their search criteria.

Then there are the window shoppers, folks who aren't sure they want anything, but might buy if they saw something that interested them. They have no strongly felt need in mind, but one could be suggested to them.

The fourth group aren't really prospects. They're lost or there by mistake. Be happy when they go away.

You don't know where your visitors are in the process when they land on your site, so you've got to plan for each possibility. You've got to help the folks who know exactly what they want get to it quickly; make them jump through too many hoops and they're gone. You've got to help the ones still mulling it over by offering pertinent information where and when they are most likely to need it, as well as persuading them you're the logical business choice. You've got to be most engaging and appealing for the window shopper.

It also helps to consider that not all your visitors are prepared or even inclined to make a decision when they first visit your site–sometimes a successful conversion is the result of multiple visits. So you'd like to give folks a reason to come back.

BUYING IS AN EMOTIONAL DECISION

It really is the piece that pulls it all together. Folks rationalize the decision to buy based on facts, but they make the decision to buy based on feelings. The single biggest motivator in buying is emotional response. And that takes place on two levels.

In part, it's the emotional response that comes when folks imagine themselves enjoying the benefits of what you offer. Put them in the driver's seat, and they are that much closer to being able to see themselves making the decision to buy.

"Ditch the features?" Absolutely not. You should make your features available and present them as corollaries to benefits. After all, some of your visitors, particularly analytic types who will pointedly look for this stuff, feel more comfortable emotionally with facts and specifications.

And that brings me to the other aspect of emotional response. Folks buy when they feel comfortable, when they feel they can trust you, when the process feels natural and reassuring, and when they come to believe that buying will make them feel good. Ignore this, and most of your visitors will bail out. Tap into it, and watch your conversion rate climb. Because, at then end of the day, it's not facts that convince customers to go with your company. It's emotion.

PACKAGE BUYING WITH SELLING

The persuasive architecture of your entire site must recognize every step of the buying decision process. Each step feeds and leads to the others. Although the process ultimately is linear, there can be feedback loops within the process as folks reevaluate information. So, it's not unusual to address multiple steps on a single page.

To successfully get your visitors to take action you must be able to see the world from their "buying" point of view. So learn how to address and package the buying process within your selling process. It will make a world of difference!

CONSUMER ADOPTION PROCESS

Adoption is an individual's decision to become a regular user of a product.

Sequence of events beginning with consumer awareness of a new product leading to trial usage and culminating in full and regular use of the new product. Over time the adoption process resembles a bell curve formed by innovators, early adopters, the majority of consumers, late adopters, and laggards.

An innovation is any good, service, or idea that is perceived by someone as new. The idea may have a long history, but it is an innovation to the person who sees it as new. Innovations take time to spread through the social system. Rogers defines the innovation diffusion process as "the spread of a new idea from its source of invention or creation to its ultimate users or adopters."

The consumer-adoption process focuses on the mental process through which an individual passes from first hearing about an innovation to final adoption.

Adopters of new products have been observed to move through five stages:

1. *Awareness*: The consumer becomes aware of the innovation but lacks information about it.
2. *Interest*: The consumer is stimulated to seek information about the innovation.
3. *Evaluation*: The consumer considers whether to try the innovation.
4. *Trial*: The consumer tries the innovation to improve his or her estimate of its value.
5. *Adoption*: The consumer decides to make full and regular use of the innovation.

The new-product marketer should facilitate movement through these stages. A portable electricdishwasher manufacturer might discover that many consumers are stuck in the interest stage;they do not buy because of their uncertainty and the large investment cost. But these same consumers would be willing to use an electric dishwasher on a trial basis for a small monthly fee.The manufacturer should consider offering a trial-use plan with option to buy.

FACTORS INFLUENCING THE ADOPTION PROCESS

People differ in their approach towards change. Some

differ in adopting new fashion, some in adopting new appliances, some doctors are hesitant to apply new medicines and still some farmers do not apply new implements. This is called adoption culture. After the early adoption, they increase the use and then others follow. Others are late adopters by nature.

Let us categorize these customers into three units:

- *One who are early adopters*: They are very quick in their response. These people are venture some and willing to try new ideas. In fact they are innovators in life and early adopters.
- *Secondly Early Majority*: They are very careful people and take time to adopt things. They tend to collect information about the change or the product, study carefully and then adopt on the basis of their merits.
- *The third ones are late majority and traditionalists*: They are the ones who adopt late and then use the product.

As marketing managers, we must study the demographics, the psychographics and media characteristics of the product and also keep the theme of advertising message on these lines. We must find the innovators of the product and also opinion leaders and keeping in view the financial stature of the consumers and their category. Then there are certain areas where product change is imminent and quicker while some areas change or innovation in the product is least desired or welcomed

CONSUMER MARKET

The consumer market is composed of individuals who buy a specific good or service. Rarely does one product interest the entire population. This statement applies even to staples, such as sugar, flour, and salt. A small percentage of households do not eat these products, so even if a company did target the entire population, not everyone would be a potential consumer. The same statistical truth applies to cultural products. However, because of the extremely fragmented nature of the cultural sector, some distinctions are in order. For example, looking at this sector as a whole, it can be said that nearly 100% of the population consumes one type of cultural product or another. Indeed, in its broadest sense, the cultural sector encompasses everything from the performing arts to heritage, compact disks, movies, book and magazine publishing, and radio and television, with each of these disciplines appropriating a more or less important share of global demand.

In Canada, for example, statistics1 show that 37.0% of families attend a performing arts event at least once a year: movies 62.2%, museums and art galleries 32.9%. In the United States the figures for cultural consumption are: classical music 15.6%, opera 4.7%, musicals 24.5%, plays 15.8%, ballet 5.8%, art museums 34.5%, and historical parks 46.9%.2 In Australia3 the figures are: musical theatre 19.3%, classical music 7.7%, festivals 21.9%, concerts 23%, and museums 27.8%. Of course, within each of these sectors, consumers cluster just as to specific poles of interest.

This leads to sharper market segmentation. The consumer makes a discriminating choice among various cultural products to acquire or consume the type of product desired. The distribution of consumers just as to various market segments differs in both time and space. Markets undergo and reflect the influence of opinion leaders, trends, tastes, and societal characteristics.

Markets also vary from country to country just as to different social structures. Over the past 40 years, various surveys focusing on the sociodemographic profile of consumers of cultural products have been carried out in nearly every European country as well as in Canada, the United States, Australia, and Japan.4 It is fascinating to note that, regardless of whether the surveys were conducted in the 1970s, 1980s, or 1990s, they all obtained the same attendance rates and the same sociodemographic profiles.

Differences in the measuring tools used can sometimes make it difficult to compare countries; nonetheless, these studies have consistently and systematically revealed strong polarization of audiences between high art and popular culture across all countries over the past four decades. They show, for example, that cultural products catering to high art attract educated consumers, whereas those catering to popular culture draw on all segments of the population, in accordance with the relative weight of each.

The proportion of university graduates making up Canadian audiences, for example, ranges between 50% and 70% for high art, compared with 10% to 25% for popular culture. By way of comparison, the overall percentage of university graduates in Canada is 25%. Similar results have been found in other countries, most notably in France5 but also in Russia, where university graduates make up 50% of performing arts audiences but only 7% of the general population. Other sociodemographic variables are also linked to attendance, including average income and type of occupation. It should be pointed out once again that this profile is based on averages. Less-educated individuals with lower income may be great consumers of culture, as is the case for students and those specialized or working in the cultural milieu.

Indeed, it is well known that, as a rule many people active in the arts are highly educated yet so ill paid that they struggle to stay above the poverty line. On the other hand, there are people with both very high salaries and very high educational levels who are not interested in the arts and gladly keep their distance. Four factors are known to influence an individual's penchant for complex cultural products: family values that encourage or discourage high art; the educational milieu and the value it places on high art; the fact of having attended performances or visited museums as a child; and amateur art practice.

A more detailed analysis of the typical cultural consumer's traits reveals other nuances based on the different disciplines. For example, dance audiences are relatively younger and even more female in composition than those of the other performing arts; similarly, more women than men read novels, although a larger proportion of men read daily newspapers. In the film sector, there are two very different segments of avid cinema-goers; one of these segments is dominated by a young clientele, while the other is made up of educated people. The majority of consumers in the film sector belong to one or the other of these two segments.

BUSINESS BUYING BEHAVIOUR

The business market is comprised of organizations that, in some form, are involved in the manufacturer, distribution or support of products or services sold or otherwise provided to other organizations.

The amount of purchasing undertaken in the business market easily dwarfs the total spending by consumers. Because the business market is so large it draws the interest of millions of companies worldwide that market exclusively to business customers.

For these marketers understanding how businesses make purchase decisions is critical to their organizations' marketing efforts.

In some ways understanding the business market is not as complicated as understanding the consumer market. For example, in certain business markets purchase decisions hinge on the outcome of a bidding process between competitors offering similar products and services.

In these cases the decision to buy is often whittled down to one concern–who has the lowest price. Thus, unlike consumer markets, where building a recognizable brand is very important, for many purchase situations in the business market this is not the case.

However, in many other ways business buying is much more complicated. For instance, the demand by businesses for products and services is affected by consumer purchases and because so many organizations may have a part in creating consumer purchases, a small swing in consumer demand can create big changes in business purchasing.

Automobile purchases are a good example. If consumer demand for cars increases many companies connected with the automobile industry will also see demand for their products and services increase. Under these conditions companies will ratchet up their operations to ensure demand is met, which invariably will lead to new purchases by a large number of companies. In fact, it is conceivable that an increase of just one or two per cent for consumer demand can increase business demand for products and services by five or more per cent. Unfortunately, the opposite is true if demand declines. Trying to predict these swings requires businesses to not only understand their immediate customers but also the end user, which as suggested, discuss, may be well down the supply chain from where the business operates.

Principles of Marketing Tutorials discusses the unique characteristics of the business market. As suggested, see that marketers must appeal to business customers in ways that are distinct from how they would approach consumers. While marketers selling to other businesses operate with most of the same marketing tools used by marketers of consumer products, how they employ these tools to reach their marketing objectives may be quite different.

SUPPLY CHAIN MARKET

The supply chain consists of mostly for-profit companies engaged in activities involving product creation and delivery. Essentially the chain represents major steps needed to manufacture a product that will eventually be sold as a final product.

Each member of the supply chain purchases products and services enabling them to carry out its business objectives. When making purchase decisions supply chain members may be motivated by such factors as: product cost, return on investment, assurance of consistent supply, reciprocity with supplying firm, and much more. Examples of purchasing occurring in the supply chain include: manufacturing and plant equipment, information technology, office supplies, professional business services, etc.

In the table we arbitrarily identify five main categories of supply chain members primarily based on the stage at which they contribute to the manufacturing process. However, it is conceivable that these categories can be further divided in order to flush out more specific activities.

Supply Chain Member	What They Do	Example
Raw Material Suppliers	These companies are generally considered the first stage in the supply chain and provide basic products through mining, harvesting, fishing, etc., that are key ingredients in the production of higher-order products.	Copper is mined and extracted from copper ore. Copper is then refined to remove impurities.
Processed Materials or Basic Component Manufacturers	Firms at this level use raw materials to produce more advanced materials or products contained within more advanced components.	Copper is purchased by electrical wire manufacturers.
Advanced Component Manufacturers	These companies use basic components to produce products that offer a significant function needed within a larger product.	Electrical wire is purchased by a manufacturer of electrical power supplies.
Product Manufacturers	This market consists of companies that purchase both basic and advanced components and then assemble these components into a final product designated for a user. These products may or may not be sold as stand-alone products. Some may be included within larger products.	Power supplies are purchased by manufacturers of desktop computers.
Support Service Firms	These companies offer services at almost any point in the supply chain and also to the business user market. Some services are directly related to the product while others focus on areas of the business not directly related to production.	Distribution companies, such as truck firms and storage facilities, assist in moving products from one supply chain member to another. However, in most cases they do not take ownership of products that pass through the supply chain.

BUSINESS USER MARKETS

Besides selling final products and services to supply chain companies, several additional user markets also make purchases either for their own consumption or they buy with the intention of redistributing to others.

Market	What They Do	Considerations When Buying	What They Buy
Government	Made up of Federal, State, Local and International governments. They use purchases to assist with the functioning of the government that may include redistributing to others.	Mostly require suppliers to be approved, meet specifications and to bid for purchases.	Defense equipment, heavy equipment for public works projects, office supplies, pharmaceuticals, etc.
Not-For-Profit	Organizations whose tax structure precludes earning profits from operations and whose missions tend to be oriented to assisting others.	Look for purchases that will fit within tight budgetary restrictions and also within the mission of the organization.	Office equipment and supplies, office rental, professional services, etc.
Reseller	Also called distributors, these companies operate in both the consumer and the business markets. Their function involves purchasing large volumes of products from manufacturers and selling these products in smaller quantities. Includes wholesalers, retailers and industrial distributors.	Seek products that are of interest to the reseller's customers. Other issues include how delivery is handled and whether the supplier offers incentives to help the reseller promote the product.	Consumer and industrial products to be redistributed to other businesses and co

In these purchase situations the buyer generally does not radically change the product from its form when it was purchased from a Product Manufacturer. While technically these markets are also part of the supply chain, members of the business user market do not, in most cases, engage or directly assist in production activities.

BUSINESS VS CONSUMER MARKETS

For marketers, the selling environment of business markets present uniquely different circumstances when compared to selling to consumers.

At the beginning of this tutorial we saw two ways in which consumer and business markets differ:

- Business markets are more likely to be price driven than brand driven, and
- Demand in business markets tends to be more volatile than consumer markets.

However, the two markets are dissimilar in other ways requiring marketers to take a different approach when selling to business customers than to consumers.

These differences include:

- How Decisions Are Made
- Existence of Experienced Purchasers
- Time Needed to Make Buying Decision
- Size of Purchases
- Number of Buyers
- Type of Promotional Effort Needed to Reach Buyer

BUYING DIFFERENCES

Buying Centre Decisions

In the consumer market a very large percentage of purchase decisions are made by a single person. As we discussed in the Consumer Buying Behaviour tutorial, there are situations in which multiple people may be involved in a consumer purchase decision, such as a child influencing a parent to choose a certain brand of cereal or a husband and wife deciding together to buy a house, but most of the time purchases are individual decisions. The business market is significantly different. While single person purchasing is not unusual, especially within a small company, a significant percentage of business buying, especially within larger organizations, requires the input of many.

In the marketing literature those associated with the purchase decision are known to be part of a Buying Centre, which consists of individuals within an organization that perform one or more of the following roles:

- *Buyer*: Responsible for dealing with suppliers and placing orders
- *Decider*: Has the power to make the final purchase decision
- *Influencer*: Has the ability to affect what is ordered such as setting order specifications
- *User*: Those who will actually use the product when it is received
- *Initiator*: Any Buying Centre member who is the first to determine that a need exists
- *Gatekeeper*: Anyone who controls access to other Buying Centre members

For marketers confronting a Buying Centre it is important to first identify who plays what role. Once identified the marketer must address the needs of each member, which may differ significantly. For instance, the Decider, who may be the company president wants to make sure the purchase will not negatively affect the company's bottom line while the Buyer wants to be assured the product will be delivered on time. Thus, the way each Buying Centre member is approached and marketed to requires careful planning in order to address the unique needs of each member.

Experienced Purchasers

As noted in the discussion of the Buying Centre, organizations often employ purchasing agents or professional buyers whose job is to negotiate the best deals for their company. Unlike consumers, who often lack information when making purchase decisions, professional buyers are generally as knowledgeable about the product and the industry as the marketer who is selling to them.

Decision Making Time

Depending on the product, business purchase decisions can drag on for an extensive period. Unlike consumer markets where impulse purchasing is rampant, the number of people involved in business purchase decisions results in decisions taking weeks, months or even years.

Size of Purchases

For products that are regularly used and frequently purchased, businesses will often buy a larger volume at one time compared to consumer purchases. Because of this business purchasers often demand price breaks for higher order levels.

Type of Promotions

Companies who primarily target consumers often use mass advertising methods to reach an often widely dispersed market. For business-to-business marketers the size of individual orders, along with a smaller number of buyers, makes person-to-person contact by sales representatives a more effective means of promotion.

TYPES OF BUSINESS PURCHASE DECISIONS

While it would appear business customers face the same four purchase situations faced by consumers, the nature of the business market has led many marketing academics to group business purchase situations into only three categories.

The reason is that the idea of a minor order may not hold as well in the business market, where buyers tend to place larger orders and where suppliers' marketing efforts are directed toward the most profitable buyers.

- *Straight Re-Purchase*: These purchase situations involve routine ordering. In most cases buyers simply reorder the same products or services that were previously purchased. In fact, many larger companies have programmed re-purchases into an automated ordering system that initiates electronic orders when inventory falls a certain pre-determined level. For the supplier benefiting from the re-purchase this situation is ideal since the purchaser is not looking to evaluate other products. For competitors who are not getting the order it may require extensive marketing efforts to persuade the buyer to consider other product or service options.

- *Modified Re-Purchase*: These purchases occur when products or services previously considered a straight re-purchase are for some reason now under a re-evaluation process. There are many reasons why a product is moved to the status of a modified re-purchase. Some of these reasons include: end of purchase contract period, change in who is involved in making the purchase, supplier is removed from an approved suppliers list, mandate from top level of organization to re-evaluate all purchasing, or strong marketing effort by competitors. In this circumstance the incumbent supplier faces the same challenges they may have faced when they initially convinced the buyer to make the purchase. For competitors the door is now open and they must work hard to make sure their message is heard by those in charge of the purchase decision.
- *New Task Purchase*: As the name suggests, these purchases are ones the buyer has never or rarely made before. In some ways new task purchases can be considered as either minor or major depending on the total cost or overall importance of the purchase. In either case the buyer will spend considerably more time evaluating alternatives. For example, if faced with a major new task purchase, which often involves complex items, such as computer systems, buildings, robotic assembly lines, etc., the purchase cycle from first recognizing the need to placement of the order may be months or even years.

7

Market Segmentation and Targeting

AN OVERVIEW

Segmentation, targeting, and positioning together comprise a three stage process.

We first:

- Determine which kinds of customers exist, then
- Select which ones we are best off trying to serve and, finally,
- Implement our segmentation by optimizing our products/services for that segment and communicating that we have made the choice to distinguish ourselves that way.

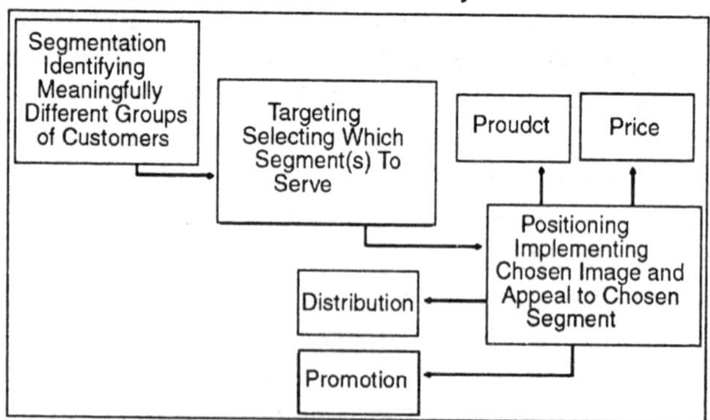

Fig. Market Segmentation and Targeting

Segmentation involves finding out what kinds of consumers with different needs exist. In the auto market, for example, some consumers demand speed and performance, while others are much more concerned about roominess and safety. In general, it holds true that "You can't be all things to all people," and experience has demonstrated that firms that specialize in meeting the needs of one group of consumers over another tend to be more profitable.

Generically, there are three approaches to marketing. In the *undifferentiated* strategy, all consumers are treated as the same, with firms not making any specific efforts to satisfy particular groups.

This may work when the product is a standard one where one competitor really can't offer much that another one can't. Usually, this is the case only for commodities. In the *concentrated* strategy, one firm chooses to focus on one of several segments that exist while leaving other segments to competitors. For example, Southwest Airlines focuses on price sensitive consumers who will forego meals and assigned seating for low prices.

In contrast, most airlines follow the *differentiated* strategy: They offer high priced tickets to those who are inflexible in that they cannot tell in advance when they need to fly and find it impractical to stay over a Saturday. These travellers—usually business travellers—pay high fares but can only fill the planes up partially. The same airlines then sell some of the remaining seats to more price sensitive customers who can buy two weeks in advance and stay over.

Note that segmentation calls for some tough choices. There may be a large number of variables that can be used to differentiate consumers of a given product category; yet, in practice, it becomes impossibly cumbersome to work with more than a few at a time. Thus, we need to determine which variables will be *most* useful in distinguishing different groups of consumers.

We might thus decide, for example, that the variables that are most relevant in separating different kinds of soft drink consumers are: light consumers.

- Preference for taste vs. low calories,
- Preference for Cola vs. non-cola taste,

- Price sensitivity—willingness to pay for brand names;
- Heavy vs.

We now put these variables together to arrive at various combinations.

Several different kinds of variables can be used for segmentation:

- *Demographic* variables essentially refer to personal statistics such as income, gender, education, location, ethnicity, and family size. Campbell's soup, for instance, has found that Western U.S. consumers on the average prefer spicier soups—thus, you get a different product in the same cans at the East and West coasts. Facing flat sales of guns in the traditional male dominated market, a manufacturer came out with the Lady Remmington, a more compact, handier gun more attractive to women. Taking this a step farther, it is also possible to segment on *lifestyle and values*."
- Some consumers want to be seen as similar to others, while a different segment wants to stand apart from the crowd.
- Another basis for segmentation is *behaviour*. Some consumers are "brand loyal"—i.e., they tend to stick with their preferred brands even when a competing one is on sale. Some consumers are "heavy" users while others are "light" users. For example, research conducted by the wine industry shows that some 80% of the product is consumed by 20% of the consumers—presumably a rather intoxicated group.
- One can also segment on *benefits sought*, essentially bypassing demographic explanatory variables. Some consumers, for example, like scented soap, while others prefer the "clean" feeling of unscented soap. Some consumers use toothpaste primarily to promote oral health, while another segment is more interested in breath freshening.

In the next step, we decide to target one or more segments. Our choice should generally depend on several factors. First, how well are existing segments served by *other* manufacturers?

It will be more difficult to appeal to a segment that is already well served than to one whose needs are not currently being served well. Secondly, how large is the segment, and how can we expect it to grow?. Thirdly, do we have strengths as a company that will help us appeal particularly to one group of consumers? Firms may already have an established reputation. While McDonald's has a great reputation for fast, consistent quality, family friendly food, it would be difficult to convince consumers that McDonald's now offers gourmet food. Thus, McD's would probably be better off targeting families in search of consistent quality food in nice, clean restaurants. Positioning involves *implementing* our targeting. For example, Apple Computer has chosen to position itself as a maker of user-friendly computers. Thus, Apple has done a lot through its advertising to promote itself, through its unintimidating icons, as a computer for "non-geeks." The Visual C software programming language, in contrast, is aimed a "techies."

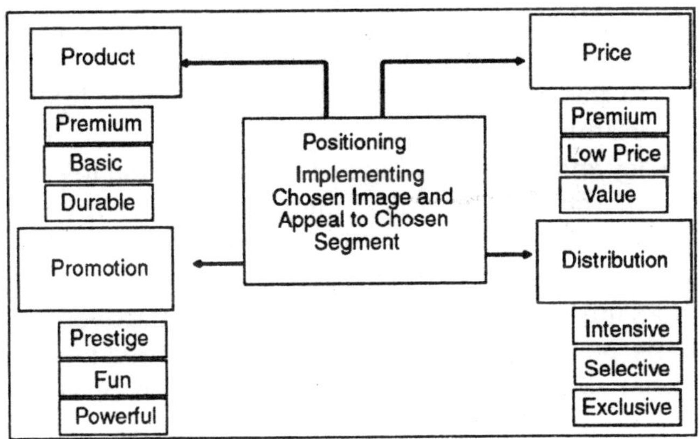

Fig. *The Discipline of Market Leaders*

That most successful firms fall into one of three categories:

- Operationally excellent firms, which maintain a strong competitive advantage by maintaining exceptional efficiency, thus enabling the firm to provide reliable service to the customer at a significantly lower cost than those of less well organized and well run competitors. The emphasis here is mostly on low cost, subject to reliable performance, and less value is put on customizing the offering for the specific customer. Wal-Mart is an example of this discipline. Elaborate logistical designs allow goods to be moved at the lowest cost, with extensive systems predicting when specific quantities of supplies will be needed.

- Customer intimate firms, which excel in serving the specific needs of the individual customer well. There is less emphasis on efficiency, which is sacrificed for providing more precisely what is wanted by the customer. Reliability is also stressed. Nordstrom's and IBM are examples of this discipline.
- Technologically excellent firms, which produce the most advanced products currently available with the latest technology, constantly maintaining leadership in innovation. These firms, because they work with costly technology that need constant refinement, cannot be as efficient as the operationally excellent firms and often cannot adapt their products as well to the needs of the individual customer. Intel is an example of this discipline.

Treacy and Wiersema suggest that in addition to excelling on one of the three value dimensions, firms must meet acceptable levels on the other two. Wal-Mart, for example, does maintain some level of customer service. Nordstrom's and Intel both must meet some standards of cost effectiveness. The emphasis, beyond meeting the minimum required level in the two other dimensions, is on the dimension of strength. *Repositioning* involves an attempt to change consumer perceptions of a brand, usually because the existing position that the brand holds has become less attractive. Sears, for example, attempted to reposition itself from a place that offered great sales but unattractive prices the rest of the time to a store that consistently offered "everyday low prices." Repositioning in practice is very difficult to accomplish. A great deal of money is often needed for advertising and other promotional efforts, and in many cases, the repositioning fails.

To effectively attempt repositioning, it is important to understand how one's brand and those of competitors are perceived. One approach to identifying consumer product perceptions is *multidimensional scaling*. Here, we identify how products are perceived on two or more "dimensions," allowing us to plot brands against each other. It may then be possible to attempt to "move" one's brand in a more desirable direction by selectively promoting certain points. There are two main approaches to multi-dimensional scaling. In the *a priori* approach, market researchers identify dimensions of interest and then ask consumers about their perceptions on each dimension for each brand.

This is useful when:

- The market researcher knows which dimensions are of interest and
- The customer's perception on each dimension is relatively clear.

In the *similarity rating* approach, respondents are not asked about their perceptions of brands on any specific dimensions. Instead, subjects are asked to rate the extent of *similarity* of different pairs of products Using a computer algorithms, the computer then identifies positions of each brand on a map of a given number of dimensions. The computer does not reveal what each dimension means—that must be left to human interpretation based on what the variations in each dimension appears to reveal. This second method is more useful when no specific product dimensions have been identified as being of particular interest or when it is not clear what the variables of difference are for the product category.

MARKET SEGMENTATION

Segmentation is the term given to the grouping of customers with similar needs by a number of different variables. Once this has been done, segments can be targeted by a number of targeting strategies. The stage that then follows is known as positioning which is the place that products or services occupy in the marketplace in relation to the competition, as perceived by the target market.

MARKET-SEGMENTATION CONCEPT

The underlying principle of market segmentation is that individual customers have different product and service needs. Mass marketing, the marketing of a single product to everyone, is rarely a viable strategy, just as it is to customise products to an individual.

MARKET SEGMENTATION PROCESS

The segmentation process is generally regarded as consisting of three stages; segmentation, targeting, and positioning.

SEGMENTATION VARIABLES

The first stage of the segmentation process involves the selection of suitable variables for grouping customers. These are also referred to as base variables or the segmentation basis. There is rarely one best way of segmenting a market and more than one variable can be used. There are a number of segmentation variables that can be used for consumer and business-to-business markets.

SEGMENTATION ANALYSIS

Research plays an important role in segmentation as segmentation analysis requires a range of data form a wide variety of sources on markets, customers' attitudes, motives and behaviour as well as competitor information.

TARGETING

Targeting is the next step in the sequential process and involves a business making choices about segment(s) on which resources are to be focused. There are three major targeting strategies: undifferentiated, concentrated, and differentiated. During this process the business must balance its resources and capabilities against the attractiveness of different segments.

POSITIONING

Positioning follows on logically from the segmentation

and targeting stages. Customer perceptions are central to the product position especially in relation to the competition's offering. The product or service has to satisfy key customer requirements and this has to be clearly communicated to customers. A tool that helps marketers understand customer perceptions of their brand is perceptual mapping and a simple 7- step approach can be used to develop a clear positioning strategy. However, a number of positioning problems can arise.

GETTING THE MOST OUT OF MARKET SEGMENTATION

Market segmentation, targeting and positioning are not always easy to apply and problems can arise for a number of reasons. There are a number of steps that can be taken to avoid these problems and, in addition, there are a set of segmentation criteria that can help.

FUTURE OF MARKET SEGMENTATION

The two key factors that will affect segmentation in the future are competitive and technological forces. In addition, there is a rising trend towards one-to-one marketing.

OBJECTIVES OF MARKET SEGMENTATION

Market segmentation is the first of three important steps in developing marketing strategy. Segmentation groups customers with similar needs and responses; targeting determines which segments to serve; positioning is about how the product should compete with others in the market.

The objectives of market segmentation are to more accurately meet the needs of selected customers in a more profitable way.

Precisely how this can be achieved will vary by company capability. For example, a single product company may be able to boost sales and cut advertising costs if they can target consumers with a high likelihood of product purchase. On the other hand, a company with several brands in a category will benefit by positioning each brand within the portfolio against a distinct set of consumer needs–ideally each brand should be sufficiently distinct so that there is little cannibalisation.

SEGMENTATION BASES

There is a large array of possible segmentation bases.

Demographics

Consumers can be grouped on the basis of characteristics such as age or household composition. This is easy to do and it is easy to reach such segments with media. But age and other demographics are only loosely related to behaviour.

Socioeconomic Characteristics

Similarly, characteristics such as income, occupation and education can be used to derive segments that are easy to reach. Such segments are indicators of behaviour such as lifestyle, price sensitivity, and brand preference.

Product Usage

Potential to use the firm's product is a behaviourally based segmentation basis. Potential could be determined by administering questions about disposition to use in a survey and respondents grouped accordingly. The problem is then how to reach the most attractive segments. This is done either by using a large-scale single source survey that asks consumers about product disposition and media usage or by relating product disposition to demographics. Both approaches are usually imperfect as behaviour is rarely strongly correlated with demographics or media usage.

Psychographics

Personality, attitudes, opinions, and life styles are often used a segmentation bases. These characteristics have some relationship to behaviour and provide insight into how to communicate with chosen segments. Reaching the chosen segments is then the issue, as discussed under product usage.

Generation

Generation, or cohort, refers to people born in the same

period of time. For example, the Baby Boomer generation can be defined as those people born between 1946 and 1955. Such cohorts share much in common. Not only are they of a similar age, but they experienced similar economic, cultural, and political influences in formative years. Thus generation is probably a better segmentation basis than age and just as easy to reach.

Benefits Sought

Some people are price sensitive, others seek quality or service. Some people are brand loyal, while others frequently switch brands. It is possible to group consumers on the basis of these factors. Note that price/quality sensitivity can vary by category. Some people are very concerned about the quality of the food they eat but will buy cheap laundry detergent. Others will feed themselves any rubbish but are fastidious about cleanliness. This is a very powerful basis for segmentation but it is not easy to buy media on this basis. These segments can be reached by the message but this is not necessarily cost effective.

Geography

There are two reasons why people who live in the same area may share similar characteristics. First, some areas have more expensive properties than others and so people with similar socioeconomic characteristics may cluster together. Second, they have similar transport and shopping options. It is easy to reach particular areas by using local newspapers, cinema, outdoor, and selective direct mail but mass media is less effective.

Geodemographic

There are several commercial geodemographic segmentation plans available, that combine demographics and geography as a segmentation basis. This approach aims to identify groups of small geographic areas that have similar demographic profiles. These tend to suffer from the fallacy of averages. Some areas may be genuinely relatively homogenous but many are not and this can be very misleading.

HOW MARKET SEGMENTATION CAN INCREASE PROFIT

Increasing profits is the major objective of companies. We can write the profit for a product down as a formula:

Profit = Volume*(Price–Variable Cost)–Marketing Costs–Fixed Costs

There are several ways in which effective segmentation can boost profits:

- By better meeting customer needs, through better positioning to chosen segments, we may be able to increase market share and hence volume.
- By better meeting needs, we may also be able to increase price without sacrificing much volume.
- By only targeting the most profitable segments, we may be able to reduce marketing costs.

METHODS OF MARKET SEGMENTATION

There is a large array of analytical techniques applicable to market segmentation..

Cluster Analysis

Cluster analysis is a set of techniques for discovering structure, or groups of individuals, within a set of data comprising measures on each individual. The measures could be, for example, an attitudinal battery. There is no dependent variable–all variables are treated equally.

Conjoint Analysis

This technique aims to decompose preference into component parts, such as brand, quality, and price. This technique views products as bundles of attributes and uses an experimental design to vary attribute levels to create product descriptions.

Survey respondents then rank the products and the analysis works out how much each attribute contributes to preference. It is a good technique for benefit segmentation.

CHAID/Regression Trees

This was called Automatic Interaction Detection for a long time and now also goes under various names used by software vendors, including Regression Tree, Answer Tree, Classification Tree and CART. It is a technique frequently employed in Data Mining and it is a useful exploratory analysis technique prior to regression analysis. It can quickly analyse a large set of candidate explanatory variables to determine the most influential variables on a dependent variable.

The basic idea is to hierarchically segment the population on the database based on a dependent variable such as bought/ did not buy a product.

The explanatory variables are categorical too, such as:

- Demographic variables;
- Attitudes;
- Previous behaviour.

Discriminant Analysis

This technique is used to quantify the relationship between segment membership and explanatory variables such as income and attitudes. It is often used after CHAID identifies candidate explanatory variables, to formally quantify and test the significance of relationships.

DEVELOPING A TARGET MARKET STRATEGY

Developing a target market strategy has three phases:

1. Analyzing consumer demand
2. Targeting the market(s)
   - Undifferentiated
   - Concentrated
   - Multisegmented
3. Developing the marketing strategy

SELECTING TARGET MARKETS

Need to aggregate consumers with similar needs. Demand patterns: Do all potential customers have similar needs/desires or are there clusters?

Types of demand patterns are:

- Homogeneous Demand-uniform, everyone demands the product for the same reason(s). Very rare in the US, staple foods...
- Clustered Demand-consumer demand classified in 2 or more identifiable clusters.

IE Automobiles:

  - Luxury
  - Cheap
  - Sporty
  - Spacious

- Diffused Demand-Product differentiation more costly and more difficult to communicate IE Cosmetic market, need to offer hundreds of shades of lipstick. Firms try to modify consumer demand to develop clusters of at least a moderate size. Or uses one MM.

TARGETING

After the process of segmentation the next step is for the organisation to decide how it is going to target these particular group(s). There are three targeting options an organisation can adopt.

UNDIFFERENTIATED MARKETING

Sometimes referred to as mass marketing the firm may decide to aim its resources at the entire market with one particular product. Coca Colas original marketing strategy was based on this form. One product aimed at the mass market in the hope that a sufficient amount of buyers would be attracted., although there are now changes in their product line to cater for growing dietary and caffeine free needs of consumers.

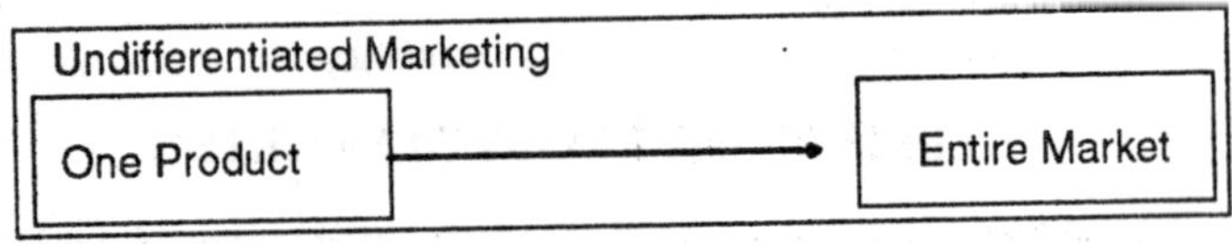

DIFFERENTIATED MARKETING STRATEGY

Where the firm decides to target several segments and

develops distinct products/services with separate marketing mix strategies aimed at the varying groups. An example of this would be airline companies offering first, business or economy class tickets, with separate marketing programmes to attract the different groups.

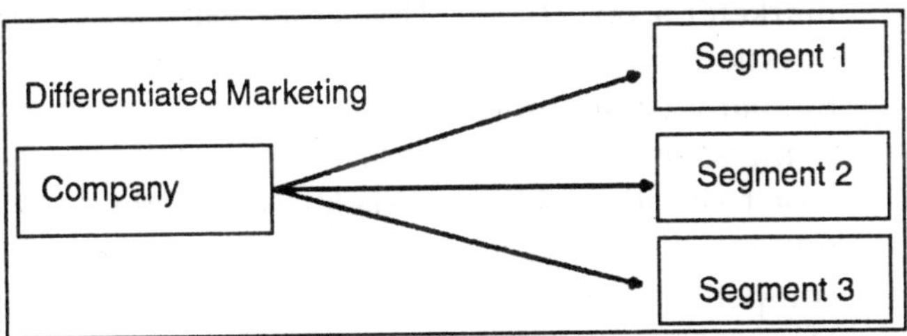

CONCENTRATED MARKETING

Where the organisation concentrates its marketing effort on one particular segment. The firm will develop a product that caters for the needs of that particular group. For example Rolls Royce cars aim its vehicles at the premium segment, same as Harrods within the UK.

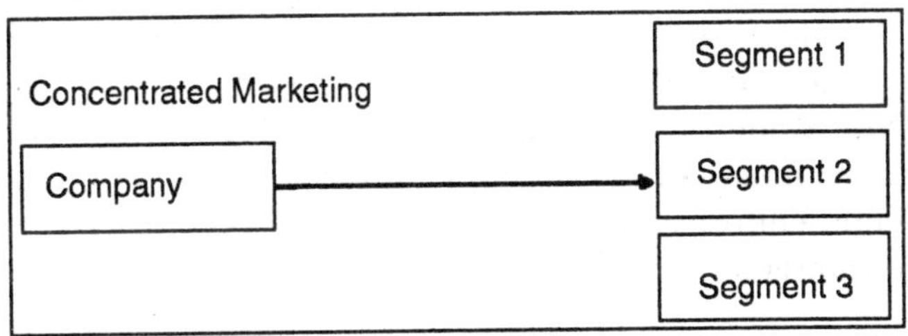

CHOOSING MARKET SEGMENTS

The second step in selecting target markets requires the marketer to critically evaluate the segments identified in Step 1 in order to select those which are most attractive. For small firms this step may not be very involving since they may lack the resources needed to do it effectively. So they are often left with using their own intuition or judgment to determine which segments are the most promising. For companies with the time and money to commit to this step, the results may identify the segments that are primary candidates for current marketing efforts and also present segments that are future targets for the company's offerings.

In determining whether a segment is worthy of being a target market, the marketer needs to address the following questions:

- Is the segment large enough to support the marketer's objectives? This is an especially critical question if the marketer is entering a market served by many competitors.
- Is the segment showing signs of growth? One of the worst situations for a marketer is to enter a market whose growth is flat or declining, especially if competitors already exist.
- Does the company have the necessary skills, knowledge and expertise to service the segment? The company should understand and be able to communicate with the customers in the segment, otherwise they may face a significant learning curve in understanding how to effectively market to a segment.
- Does the segment meet the mission of the company? The segment should not extend too far beyond the direction the company has chosen to take.

Once one or more segments have been identified the marketer must choose the most attractive option(s) for their marketing efforts. At this point the choice becomes the firm's target market(s).

8

Product Management

INTRODUCTION

Product management is an organizational lifecycle function within a company dealing with the planning or forecasting or marketing of a product or products at all stages of the product lifecycle.

Product management and product marketing are different yet complementary efforts with the objective of maximizing sales revenues, market share, and profit margins. The role of product management spans many activities from strategic to tactical and varies based on the organizational structure of the company. Product management can be a function separate on its own and a member of marketing or engineering.

While involved with the entire product lifecycle, product management's main focus is on driving new product development. Product Development and Management Association, superior and differentiated new products - ones that deliver unique benefits and superior value to the customer - is the number one driver of success and product profitability.

CHARACTERISTICS

Depending on the company size and history, product management has a variety of functions and roles. Sometimes there is a product manager, and sometimes the role of product manager is held by others. Frequently there is Profit and Loss responsibility as a key metric for evaluating product manager performance. In some companies, the product management function is the hub of many other activities around the product.

In others, it is one of many things that need to happen to bring a product to market.

Product management often serves an inter-disciplinary role, bridging gaps within the company between teams of different expertise, most notably between engineering-oriented teams and business-oriented teams. For example product managers often translate business objectives set for a product by Marketing or Sales into engineering requirements. Conversely they may work to explain the capabilities and limitations of the finished product back to Marketing and Sales. Product Managers may also have one or more direct reports such as a Product Executive who can manage operational tasks or a Change Manager who can oversee new initiatives.

Product Planning

- Identifying new product candidates
- Gathering market requirements
- Determine business-case and feasibility
- Scoping and defining new products at high level
- Evangelizing new products within the company
- Building product roadmaps, particularly Technology roadmaps
- Working to a critical path and ensuring all products are produced on schedule
- Ensuring products are within price margins and up to spec
- Product Life Cycle considerations
- Product differentiation
- Detailed Product planning
- 7 functions of marketing

Product Marketing

- Product positioning and outbound messaging
- Promoting the product externally with press, customers, and partners
- Bringing new products to market
- Monitoring the competition
- more detail on Product marketing

PRODUCT DIFFERENTIATION

Product differentiation is a business level strategy in which firms attempt to create and exploit differences between their products and those offered by competitors. These differences may lead to competitive advantage if customers perceive the difference and have a preference for the difference.

A product differentiation strategy requires that a firm be able to effectively communicate with customers through advertising, public relations, sponsoring of events, etc. In fact, advertising usually plays a critical role in an effective product differentiation strategy.

Ironically, a firm does not have to be able to create a product with actual differences if it can convince customers that differences exist. Firms that do create products with actual differences have a much easier time convincing customers that those differences exist. Nike's capabilities lie primarily in design and marketing. The vast majority of Nike's production of shoes and clothing is outsourced to other firms. Nike's base of differentiation is not proprietary high-tech manufacturing of superior athletic shoes. Rather, Nike's base of differentiation is a well-orchestrated marketing effort that has spanned decades.

BASES OF DIFFERENTIATION

The notion of a base of differentiation is important because it allows a firm to focus its efforts on creating and exploiting a particular difference between its products and competitors' products. Managers need to understand their own bases of differentiation and the bases of differentiation of competitors so that they can make informed strategic choices. Almost anything could be a base of differentiation. The key is that some set of customers must find value in the base of differentiation.

Everything from tangible product characteristics to abstract intangible concepts like national or regional pride could potentially be a base of differentiation. Managers can create and exploit bases of differentiation from a seemingly infinite number of ideas. For example, "freedom fries" became a base of differentiation among some restaurants as a form of protest against the French who refused to join the U.S. in its war against Saddam Hussein's government in Iraq. The name change from French fries to freedom fries was the idea of small but very patriotic restaurateur.

This' base of differentiation was short-lived as the attention of Americans shifted from the lack of French participation to the war itself.

Attributes of the Product or Service

- Preferences are created by actual differences in the tangible product or service offered by the focal firm vis-à-vis competitors' offerings
- Product features
- Product complexity
- Timing of product introduction
- Location

Relationship Between the Focal Firm and its Customers

- Preferences are created as the focal firm develops and exploits relationships with customers based on what the focal firm's target customers want
- Product customization
- Consumer marketing
- Product reputation

Linkages Within or Between Firms

- Preferences are created as the focal firm combines the competencies of different functions within or across organizations to produce tangible and/or intangible differences between the focal firm's offerings and those of competitors
- Linkages among functions within the focal firm
- Linkages with other firms
- Product mix
- Distribution channels
- Service and support

VALUE OF DIFFERENTIATION

Neutralizing Threats. Here is a brief description of how product differentiation can neutralize the threats of the forces in the Five Forces Model along with an example of each one. If the focal firm's product differentiation strategy is effective:

Threat of Entry

- Would-be entrants face the costs of overcoming customers' preferences for the focal firm's products and/or services
- *Example*: Toyota was protected from Hyundai's entry into the U.S. market because Hyundai had to enter at a low price and advertise heavily to attract customers away from Toyota's well-established Corolla.

Threat of Rivalry

- Customers have, to some extent, segmented themselves based on their preferences for the products of the several competing firms in a market. Thus, the rivalry is generally lower among firms competing in a market of differentiated products.
- *Example*: Allen Edmonds men's dress shoes sell for around $300. Most models have thick leather soles that conform comfortably to the foot. Once a customer wears Allen Edmonds shoes, he tends to be very loyal to the brand. Cole Hahn is a competitor at the high end of the market. Some people prefer Cole Hahn, some prefer Allen Edmonds and once the customer decides on a preference, there is little competition remaining between Cole Hahn and Allen Edmonds. Product differentiation attenuates rivalry for Allen Edmonds because competition for customers is minimized due to customers' selfselected segmentation.

Threat of Substitutes

- Customers will find the focal firm's products and

services substantially more attractive than substitute products

- *Example*: Printing digital photographs on a personal printer at home may be viewed as a substitute for professional printing at a photo shop. Photo shops that advertise that their digital prints are superior to what can be printed at home are attempting to create a preference for their product. Shops that successfully convince customers that their product is superior are insulated from the competitive pressure of the in-home substitute.

Threat of Suppliers

- The power of suppliers may be mitigated in two ways. First, the focal firm will likely be able to pass supplier price increases along to customers who have a preference for the focal firm's differentiated product. Second, a firm that enjoys the strong preference of customers will usually have more bargaining power with suppliers compared to competitors that do not have differentiated products and services.
- *Example*: Recent spikes in the price of beef are easily passed on to customers of high-end steak houses like Ruth's Chris and Spencer's. McDonald's, Wendy's, and Burger King's customers are more sensitive to price increases that make the $.99 burger a thing of the past.

Threat of Buyers

- The power of buyers is reduced because the focal firm enjoys a quasimonopoly. By definition, if a firm has a highly differentiated product, then the firm is the only firm in that market that can offer that particular product. Customers with a preference for the focal firm's products and services must buy from the focal firm, thus reducing the power of buyers.
- Daimler-Chrysler's Crossfire sports car has allowed

dealers to enjoy a quasi-monopoly as evidenced by the "local market adjustment" that dealers are able to tack onto the price of the car. The car is different from other cars and a set of customers has a strong preference for the car. There are a limited number of the cars being built. These factors serve to greatly reduce the power of buyers of the Crossfire.

Exploiting Opportunities

A product differentiation strategy can be used to exploit opportunities in several different ways. The textbook focuses on how product differentiation can be used to exploit opportunities based on the type of industry in which the focal firm operates. In addition to industry-type opportunities, there are many other opportunities that arise in the external environment that firms can exploit. In a sense, a firm is exploiting an opportunity in the external environment any time it is able to fill some customer need in a new or different way.

PRODUCT DIFFERENTIATION AND COMPETITIVE ADVANTAGE

Having established the *V*alue of product differentiation, we next consider the *R*areness and *I*mitability of product differentiation. The answer to the question of rareness can safely be assumed to be affirmative at this point in the analysis. The assumption is that the focal firm has established a differentiated product, which implies that the product is rare. We therefore turn our attention to the question of imitability. If a product differentiation strategy is costly to imitate, the focal firm can reasonably expect to enjoy a competitive advantage.

Easy to Duplicate

Product Features:

- Are easy for competitors to observe
- Unless there is a patent, competitors face little cost in imitation
- May lead to temporary competitive advantage until competitors are able to imitate

- *Example*: Wrinkle-free, 100% cotton in shirts, blouses, and pants is a product feature that has been rapidly duplicated. This innovation meant that customers could enjoy the feel of 100% cotton without having to iron or professionally launder their clothing. Nordstrom was an early adopter with its SmartCare line. Most other department stores now have their own line of all cotton clothing that is wrinkle-free.

IMPLEMENTING A PRODUCT DIFFERENTIATION STRATEGY

The Organization question of the VRIO Model is perhaps even more important with a product differentiation strategy than with a cost leadership strategy because of the relationship between the focal firm and customers.

A successful differentiation strategy depends on creating customer preferences for the products and/or services of the focal firm.

Customer preferences are heavily influenced by customers' experiences in interacting with the focal firm. The focal firm must be able to respond quickly and accurately to customer needs.

Customers need to'feel' that the focal firm is catering to their needs. Organizational structure, management control systems, and compensation policies can all be managed to encourage customers to have a preference for the focal firm's products and/or services.

Organizational Structure

At the business level, the U-Form is used to implement product differentiation strategies just as it is to implement cost leadership strategies.

However, there are some important differences in the way the structure is used. The U-Form is used in a cost leadership strategy to exploit the efficiencies inherent in the structure due to specialization. With a product differentiation strategy, the specialization of the U-Form structure is exploited through cross-functional teams.

Management Controls

The main idea behind using management controls in the implementation of a product differentiation strategy is that of flexibility.

Not only must managers and employees have the freedom to be flexible, they should also be encouraged to be creative and adaptable. Decision making is usually more decentralized in a product differentiation strategy as compared to a cost leadership strategy.

This decentralization means that managers can make decisions and take actions that allow the focal firm to differentiate its products and/or services through a high degree of responsiveness to customers. As a matter of firm policy, decision making guidelines are broader-allowing greater flexibility. Also, managers and employees should explicitly be given the freedom and encouragement to experiment with new ideas. Managers and employees need to know that if experimentation leads to failure they will not be punished for having tried.

Compensation Policies

Compensation policies can be used to help exploit the U-form structure and reinforce the broader management controls. In the simplest of terms, compensation policies should be structured to reward managers and employees for cooperating within cross functional teams and being creative in the process. Compensation policies can be especially effective with regard to experimentation and risk taking. Promised rewards for successful experimentation and the promised absence of punishment for failed experimentation provide strong incentive to be creative.

PRODUCT LIFE CYCLE

A product's life cycle can be divided into several stages characterized by the revenue generated by the product. If a curve is drawn showing product revenue over time, it may take one of many different shapes, an example of which is shown below:

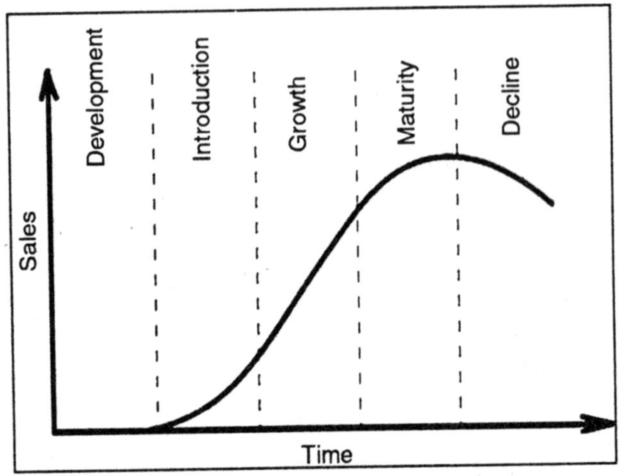

Fig. Product Life Cycle Curve

The life cycle concept may apply to a brand or to a category of product. Its duration may be as short as a few months for a fad item or a century or more for product categories such as the gasoline-powered automobile.

Product development is the incubation stage of the product life cycle. There are no sales and the firm prepares to introduce the product. As the product progresses through its life cycle, changes in the marketing mix usually are required in order to adjust to the evolving challenges and opportunities.

INTRODUCTION STAGE

When the product is introduced, sales will be low until customers become aware of the product and its benefits. Some firms may announce their product before it is introduced, but such announcements also alert competitors and remove the element of surprise. Advertising costs typically are high during this stage in order to rapidly increase customer awareness of the product and to target the early adopters. During the introductory stage the firm is likely to incur additional costs associated with the initial distribution of the product. These higher costs coupled with a low sales volume usually make the introduction stage a period of negative profits.

During the introduction stage, the primary goal is to establish a market and build primary demand for the product class.

The following are some of the marketing mix implications of the introduction stage:

- *Product*: One or few products, relatively undifferentiated
- *Price*: Generally high, assuming a skim pricing strategy for a high profit margin as the early adopters buy the product and the firm seeks to recoup development costs quickly. In some cases a penetration pricing strategy is used and introductory prices are set low to gain market share rapidly.
- *Distribution*: Distribution is selective and scattered as the firm commences implementation of the distribution plan.
- *Promotion*: Promotion is aimed at building brand awareness. Samples or trial incentives may be directed toward early adopters. The introductory promotion also is intended to convince potential resellers to carry the product.

GROWTH STAGE

The growth stage is a period of rapid revenue growth. Sales increase as more customers become aware of the product and its benefits and additional market segments are targeted. Once the product has been proven a success and customers begin asking for it, sales will increase further as more retailers become interested in carrying it. The marketing team may expand the distribution at this point. When competitors enter the market, often during the later part of the growth stage, there may be price competition and/or increased promotional costs in order to convince consumers that the firm's product is better than that of the competition. During the growth stage, the goal is to gain consumer preference and increase sales.

The marketing mix may be modified as follows:

- *Product*: New product features and packaging options; improvement of product quality.

- *Price*: Maintained at a high level if demand is high, or reduced to capture additional customers.
- *Distribution*: Distribution becomes more intensive. Trade discounts are minimal if resellers show a strong interest in the product.
- *Promotion*: Increased advertising to build brand preference.

MATURITY STAGE

The maturity stage is the most profitable. While sales continue to increase into this stage, they do so at a slower pace. Because brand awareness is strong, advertising expenditures will be reduced. Competition may result in decreased market share and/or prices. The competing products may be very similar at this point, increasing the difficulty of differentiating the product. The firm places effort into encouraging competitors' customers to switch, increasing usage per customer, and converting non-users into customers. Sales promotions may be offered to encourage retailers to give the product more shelf space over competing products.

During the maturity stage, the primary goal is to maintain market share and extend the product life cycle.

Marketing mix decisions may include:

- *Product*: Modifications are made and features are added in order to differentiate the product from competing products that may have been introduced.
- *Price*: Possible price reductions in response to competition while avoiding a price war.
- *Distribution*: New distribution channels and incentives to resellers in order to avoid losing shelf space.
- *Promotion*: Emphasis on differentiation and building of brand loyalty. Incentives to get competitors' customers to switch.

DECLINE STAGE

Eventually sales begin to decline as the market becomes saturated, the product becomes technologically obsolete, or customer tastes change. If the product has developed brand loyalty, the profitability may be maintained longer. Unit costs may increase with the declining production volumes and eventually no more profit can be made.

During the decline phase, the firm generally has three options:

- Maintain the product in hopes that competitors will exit. Reduce costs and find new uses for the product.
- Harvest it, reducing marketing support and coasting along until no more profit can be made.
- Discontinue the product when no more profit can be made or there is a successor product.

The marketing mix may be modified as follows:

- *Product*: The number of products in the product line may be reduced. Rejuvenate surviving products to make them look new again.
- *Price*: Prices may be lowered to liquidate inventory of discontinued products. Prices may be maintained for continued products serving a niche market.
- *Distribution*: Distribution becomes more selective. Channels that no longer are profitable are phased out.
- *Promotion*: Expenditures are lower and aimed at reinforcing the brand image for continued products.

LIMITATIONS

The term "life cycle" implies a well-defined life cycle as observed in living organisms, but products do not have such a predictable life and the specific life cycle curves followed by different products vary substantially. Consequently, the life cycle concept is not well-suited for the forecasting of product sales. Furthermore, critics have argued that the product life cycle may become self-fulfilling. For example, if sales peak and then decline, managers may conclude that the product is in the decline phase and therefore cut the advertising budget, thus precipitating a further decline.

Nonetheless, the product life cycle concept helps marketing managers to plan alternate marketing strategies to address the challenges that their products are likely to face. It also is useful for monitoring sales results over time and comparing them to those of products having a similar life cycle.

PRODUCT LIFECYCLE MANAGEMENT

Product lifecycle management, sometimes "product life cycle management", represents an all-encompassing vision for managing all data relating to the design, production, support and ultimate disposal of manufactured goods.

PLM concepts were first introduced where safety and control have been extremely important, notably the aerospace, medical device, military and nuclear industries. These industries originated the discipline of configuration management, which evolved into electronic data management systems, which then further evolved to product data management.

Over the last ten years, manufacturers of instrumentation, industrial machinery, consumer electronics, packaged goods and other complex engineered products have discovered the benefits of PLM solutions and are adopting efficient PLM software in increasing numbers.

PLM SOLUTIONS

PLM can be thought of as both:

- A repository for all information that affects a product, and
- *A communication process between product stakeholders*: Principally marketing, engineering, manufacturing and field service.

The PLM system is the first place where all product information from marketing and design comes together, and where it leaves in a form suitable for production and support.

A few analysts use "PLM" as an umbrella term that includes engineering CAD. But product information creation tools include word processors; spreadsheet and graphics prigrammes; requirements analysis and market assessment tools; field trouble reports; and even emails or other correspondence. In our view, a PLM tool focuses exclusively on managing data that covers the breadth of a product's lifecycle, without regard to how that data is developed.

The essential elements of PLM:

- Manages design and process documents

- Constructs and controls bill of material records
- Offers an electronic file repository
- Includes built-in and custom part and document metadata
- Identifies materials content for environmental compliance
- Permits item-focused task assignments
- Enables workflow and process management for approving changes
- Controls multi-user secured access, including "electronic signature"
- Exports data for downstream ERP systems

LIMITATIONS

The PLC model is of some degree of usefulness to marketing managers, in that it is based on factual assumptions. Nevertheless, it is difficult for marketing management to gauge accurately where a product is on its PLC graph. A rise in sales per se is not necessarily evidence of growth. A fall in sales per se does not typify decline. Furthermore, some products do not experienced a decline. Coca Cola and Pepsi are examples of two products that have existed for many decades, but are still popular products all over the world. Both modes of cola have been in maturity for some years.

Another factor is that differing products would possess different PLC "shapes". A fad product would hold a steep sloped growth stage, a short maturity stage, and a steep sloped decline stage. A product such as Coca Cola and Pepsi would experience growth, but also a constant level of sales over a number of decades. It can probably be said that a given product may hold a unique PLC shape, and the typical PLC model can only be used as a rough guide for marketing management. This is why its called the product life cycle.

DIFFUSION (BUSINESS)

Diffusion is the process by which a new idea or new product is accepted by the market. The rate of diffusion is the speed that the new idea spreads from one consumer to the next.

Adoption is similar to diffusion except that it deals with the psychological processes an individual goes through, rather than an aggregate market process. In economics it is more often named "technological change".

THEORIES

There are several theories that purport to explain the mechanics of diffusion:

- *The two-step hypothesis*: Information and acceptance flows, via the media, first to opinion leaders, then to the general population
- *The trickle-down effect*: Products tend to be expensive at first, and therefore only accessible to the wealthy social strata - in time they become less expensive and are diffussed to lower and lower strata
- *The Everett Rogers Diffusion of innovations theory*: For any given product category, there are five categories of product adopters:
  - *Innovators*: Venturesome, educated, multiple info sources;
  - *Early adopters*: Social leaders, popular, educated;
  - *Early majority*: Deliberate, many informal social contacts;
  - *Late majority*: Skeptical, traditional, lower socio-economic status;
  - *Laggards*: Neighbours and friends are main info sources, fear of debt.
- *Crossing the Chasm model developed by Geoffrey Moore*: This is basically a modification of Everett Rogers' theory applied to technology markets and with a chasm added. Moore, the marketer should focus on one group of customers at a time, using each group as a base for marketing to the next group. The most difficult step is making the transition between visionaries and pragmatists. This is the chasm that he refers to. If successful, a firm can create a bandwagon effect in which the momentum builds and the product becomes a de facto standard.

- *Technology driven models*: These are particularly relevant to software diffusion. The rate of acceptance of technology is determined by factors such as ease of use and usefulness.

RATE

Everett M. Rogers, the rate of diffusion is influenced by:

- The product's perceived advantage or benefit.
- Riskiness of purchase.
- Ease of product use - complexity of the product.
- Immediacy of benefits.
- Observability.
- Trialability.
- Price.
- Extent of behavioural changes required.
- Return on investment in the case of industrial products.

Models

There are several types of diffusion rate models:

- *Penetration models*: Use test market data to develop acceptance equations of expected sales volume as a function of time. Three examples of penetration models are:
  - Bass trial only model
  - Bass declining trial model
  - Fourt and Woodlock model
- *Trial/Repeat models*: Number of repeat buyers is a function of the number of trial buyers.
- *Deterministic models*: Assess number of buyers at various states of acceptance - later states are determined from calculations to previous states.
- *Stochastic models*: Recognize that many elements of the diffusion process are unknown but explicitly incorporate probabilistic terms.

TECHNOLOGY LIFECYCLE

Most new technologies follow a similar technology

lifecycle. This is similar to a product life cycle, but applies to an entire technology, or a generation of a technology.

There is usually technology hype at the introduction of any new technology, but only after some time has passed can it be judged as mere hype or justified true acclaim. Because of the logistic curve nature of technology adoption, it is difficult to see at in the early stages whether the hype is excessive.

The two errors commonly committed in the early stages of a technology's development are:

1. Fitting an exponential curve to the first part of the growth curve, and assuming eternal exponential growth
2. Fitting a linear curve to the first part of the growth curve, and assuming that takeup of the new technology is disappointing

Similarly, in the later stages, the opposite mistakes can be made relating to the possibilities of technology maturity and market saturation.

DISRUPTIVE TECHNOLOGY

Disruptive innovation is a term used in business and technology literature to describe innovations that improve a product or service in ways that the market does not expect, typically by lowering price or designing for a different set of consumers.

In contrast to "disruptive innovation", a "sustaining" innovation does not have an effect on existing markets. Sustaining innovations may be either "discontinuous" or "continuous". Transformational innovations are not always disruptive. Although the automobile was a transformational innovation, it was not a disruptive innovation, because early automobiles were expensive luxury items that did not disrupt the market for horse-drawn vehicles. However, they did transform the transportation industry along an important technological vector. The market for transportation essentially remained intact until the debut of the lower priced Ford Model T in 1908 by making higher speed, motorized transportation available to the masses.

THE THEORY

Christensen distinguishes between "low-end disruption" which targets customers who do not need the full performance valued by customers at the high end of the market and "new-market disruption" which targets customers who have needs that were previously unserved by existing incumbents.

"Low-end disruption" occurs when the rate at which products improve exceeds the rate at which customers can adopt the new performance. Therefore, at some point the performance of the product overshoots the needs of certain customer segments. At this point, a disruptive technology may enter the market and provide a product which has lower performance than the incumbent but which exceeds the requirements of certain segments, thereby gaining a foothold in the market.

In low-end disruption, the disruptor is focused initially on serving the least profitable customer, who is happy with a good enough product. This type of customer is not willing to pay premium for enhancements in product functionality. Once the disruptor has gained foot hold in this customer segment, it seeks to improve its profit margin.

To get higher profit margins, the disruptor needs to enter the segment where the customer is willing to pay a little more for higher quality. To ensure this quality in its product, the disruptor needs to innovate.

The incumbent will not do much to retain its share in a not so profitable segment, and will move up-market and focus on its more attractive customers. After a number of such encounters, the incumbent is squeezed into smaller markets than it was previously serving.

And then finally the disruptive technology meets the demands of the most profitable segment and drives the established company out of the market.

"New market disruption" occurs when a product fits a new or emerging market segment that is not being served by existing incumbents in the industry.

The Linux operating system when introduced was inferior in performance to other server operating systems like Unix and

Windows NT. But the Linux OS is inexpensive compared to other server operating systems. After years of improvements Linux is now installed in 87.8% of the worlds 500 fastest supercomputers.

BUSINESS IMPLICATIONS

Disruptive technologies are not always disruptive to customers, and often take a long time before they are significantly disruptive to established companies. They are often difficult to recognize.

Indeed, as Christensen points out and studies have shown, it is often entirely rational for incumbent companies to ignore disruptive innovations, since they compare so badly with existing technologies or products, and the deceptively small market available for a disruptive innovation is often very small compared to the market for the established technology.

Even if a disruptive innovation is recognized, existing businesses are often reluctant to take advantage of it, since it would involve competing with their existing technological approach.

Christensen recommends that existing firms watch for these innovations, invest in small firms that might adopt these innovations, and continue to push technological demands in their core market so that performance stays what disruptive technologies can achieve.

Disruptive technologies, too, can be subtly disruptive, rather than prominently so. Examples include digital photography and IP/Internet telephony, where the replacement technology does not, and sometimes cannot practically replace all of the non-obvious attributes of the older system.

LIFE-CYCLE COST ANALYSIS

Life-cycle cost analysis is a method for assessing the total cost of facility ownership. It takes into account all costs of acquiring, owning, and disposing of a building or building system.

LCCA is especially useful when project alternatives that

fulfill the same performance requirements, but differ with respect to initial costs and operating costs, have to be compared in order to select the one that maximizes net savings. For example, LCCA will help determine whether the incorporation of a high-performance HVAC or glazing system, which may increase initial cost but result in dramatically reduced operating and maintenance costs, is cost-effective or not. LCCA is not useful for budget allocation.

Lowest life-cycle cost is the most straightforward and easy-to-interpret measure of economic evaluation. Some other commonly used measures are Net Savings, Savings-to-Investment Ratio, Internal Rate of Return, and Payback Period. They are consistent with the Lowest LCC measure of evaluation if they use the same parametres and length of study period.

Building economists, certified value specialists, cost engineers, architects, quantity surveyors, operations researchers, and others might use any or several of these techniques to evaluate a project. The approach to making cost-effective choices for building-related projects can be quite similar whether it is called cost estimating, value engineering, or economic analysis.

DESCRIPTION

Life-Cycle Cost Analysis Method

The purpose of an LCCA is to estimate the overall costs of project alternatives and to select the design that ensures the facility will provide the lowest overall cost of ownership consistent with its quality and function. The LCCA should be performed early in the design process while there is still a chance to refine the design to ensure a reduction in life-cycle costs.

The first and most challenging task of an LCCA, or any economic evaluation method, is to determine the economic effects of alternative designs of buildings and building systems and to quantify these effects and express them in dollar amounts.

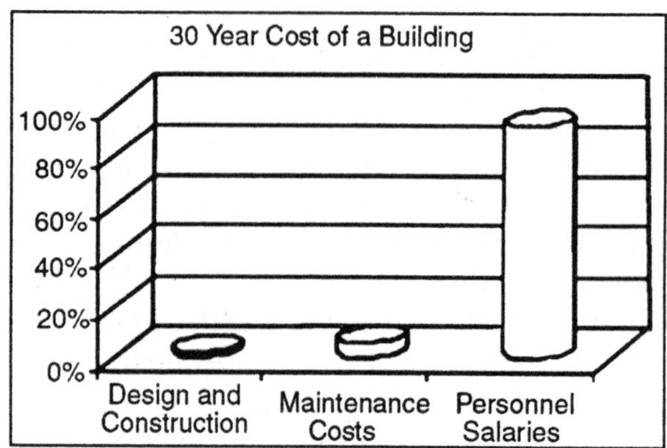

Viewed over a 30 year period, initial building costs account for approximately just 2% of the total, while operations and maintenance costs equal 6%, and personnel costs equal 92%.

Costs

There are numerous costs associated with acquiring, operating, maintaining, and disposing of a building or building system.

Building-related costs usually fall into the following categories:

- *Initial Costs*: Purchase, Acquisition, Construction Costs
- Fuel Costs
- Operation, Maintenance, and Repair Costs
- Replacement Costs
- *Residual Values*: Resale or Salvage Values or Disposal Costs
- *Finance Charges*: Loan Interest Payments
- Non-Monetary Benefits or Costs

Only those costs within each category that are relevant to the decision and significant in amount are needed to make a valid investment decision. Costs are relevant when they are different for one alternative compared with another; costs are significant when they are large enough to make a credible difference in the LCC of a project alternative. All costs are entered as base-year amounts in today's dollars; the LCCA method escalates all amounts to their future year of occurrence and discounts them back to the base date to convert them to present values.

Initial Costs

Initial costs may include capital investment costs for land acquisition, construction, or renovation and for the equipment needed to operate a facility.

Land acquisition costs need to be included in the initial cost estimate if they differ among design alternatives. This would be the case, for example, when comparing the cost of renovating an existing facility with new construction on purchased land.

Construction costs: Detailed estimates of construction costs are not necessary for preliminary economic analyses of alternative building designs or systems. Such estimates are usually not available until the design is quite advanced and the opportunity for cost-reducing design changes has been missed.

LCCA can be repeated throughout the design process if more detailed cost information becomes available. Initially, construction costs are estimated by reference to historical data from similar facilities. Alternately, they can be determined from government or private-sector cost estimating guides and databases. The Tri-Services Parametric Estimating System contained in the National Institute of Building Sciences Construction Criteria Base developed models of different facility types by determining the critical cost parametres and relating these values through algebraic formulas to predict costs of a wide range of building systems, subsystems, and assemblies. The TPES models can be adapted to facilities beyond those included in the base modeling system by using SuccessEstimator, a software package available from U.S. Cost.

Detailed cost estimates are prepared at the submittal stages of design based on quantity take-off calculations. These estimates rely on cost databases such as the Commercial Unit Price Book or the R. S. Means Building Construction Cost Database.

Testing organizations such as ASTM International and trade organizations have reference data for materials and products they test or represent.

Energy and Water Costs

Operational expenses for energy, water, and other utilities are based on consumption, current rates, and price projections. Because energy, and to some extent water consumption, and building configuration and building envelope are interdependent, energy and water costs are usually assessed for the building as a whole rather than for individual building systems or components.

Energy usage: Energy costs are often difficult to predict accurately in the design phase of a project. Assumptions must be made about use profiles, occupancy rates, and schedules, all of which impact energy consumption. At the initial design stage, data on the amount of energy consumption for a building can come from engineering analysis or from computer prigrammes such as Energy-10, or eQuest. ENERGY PLUS, DOE-2.1E and BLAST require more detailed input not usually available until later in the design process. Other software packages, such as the proprietary prigrammes TRACE, ESPRE, and HAP have been developed to assist in mechanical equipment selection and sizing and are often distributed by manufacturers.

When selecting a prigramme, it is important to consider whether you need annual, monthly, or hourly energy consumption figures and whether the prigramme adequately tracks savings in energy consumption when design changes or different efficiency levels are simulated.

Energy prices: Quotes of current energy prices from local suppliers should take into account the rate type, the rate structure, summer and winter differentials, block rates, and demand charges to obtain an estimate as close as possible to the actual energy cost.

Energy price projections: Energy prices are assumed to increase or decrease at a rate different from general price inflation. This differential energy price escalation needs to be taken into account when estimating future energy costs. Energy price projections can be obtained either from the supplier or from energy price escalation rates published annually on April 1 by DOE in Discount Factors for Life-Cycle Cost Analysis.

Water Costs: Water costs should be handled much like energy costs. There are usually two types of water costs: water usage costs and water disposal costs. DOE does not publish water price projections.

Operation, Maintenance, and Repair Costs

Non-fuel operating costs, and maintenance and repair costs are often more difficult to estimate than other building expenditures. Operating schedules and standards of maintenance vary from building to building; there is great variation in these costs even for buildings of the same type and age. It is therefore especially important to use engineering judgment when estimating these costs.

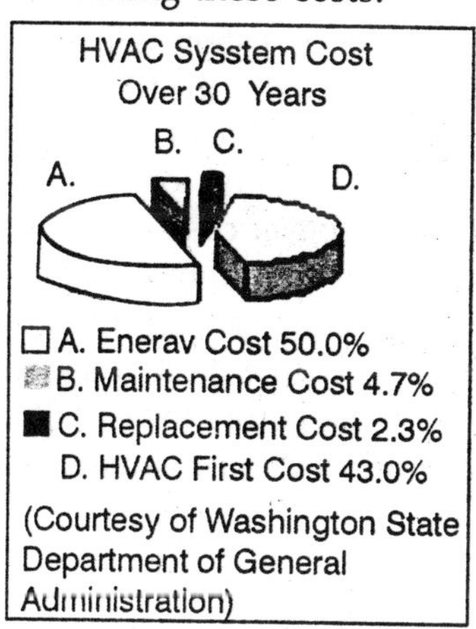

(Courtesy of Washington State Department of General Administration)

Supplier quotes and published estimating guides sometimes provide information on maintenance and repair costs. Some of the data estimation guides derive cost data from statistical relationships of historical data and report, for example, average owning and operating costs per square foot, by age of building, geographic location, number of stories, and number of square feet in the building. The Whitestone

Research Building Maintenance and Repair Cost Reference gives annualized costs for building systems and elements as well as service life estimates for specific building components. The U.S. Army Corps of Engineers, Huntsville Division, provides access to a customised OM&R database for military construction.

Replacement Costs

The number and timing of capital replacements of building systems depend on the estimated life of the system and the length of the study period. Use the same sources that provide cost estimates for initial investments to obtain estimates of replacement costs and expected useful lives. A good starting point for estimating future replacement costs is to use their cost as of the base date. The LCCA method will escalate base-year amounts to their future time of occurrence.

Residual Values

The residual value of a system is its remaining value at the end of the study period, or at the time it is replaced during the study period. Residual values can be based on value in place, resale value, salvage value, or scrap value, net of any selling, conversion, or disposal costs. As a rule of thumb, the residual value of a system with remaining useful life in place can be calculated by linearly prorating its initial costs. For example, for a system with an expected useful life of 15 years, which was installed 5 years before the end of the study period, the residual value would be approximately 2/3 (=(15-10)/15) of its initial cost.

Other Costs

Finance charges and taxes: For federal projects, finance charges are usually not relevant. Finance charges and other payments apply, however, if a project is financed through an Energy Savings Performance Contract or Utility Energy Services Contract. The finance charges are usually included in the contract payments negotiated with the Energy Service Company or the utility.

Non-monetary benefits or costs: Non-monetary benefits or costs are project-related effects for which there is no objective way of assigning a dollar value. Examples of non-monetary effects may be the benefit derived from a particularly quiet HVAC system or from an expected, but hard-to-quantify productivity gain due to improved lighting. By their nature, these effects are external to the LCCA, but if they are significant they should be considered in the final investment decision and included in the project documentation.

To formalize the inclusion of non-monetary costs or benefits in your decision making, you can use the analytical hierarchy process, which is one of a set of multi-attribute decision analysis methods that consider non-monetary attributes in addition to common economic evaluation measures when evaluating project alternatives.

ASTM E 1765 Standard Practice for Applying Analytical Hierarchy Process to Multi-attribute Decision Analysis of Investments Related to Buildings and Building Systems published by ASTM International presents a procedure for calculating and interpreting AHP scores of a project's total overall desirability when making building-related capital investment decisions. A source of information for estimating productivity costs, for example, is the WBDG Productive Branch.

Parametres for Present-Value Analysis

Discount Rate

In order to be able to add and compare cash flows that are incurred at different times during the life cycle of a project, they have to be made time-equivalent. To make cash flows time-equivalent, the LCC method converts them to present values by discounting them to a common point in time, usually the base date. The interest rate used for discounting is a rate that reflects an investor's opportunity cost of money over time, meaning that an investor wants to achieve a return at least as high as that of her next best investment. Hence, the discount rate represents the investor's minimum acceptable rate of return.

The discount rate for federal energy and water conservation projects is determined annually by FEMP; for other federal projects, those not primarily concerned with energy or water conservation, the discount rate is determined by OMB. These discount rates are real discount rates, not including the general rate of inflation.

Cost Period(s)

Length of study period: The study period begins with the base date, the date to which all cash flows are discounted. The study period includes any planning/construction/ implementation period and the service or occupancy period. The study period has to be the same for all alternatives considered.

Service period: The service period begins when the completed building is occupied or when a system is taken into service. This is the period over which operational costs and benefits are evaluated. In FEMP analyses, the service period is limited to 40 years.

Contract period: The contract period in ESPC and UESC projects lies within the study period. It starts when the project is formally accepted, energy savings begin to accrue, and contract payments begin to be due. The contract period generally ends when the loan is paid off.

Discounting Convention

In OMB and FEMP studies, all annually recurring cash flows are discounted from the end of the year in which they are incurred; in MILCON studies they are discounted from the middle of the year. All single amounts are discounted from their dates of occurrence.

Treatment of Inflation

An LCCA can be performed in constant dollars or current dollars. Constant-dollar analyses exclude the rate of general inflation, and current-dollar analyses include the rate of general inflation in all dollar amounts, discount rates, and price escalation rates. Both types of calculation result in identical present-value life-cycle costs. Constant-dollar analysis is recommended for all federal projects, except for projects financed by the private sector. The constant-dollar method has the advantage of not requiring an estimate of the rate of inflation for the years in the study period. Alternative financing studies are usually performed in current dollars if the analyst wants to compare contract payments with actual operational or energy cost savings from year to year.

Life-Cycle Cost Calculation

After identifying all costs by year and amount and discounting them to present value, they are added to arrive at total life-cycle costs for each alternative:

LCC = I + Repl – Res + E + W + OM&R + O LCC = Total LCC in present-value dollars of a given alternative I = PV investment costs Repl = PV capital replacement costs Res = PV residual value less disposal costs E = PV of energy costs W = PV of water costs OM&R = PV of non-fuel operating, maintenance and repair costs O = PV of other costs

Supplementary Measures

Supplementary measures of economic evaluation are Net Savings, Savings-to-Investment Ratio, Adjusted Internal Rate of Return, and Simple Payback or Discounted Payback. They are sometimes needed to meet specific regulatory requirements. For example, the FEMP LCC rules require the use of either the SIR or AIRR for ranking independent projects competing for limited funding. Some federal prigrammes require a Payback Period to be computed as a screening measure in project evaluation. NS, SIR, and AIRR are consistent with the lowest LCC of an alternative if computed and applied correctly, with the same time-adjusted input values and assumptions. Payback measures, either SPB or DPB, are only consistent with LCCA if they are calculated over the entire study period, not only for the years of the payback period.

All supplementary measures are relative measures, i.e., they are computed for an alternative relative to a base case.

NS = Net Savings: operational savings less difference in capital investment costs SIR = Savings-to-Investment Ratio: ratio of operational savings to difference in capital investment costs AIRR = Adjusted Internal Rate of Return: annual yield from an alternative over the study period, taking into account reinvestment of interim returns at the discount rate SPB = Simple Payback: time required for the cumulative savings from an alternative to recover its initial investment cost and other accrued costs, without taking into account the time value of money DPB = Discounted Payback: time required for the cumulative savings from an alternative to recover its initial investment cost and other accrued costs, taking into account the time value of money

Evaluation Criteria

Lowest LCC NS > 0 SIR > 1 AIRR > discount rate SPB, DPB < than study period

Uncertainty Assessment in Life-Cycle Cost Analysis

Decisions about building-related investments typically involve a great deal of uncertainty about their costs and potential savings. Performing an LCCA greatly increases the likelihood of choosing a project that saves money in the long run. Yet, there may still be some uncertainty associated with the LCC results. LCCAs are usually performed early in the design process when only estimates of costs and savings are available, rather than certain dollar amounts. Uncertainty in input values means that actual outcomes may differ from estimated outcomes.

There are techniques for estimating the cost of choosing the "wrong" project alternative. Deterministic techniques, such as sensitivity analysis or breakeven analysis, are easily done without requiring additional resources or information. They produce a single-point estimate of how uncertain input data affect the analysis outcome. Probabilistic techniques, on the other hand, quantify risk exposure by deriving probabilities of achieving different values of economic worth from probability distributions for input values that are uncertain. However, they have greater informational and technical requirements than do deterministic techniques. Whether one or the other technique is chosen depends on factors such as the size of the project, its importance, and the resources available. Since sensitivity analysis and break-even analysis are two approaches that are simple to perform, they should be part of every LCCA.

Sensitivity Analysis

Sensitivity analysis is the technique recommended for energy and water conservation projects by FEMP.

Sensitivity analysis is useful for:

- Identifying which of a number of uncertain input values has the greatest impact on a specific measure of economic evaluation,
- Determining how variability in the input value affects the range of a measure of economic evaluation, and
- Testing different scenarios to answer "what if" questions.

To identify critical parametres, arrive at estimates of upper and lower bounds, or answer "what if" questions, simply change the value of each input up or down, holding all others constant, and recalculate the economic measure to be tested.

Break-even Analysis

Decision-makers sometimes want to know the maximum cost of an input that will allow the project to still break even, or conversely, what minimum benefit a project can produce and still cover the cost of the investment. To perform a break-even analysis, benefits and costs are set equal, all variables are specified, and the break-even variable is solved algebraically.

Sensitivity analysis and break-even analysis, and a number of other approaches to risk and uncertainty assessment, both deterministic and probabilistic, are described in detail in Techniques for Treating Uncertainty and Risk in the Economic Evaluation of Building Investments, by Harold Marshall, NIST Special Publication 757, September 1988..

Design and Analysis Tools

The use of computer prigrammes can considerably reduce the time and effort spent on formulating the LCCA, performing the computations, and documenting the study.

Listed are several LCCA-related software prigrammes:

- Building Life-Cycle Cost Prigramme—Economic analysis tool developed by the National Institute of Standards and Technology for the U.S. Department of Energy Federal Energy Management Prigramme.
- ECONPACK for Windows—An economic analysis tool developed by the U.S. Army Corps of Engineers in support of DOD funding requests.
- Energy-10—Cost estimating prigramme available from the Sustainable Buildings Industry Council.
- SuccessEstimator Estimating and Cost Management System—Cost estimating tool available from U.S. Cost.

APPLICATION

LCCA can be applied to any capital investment decision in which relatively higher initial costs are traded for reduced future cost obligations.

It is particularly suitable for the evaluation of building design alternatives that satisfy a required level of building performance but may have different initial investment costs, different operating and maintenance and repair costs, and possibly different lives.

LCCA provides a significantly better assessment of the long-term cost-effectiveness of a project than alternative economic methods that focus only on first costs or on operating-related costs in the short run.

LCCA can be performed at various levels of complexity. Its scope might vary from a "back-of-the-envelope" study to a detailed analysis with thoroughly researched input data, supplementary measures of economic evaluation, complex uncertainty assessment, and extensive documentation. The extensiveness of the effort should be tailored to the needs of the project.

PRODUCT DECISIONS

Marketers think of a product as a bundle of physical, service, and symbolic characteristics expected to yield benefits to the consumer. Products may range from goods to services, although most products will have some degree of both characteristics.

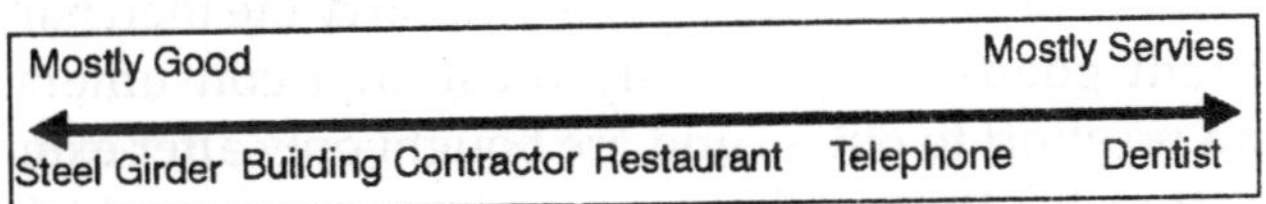

A product item is a specific version of a product that has a unique designation in the seller's list of products. A product line is a series of related product items. A product mix is the company's total assortment of product items.

The product mix may be described by three characteristics:

- Width: the number of product lines
- Depth: the average number of items per line
- *Consistency*: how closely related the product lines are

American Brands, for example, has five major product lines: tobacco products, distilled spirits, office products, home improvement and hardware, and golf and leisure. The tobacco line itself consists of several lines: cigarettes, cigars, pipe tobacco, and roll-your-own supplies. The home improvement and hardware line includes Master Lock and Moen products. A particular style of kitchen faucet would be a product item within the Moen line.

There are several ways to classify products. A popular way is to think of four categories based on the amount of effort a consumer might be expected to expend on obtaining the product: convenience, shopping, specialty, and unsought. In general, a person will expend little effort to obtain a convenience product, so marketers will focus on maximizing product availability via distribution and will try to build brand identity and competitive prices. Shopping products are items people do not buy as frequently, expending a moderate amount of effort to obtain the item and/or compare different alternatives. Distribution can be more selective, and marketers will attempt to build brand differentiation through promotion and the type of outlet carrying the merchandise. If consumers do not believe there really are brand differences, then price will be very important.

Specialty products are not bought very often and will usually be more expensive items. Consumers will expend maximum effort to obtain what they want. Marketers want to build an image of exclusiveness through promotion and distribution; only exclusive outlets will carry the merchandise. Unsought goods are generally those that consumers will expend no effort to obtain and are bought only after extensive promotion by the marketer. Life insurance might be an example of an unsought good.

There are thousands of "new" products introduced every year. It has been estimated that only about 10 per cent of these are new in the sense that they did not exist before. More than half of "new" products are really product modifications or product improvement.

Consumers tend to perceive "newness" based on the amount of behaviour change necessary to use the product:

- Discontinuous innovation: pioneering products so new that no previous product performed an equivalent function; necessitate new consumption or usage patterns
- Dynamically continuous innovation: changes and improvements that do not strikingly change buying and usage patterns; these occupy the middle range on the continuum of newness
- Continuous innovations: ongoing, commonplace changes, such as minor product alterations or imitative products

Although definitions of success and failure vary, there is no doubt that the majority of new products are not successes.

Common reasons for failure include:

- Inadequate product superiority or uniqueness, as when a "me too" product does not offer a relative advantage
- Inadequate or inferior planning, such as failing to do proper marketing research to understand consumers'

needs or failure to develop realistic estimates of demand

- Poor execution, which may occur when management believes the product is so good it will succeed without resources to support it
- Technical problems, as when a product fails because of design or production problems
- Poor timing, as when a company enters a market too early or too late in the product life cycle or when the marketing environment changes

The typical process for developing new products looks like this:

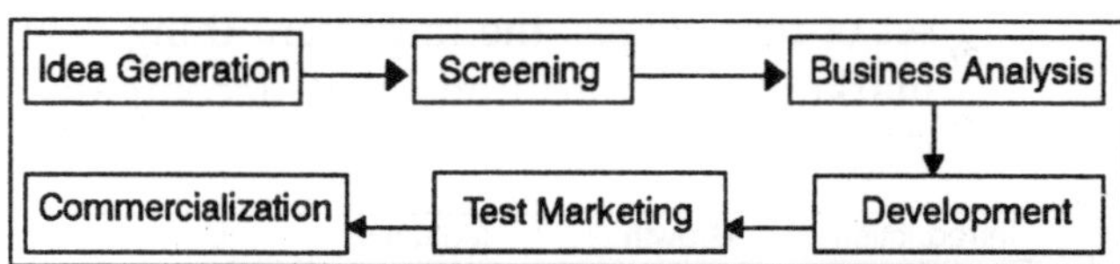

Step 1: *Idea Generation*: Perfom a continuous, systematic search for new ideas. Sources of ideas include scientists, consumers, salespeople, top management, and competitors.

Step 2: *Screening*: Delete from further consideration those ideas that are not consistent with company objectives and resources or with the market needs that the company tries to serve. Common tools include screening checklists and concept testing.

Step 3: *Business Analysis*: Do financial and marketing analyses to see whether the product idea appears to be profitable and what type of marketing efforts it will require.

Step 4: *(Product) Development*: See if the idea can actually be realised. Is it technically and commercially feasible? This stage often involves a host of other decisions, such as package design, brand name selection, trademark registration, etc.

Step 5: *Test Marketing*: Put the product on the market in limited areas to gauge market reaction. The amount of test marketing needed varies by product. Generally little or no test marketing is done when development costs are low, management is very confident, the innovation is a minor product modification or is an imitative product, and/or the product is a high-ticket item.

Step 6: *Commercialization*: Introduce and market the new product. Decisions include when, where, to whom, and how. Once a product is launched, it enters a product life cycle. The PLC describes how a typical new product category follows a set of four stages, the important thing being the marketing implications that accompany each stage.

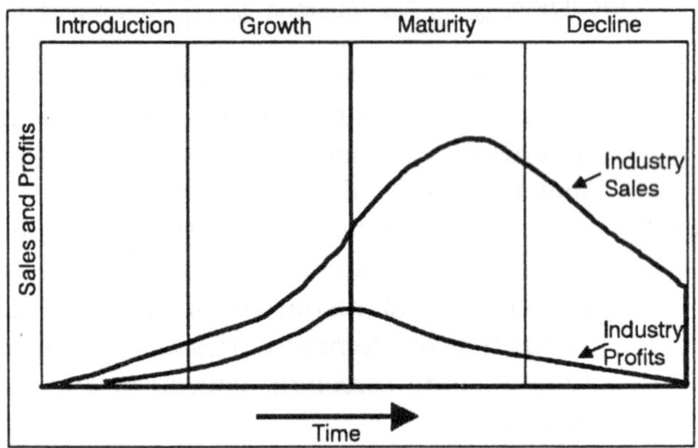

In the introduction stage, the firm faces little if any direct competition for its new product. The objective is to gain awareness and acceptance in the market both by consumers and by middlemen who might carry the product. Price is typically set high, both to take advantage of the fact that the earliest buyers of a new product are often willing to pay premium prices for something new and to begin to regain some of the investment expenses incurred in developing the product. Sometimes, especially if competition might be expected early, a low price is used to discourage competition from entering. Promotion is designed to inform and educate the market about the new product. Distribution is limited to those few middlemen who might be willing to accept a new product. In the growth stage, competitors enter the market with their own versions of the product, and competition often is based on real product differences. The strategic focus now becomes building market share and establishing product differentiation. Price tends to remain high but will fall toward the end of the stage as it becomes more of a competitive tool. Distribution will expand considerably, and the tone of promotion shifts to being more persuasive, stressing product differences.

The maturity stage is marked by stable sales and high total industry profits. Many competitors dominate the market, although many more marginal ones that entered during the growth stage have left. The objective now is maintaining the market built in the growth stage. Although firms will have full product lines with many variations, real product differences are fewer. Price tends to fall, being used more competitively. Distribution will be at its maximum. Promotion is of a "reminder" nature.

In the decline stage, sales are falling, as are profits. Firms begin to exit the industry, and the objective now becomes one of trying to pull as much profit as possible from the product in its waning days. The product lines are pruned, with only the few best versions remaining. Both promotion and distribution are reduced as much as possible to help pare back costs. Because the maturity stage is the most profitable, firms will derive strategies for prolonging it as much as possible through either product or market modifications.

Product modifications may include the following:

- *Quality improvements*: Quality is defined by *consumers* and measures how well a product does what it is supposed to do. Marketers need to
  - Provide the desired level of quality,
  - Work constantly to improve quality, and
  - Accurately communicate quality to market.
- *Design improvements*: Styling, aesthetics, and/or function of a product is altered to offer more convenience, safety, efficiency, or versatility.

- *Style improvements*: The aesthetic appeal of the product is increased, especially with an eye toward creating a unique look.

The Product Life Cycle results from a diffusion process that is the the sequence of acceptance of new products by the members of a community or social system.

Five groups are visible in the diffusion process, based on the speed with which they adopt an innovation:

- Innovators initially purchase a new product. They are motivated by novelty and tend to be younger, more affluent, better educated, and confident about their decision-making ability.
- Early Adopters are similar to innovators. They are motivated more by improvement than novelty and are generally considered the most important group because of their opinion leadership qualities—others will follow them.
- Early Majority members are aware of and willing to accept change. They tend to be average in age, affluence, and education.
- Late Majority members are less aware of and less willing to accept change. They may be of an older average age and a little below average in affluence and education; they tend to be conservative and traditional.
- Laggards are the last group to adopt a product. They are generally the oldest, most conservative group.

Part of the "product decision area" involves branding, packaging, and labeling. Both consumers and marketers rely on branding. Think how much easier it is to buy products based on your familiarity with the brand—it certainly makes the search and evaluation stages much simpler than when buying a brand you aren't familiar with. For consumers, benefits include quality assurance, a reduced search/selection time, a known quantity, and prestige. For marketers, benefits include differentiation of their product from competitors', improved brand identity, and more effective marketing communications.

There are several terms to be familiar with:

- *Brand*: A name, term, sign, symbol, design, or combination thereof used to identify and differentiate a company's products from competitors'
- *Brand name*: The element of the brand that can be vocalized
- *Brand mark*: The element of the brand that cannot be vocalized
- *Trademark*: A brand or part of a brand that is registered with the U.S. Patent and Trademark office. This provides the owner of the brand with legal protection for excluding competitors from use of the same or very similar name or logo.
- *Service mark*: the "trademark" for services

Marketers must choose from several brand strategies. One choice involves the sponsor of the brand. A national brand is owned by a manufacturer who then bears the cost of marketing the brand. A distributor or private brand is owned by a retailer or wholesaler, although the product generally is made by a well-known manufacturer. The retailer or wholesaler is responsible for any marketing of the brand. A generic brand has no visible brand name—ownership cannot be determined, and usually no marketing outside of distribution is done.

Another decision is "family vs. individual" branding. In a family, one name is used for a set of products, such as the Craftsman name on a variety of tools. A variation on this is licensing, where the owner of a trademark permits others to use it on various products. In multibranding, each product has its own name, such as with Procter and Gamble's Tide, Cheer, and Ivory Snow laundry detergents. In a combination strategy, combined family and individual brands are used, such as with Kellogg's Frosted Flakes and Kellogg's Corn Flakes. As with other marketing decisions, there is no one best way; each strategy carries certain advantages and drawbacks. Ideally, marketers try to build "brand equity," which reflects the value a brand has beyond its basic functional value. Brand equity has a financial dimension to it that results from having a large enough part of the market desiring that brand above others.

Typically, brand equity results from a long-term strategy that leads a market to that point in a series of stages:

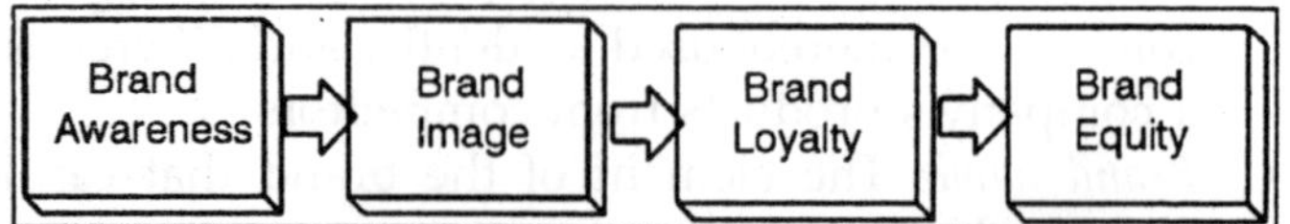

First, the market must realise that the brand exists in the marketplace. Next, the marketer builds strong, positive associations with the brand. From that comes preference, where the ideal is for the consumer to buy that brand exclusively. From long-term use comes consumer identification with the brand. The importance of packaging and labeling differs by product. Packaging may serve various functions. For many consumer products, especially those typically bought in self-serve environments, promotion is a critical element in helping the consumer identify the product and in increasing the product's visibility in a retail setting.

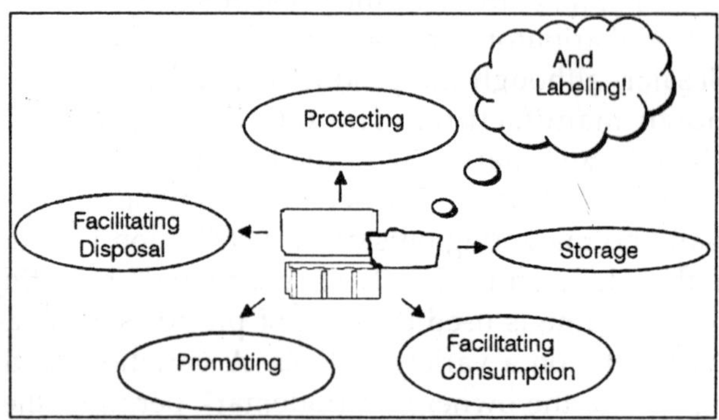

Services differ from goods in several distinct ways. *The diagram shows these key differences:*

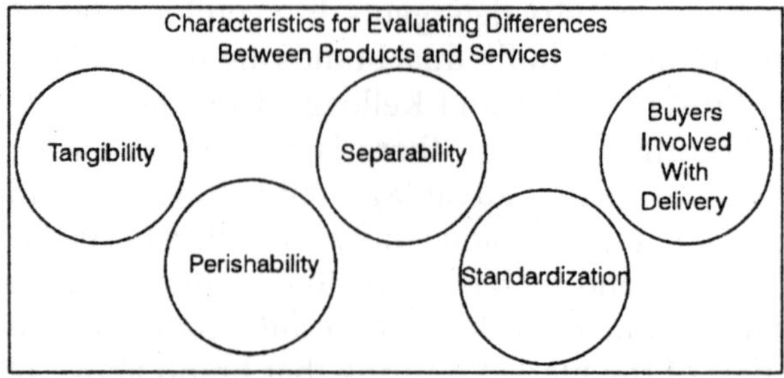

Goods are tangible; services are intangible. Although some goods have very short lifespans, they can be stored for at least a while before consumption; if services are not used when available, they are unrecoverable. Goods can be separated from their makers, but services cannot be separated from the provider.

Goods may be made just as to a standard procedure that makes consistency of output; service delivery is difficult to standardize, so delivery is always, to some degree, inconsistent. Finally, goods may be bought from someone other than the actual producer; with services, the buyer is directly involved with the process: the dental hygienist cannot clean your teeth without you being there.

Because of these differences, the marketing mix elements must be modified for services:

- *Product*: Can be classified like goods. Same marketing mix ideas would then apply. Things like packaging and labeling are of minimal or no importance.
- *Pricing*: Harder to determine because cost of "production" is often more difficult to determine. Price negotiation may be more prevalent for services.
- *Place*: Channels are usually short. Storage, transportation, and inventory are of minimal or no concern.
- *Promotion*: Can be "tangibilized" by linking service to a specific benefit. Creation of a favourable image is critical. Desire for "personal relationship" with provider increases importance of personal selling.

The intangibility of services makes it very difficult for consumers to judge the quality of the service.

Hence, consumers rely on a variety of indicators to suggest quality:

- *Reliability*: Is the service likely to be delivered as expected?
- *Tangibles*: What are the physical characteristics of the place of delivery?
- *Responsiveness*: How willing is the provider to deliver the service?

- *Empathy*: How willing is the provider to take time to determine the exact nature of the service desired?
- *Assurance*: How confident does the consumer feel that the service will be provided as expected?

PRODUCT MIX

Product mix is a combination of products manufactured or traded by the same business house to reinforce their presence in the market, increase market share and increase the turnover for more profitability.

Normally the product mix is within the synergy of other products for a medium size organization. However large groups of Industries may have diversified products within core competency.

Larsen and Toubro Ltd, Godrej, Reliance in India are some of the examples. One of the realities of business is that most firms deal with multi-products.This helps a firm diffuse its risk across different product groups/Also it enables the firm to appeal to a much larger group of customers or to different needs of the same customer group.

So when Videocon chose to diversify into other consumer durables like music systems,washing machines and refrigerators,it sought to satisfy the needs of the middle and upper middle income group of consumers. Likewise, Bajaj Electricals.a household name in India, has almost ninety products in i8ts portfolio ranging from low value items like bulbs to high priced consumer durables like mixers and luminaires and lighting projects.The number of products carried by a firm at a given point of time is called its product mix. This product mix contains product lines and product items.In other words it's a composite of products offered for sale by a firm.

PRODUCT MIX DECISIONS

Often firms take decisions to change their product mix. These decisions are dictated by the factors and also by the changes occurring in the market place. Like the changing life-styles of Indian consumers led BPL-Sanyo to launch an entire range of white goods like refrigerators, washing machines, and microwave ovens.It also motivate the firm to launch other entertainment electronics.

Rahejas, a well-known builders firm in Bombay, took a major decision to convert one of its theatre buildings in the western suburbs of Bombay into a large garments and accessories store for men,women and children, perhaps the first of its kind in India to have almost all products required by these customer groups Competition from low priced washing powders forced Hindustan Levers to launch different brands of detergent powder at different price levels positioned at different market segments.Customer preferences for herbs, mainly shikakai motivated Lever to launch black Sunsilk Shampoo,which has shikakai.Also,low purchasing power. and cultural bias against shampoo market made Hindustan Lever consider smaller packaging mainly sachets, for single use.So, it is the changes or anticipated changes in the market place that motivates a firm to consider changes in its product mix.

NEW PRODUCT DEVELOPMENT

In business and engineering, new product development is the term used to describe the complete process of bringing a new product or service to market. There are two parallel paths involved in the NPD process: one involves the idea generation, product design and detail engineering; the other involves market research and marketing analysis. Companies typically see new product development as the first stage in generating and commercializing new products within the overall strategic process of product life cycle management used to maintain or grow their market share.

PROCESS

- Idea Generation is often called the "fuzzy front end" of the NPD process
  - Ideas for new products can be obtained from basic research using a SWOT analysis, Market and consumer trends, company's R&D department, competitors, focus groups, employees,

salespeople, corporate spies, trade shows, or Ethnographic discovery methods may also be used to get an insight into new product lines or product features.

  - Idea Generation or Brainstorming of new product, service, or store concepts - idea generation techniques can begin when you have done your OPPORTUNITY ANALYSIS to support your ideas in the Idea Screening Phase.

- Idea Screening
  - The object is to eliminate unsound concepts prior to devoting resources to them.
  - The screeners should ask several questions:
    a. Will the customer in the target market benefit from the product?
    b. What is the size and growth forecasts of the market segment/target market?
    c. What is the current or expected competitive pressure for the product idea?
    d. What are the industry sales and market trends the product idea is based on?
    e. Is it technically feasible to manufacture the product?
    f. Will the product be profitable when manufactured and delivered to the customer at the target price?
- Concept Development and Testing
  - Develop the marketing and engineering details
    a. Investigate intellectual property issues and search patent data bases
    b. Who is the target market and who is the decision maker in the purchasing process?
    c. What product features must the product incorporate?
    d. What benefits will the product provide?
    e. How will consumers react to the product?
    f. How will the product be produced most cost effectively?

g. Prove feasibility through virtual computer aided rendering, and rapid prototyping
h. What will it cost to produce it?

- Testing the Concept by asking a sample of prospective customers what they think of the idea. Usually via Choice Modelling.

- Business Analysis
  - Estimate likely selling price based upon competition and customer feedback
  - Estimate sales volume based upon size of market and such tools as the Fourt-Woodlock equation
  - Estimate profitability and breakeven point
- Beta Testing and Market Testing
  - Produce a physical prototype or mock-up
  - Test the product in typical usage situations
  - Conduct focus group customer interviews or introduce at trade show
  - Make adjustments where necessary
  - Produce an initial run of the product and sell it in a test market area to determine customer acceptance
- Technical Implementation
  - New prigramme initiation
  - Finalize Quality management system
  - Resource estimation
  - Requirement publication
  - Publish technical communications such as data sheets
  - Engineering operations planning
  - Department scheduling
  - Supplier collaboration
  - Logistics plan
  - Resource plan publication
  - Prigramme review and monitoring
  - Contingencies - what-if planning
- Commercialization
  - Launch the product
  - Produce and place advertisements and other promotions

  - Fill the distribution pipeline with product
  - Critical path analysis is most useful at this stage
- New Product Pricing
  - Impact of new product on the entire product portfolio
  - Value Analysis
  - Competition and alternative competitive technologies
  - Differing value segments
  - Product Costs
  - Forecast of unit volumes, revenue, and profit

These steps may be iterated as needed. Some steps may be eliminated. To reduce the time that the NPD process takes, many companies are completing several steps at the same time. Most industry leaders see new product development as a *proactive* process where resources are allocated to identify market changes and seize upon new product opportunities before they occur. Many industry leaders see new product development as an ongoing process in which the entire organization is always looking for opportunities.

Great amounts of uncertainty and change may exist, which makes it difficult or impossible to plan the complete project before starting it. In this case, a more flexible approach may be advisable.

Because the NPD process typically requires both engineering and marketing expertise, cross-functional teams are a common way of organizing projects. The team is responsible for all aspects of the project, from initial idea generation to final commercialization, and they usually report to senior management. In those industries where products are technically complex, development research is typically expensive, and product life cycles are relatively short, strategic alliances among several organizations helps to spread the costs, provide access to a wider skill set, and speeds the overall process. Also, notice that because engineering and marketing expertise are usually both critical to the process, choosing an appropriate blend of the two is important. Observe that this substance is slanted more toward the marketing side.

People respond to new products in different ways. The adoption of a new technology can be analysed using a variety of diffusion theories such as the Diffusion of innovations theory.

A new product pricing process is important to reduce risk and increase confidence in the pricing and marketing decisions to be made. Bernstein and Macias describe an integrated process that breaks down the complex task of new product pricing into manageable elements.

FUZZY FRONT END

The Fuzzy Front End is the messy "getting started" period of new product development processes. It is in the front end where the organization formulates a concept of the product to be developed and decides whether or not to invest resources in the further development of an idea. It is the phase between first consideration of an opportunity and when it is judged ready to enter the structured development process. It includes all activities from the search for new opportunities through the formation of a germ of an idea to the development of a precise concept. The Fuzzy Front End ends when an organization approves and begins formal development of the concept.

Although the Fuzzy Front End may not be an expensive part of product development, it can consume 50% of development time and it is where major commitments are typically made involving time, money, and the product's nature, thus setting the course for the entire project and final end product. Consequently, this phase should be considered as an essential part of development rather than something that happens "before development," and its cycle time should be included in the total development cycle time.

Koen et al. distinguish five different front-end elements:

1. Opportunity Identification
2. Opportunity Analysis
3. Idea Genesis
4. Idea Selection
5. Concept and Technology Development

The first element is the opportunity identification. In this element, large or incremental business and technological chances are identified in a more or less structured way. Using the guidelines established here, resources will eventually be allocated to new projects.... which then lead to a structured NPPD strategy. The second element is the opportunity analysis. It is done to translate the identified opportunities into implications for the business and technology specific context of the company. Here extensive efforts may be made to align ideas to target customer groups and do market studies and/ or technical trials and research..

The third element is the idea genesis, which is described as evolutionary and iterative process progressing from birth to maturation of the opportunity into a tangible idea. The process of the idea genesis can be made internally or come from outside inputs, e.g. a supplier offering a new material/ technology, or from a customer with an unusual request. The fourth element is the idea selection. Its purpose is to choose whether to pursue an idea by analyzing its potential business value. The fifth element is the concept and technology development. During this part of the front-end, the business case is developed based on estimates of the total available market, customer needs, investment requirements, competition analysis and project uncertainty. Some organizations consider this to be the first stage of the NPPD process. The Fuzzy Front End is also described in literature as "Front End of Innovation", "Phase 0", "Stage 0" or "Pre-Project-Activities".

A universally acceptable definition for Fuzzy Front End or a dominant framework has not been developed so far. It is the Fuzzy Front End generally consists of three tasks: strategic planning, concept generation, and, especially, pre-technical evaluation. These activities are often chaotic, unpredictible, and unstructured. In comparison, the subsequent new product development process is typically structured, predictable, and formal. The term *Fuzzy Front End* was first popularized by Smith and Reinertsen, R.G.Cooper describes the early stages of NPPD as a four step process in which ideas are generated

- Subjected to a preliminary technical and market assessment
- And merged to coherent product concepts
- Which are finally judged for their fit with existing product strategies and portfolios
- Cooper and Edgett affirm that vital predevelopment activities include:
  - Preliminary market assessment.
  - Technical assessment.
  - Source-of-supply-assessment:suppliers and partners or alliances.
  - Market research: market size and segmentation analysis,VoC research.
  - Product concept testing
  - Value-to-the customer assessment
  - Product definition
  - Business and financial analysis.

These activities yield vital information to make a Go/No-Go to Development decision.

In the in-depth study by Khurana and Rosenthal front-end activities include:

- Product strategy formulation and communication,
- Opportunity identification and assessment,
- Idea generation,
- Product definition,
- Project planning, and
- Executive reviews.

Economical analysis, benchmarking of competitive products,and modeling and prototyping are also important activities during the front-end activities.

The outcomes of FFE are the:

- Mission statement
- Customer needs
- Details of the selected concept
- Product definition and specifications
- Economic analysis of the product
- The development schedule
- Project staffing and the budget, and a
- Business plan aligned with corporate strategy.

Husig, Kohn and Huskela was proposed a conceptual model of Front-End Process which includes early Phases of Innovation Process.

This model is structured in three phases and three gates:

- *Phase 1*: Environmental screening or opportunity identification stage in which external changes will be analysed and translated into potential business opportunities.
- *Phase 2*: Preliminary definition of an idea or concept.
- *Phase 3*: Detailed product, project or concept definition, and Business planning.

The gates are:

- Opportunity screening;
- Idea evaluation;
- Go/No-Go for development.

The final gate leads to a dedicated new product development project. Many professionals and academics consider that the general features of Fuzzy Front End make difficult to see the FFE as a structured process,but rather as a set of interdependent activities. However, Husig et al.,2005 argue that front-end not need to be fuzzy,but can be handled in a structured manner. Peter Koen argue that in the FFE for incremental,platform and radical projects,three separate strategies and processes are typically involved. The traditional Stage Gate process was designed for incremental product development,namely for a single product.The FFE for developing a new platform must start out with a strategic vision of where the company wants to develop products and this will lead to a family of products. Projects for breakthrough products start out with a similar strategic vision,but are associated with technologies which require new discoveries.It is worth mentioning what are incremental,platform and breakthrough products.

Incremental products are considered to be cost reductions, improvements to existing product lines,additions to existing platforms and repositioning of existing products introduced in markets. *Breakthrough products* are new to the company or new to the world and offer a 5-10 times or greater improvement in performance combined with a 30-50% or greater reduction in costs. *Platform products* establish a basic architecture for a next generation product or process and are substantially larger in scope and resources than incremental projects.

PLANNED OBSOLESCENCE

Planned obsolescence or built-in obsolescence is the process of a product becoming obsolete or non-functional after a certain period or amount of use in a way that is planned or designed by the manufacturer. Also known as "Designed to Fail".

Planned obsolescence has potential benefits for a producer because the product fails and the consumer is under pressure to purchase again, whether from the same manufacturer or from a competitor which might also rely on planned obsolescence. The purpose of planned obsolescence is to hide the real cost per use from the consumer, and charge a higher price than they would otherwise be willing to pay.

For an industry, planned obsolescence stimulates demand by encouraging purchasers to buy sooner if they still want a functioning product. Built-in obsolescence is in many different products, from vehicles to light bulbs, from buildings to proprietary software.

There is, however, the potential backlash of consumers who learn that the manufacturer invested money to make the product obsolete faster; such consumers might turn to a producer that offers a more durable alternative.

Planned obsolescence was first developed in the 1920s and 1930s when mass production had opened every minute aspect of the production process to exacting analysis.

Estimates of planned obsolescence can influence a company's decisions about product engineering. Therefore the company can use the least expensive components that satisfy product lifetime projections. Such decisions are part of a broader discipline known as value engineering.

The use of planned obsolescence is not always easy to pinpoint, and it is complicated by related problems, such as competing technologies or creeping featurism which expands functionality in newer product versions.

PRODUCT LINING

Product lining is the marketing strategy of offering for sale several related products. Unlike product bundling, where several products are combined into one, lining involves offering several related products individually. A line can comprise related products of various sizes, types, colours, qualities, or prices. Line depth refers to the number of product variants in a line. Line consistency refers to how closely related the products that make up the line are. Line vulnerability refers to the percentage of sales or profits that are derived from only a few products in the line.

The number of different product lines sold by a company is referred to as width of product mix. The total number of products sold in all lines is referred to as length of product mix. If a line of products is sold with the same brand name, this is referred to as family branding. When you add a new product to a line, it is referred to as a line extension. When you add a line extension that is of better quality than the other products in the line, this is referred to as trading up or brand leveraging. When you add a line extension that is of lower quality than the other products of the line, this is referred to as trading down. When you trade down, you will likely reduce your brand equity. You are gaining short-term sales at the expense of long term sales.

Image anchors are highly promoted products within a line that define the image of the whole line. Image anchors are usually from the higher end of the line's range. When you add a new product within the current range of an incomplete line, this is referred to as line filling.

Price lining is the use of a limited number of prices for all your product offerings. This is a tradition started in the old five and dime stores in which everything cost either 5 or 10 cents. Its underlying rationale is that these amounts are seen as suitable price points for a whole range of products by prospective customers. It has the advantage of ease of administering, but the disadvantage of inflexibility, particularly in times of inflation or unstable prices.

There are many important decisions about product and service development and marketing. In the process of product development and marketing we should focus on strategic decisions about product attributes, product branding, product packaging, product labeling and product support services. But product strategy also calls for building a product line.

PROJECT PORTFOLIO MANAGEMENT

Project Portfolio Management is about more than running multiple projects. Each portfolio of projects needs to be assessed in terms of its business value and adherence to strategy. The portfolio should be designed to achieve a defined business objective or benefit. Project management guru Bob Buttrick summarised it when he said; "Directing the individual project correctly will ensure it is done right. Directing 'all the projects' successfully will ensure we are doing the right projects."

While at individual project level it is important to know how each project is performing, the impact of each project on the portfolio is just as important.

The following questions should be asked:

- Does each project contribute to the overall achievement of the portfolio?
- How well is each project performing?
- Will any project have a negative impact on other projects to come?
- What projects in the portfolio are dependent on others?
- Will the successful delivery of all projects deliver the desired objective or benefit?

Working at portfolio level is about working with summary or key data. It is important to avoid information overload. The detail of each project should be kept at the project team level, administered by the individual project managers. Key information should be rolled up and presented at each level within the organisation as appropriate. At executive, VP level you are likely to be providing a summary of performance, progress, a measurement of estimates against actuals and costs.

Within almost all project portfolio management systems there is a project evaluation process. This process is used to evaluate the projects at various points during their lifecycle. At the beginning of each stage, often called a 'gate,' the responsible party evaluates the business case, asking whether it is still relevant and able to deliver the defined organisational objectives. If the answer is no, then the project should be stopped. This way the organisation can ensure that they stay focussed on delivering a strategy, goal or other defined benefit and that resources are deployed where they will offer the best return.

Project portfolio management asks the following questions:

- Are we doing the right things?
- Are we doing them the right way?
- Are we doing them well?
- Are we getting the benefits?

If the answer to any of these questions is no, immediate action is required to bring the portfolio back on track.

BCG GROWTH-SHARE MATRIX

The BCG Growth-Share Matrix is a portfolio planning model developed by Bruce Henderson of the Boston Consulting Group in the early 1970's.

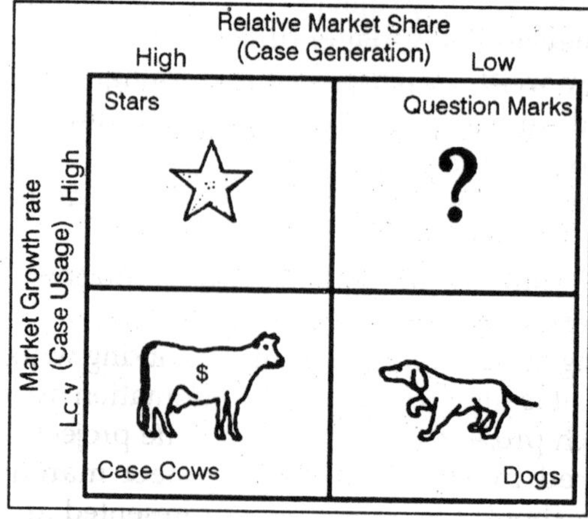

Fig. BCG Growth-Share Matrix

It is based on the observation that a company's business units can be classified into four categories based on combinations of market growth and market share relative to the largest competitor, hence the name "growth-share". Market growth serves as a proxy for industry attractiveness, and relative market share serves as a proxy for competitive advantage. The growth-share matrix thus maps the business unit positions within these two important determinants of profitability.

This framework assumes that an increase in relative market share will result in an increase in the generation of cash. This assumption often is true because of the experience curve; increased relative market share implies that the firm is moving forward on the experience curve relative to its competitors, thus developing a cost advantage. A second assumption is that a growing market requires investment in assets to increase capacity and therefore results in the consumption of cash. Thus the position of a business on the growth-share matrix provides an indication of its cash generation and its cash consumption.

Henderson reasoned that the cash required by rapidly growing business units could be obtained from the firm's other business units that were at a more mature stage and generating significant cash. By investing to become the market share leader in a rapidly growing market, the business unit could move along the experience curve and develop a cost advantage. From this reasoning, the BCG Growth-Share Matrix was born.

The four categories are:

- *Dogs*: Dogs have low market share and a low growth rate and thus neither generate nor consume a large amount of cash. However, dogs are cash traps because of the money tied up in a business that has little potential. Such businesses are candidates for divestiture.
- *Question marks*: Question marks are growing rapidly and thus consume large amounts of cash, but because they have low market shares they do not generate much cash. The result is a large net cash

comsumption. A question mark has the potential to gain market share and become a star, and eventually a cash cow when the market growth slows. If the question mark does not succeed in becoming the market leader, then after perhaps years of cash consumption it will degenerate into a dog when the market growth declines. Question marks must be analysed carefully in order to determine whether they are worth the investment required to grow market share.

- *Stars*: Stars generate large amounts of cash because of their strong relative market share, but also consume large amounts of cash because of their high growth rate; therefore the cash in each direction approximately nets out. If a star can maintain its large market share, it will become a cash cow when the market growth rate declines. The portfolio of a diversified company always should have stars that will become the next cash cows and ensure future cash generation.
- *Cash cows*: As leaders in a mature market and thus generate more cash than they consume. Such business units should be"milked", extracting the profits and investing as little cash as possible. Cash cows provide the cash required to turn question marks into market leaders, to cover the administrative costs of the company, to fund research and development, to service the corporate debt, and to pay dividends to shareholders. Because the cash cow generates a relatively stable cash flow, its value can be determined with reasonable accuracy by calculating the present value of its cash stream using a discounted cash flow analysis.

Under the growth-share matrix model, as an industry matures and its growth rate declines, a business unit will become either a cash cow or a dog, determined soley by whether it had become the market leader during the period of high growth.

While originally developed as a model for resource allocation among the various business units in a corporation, the growth-share matrix also can be used for resource allocation among products within a single business unit. Its simplicity is its strength.

LIMITATIONS

The growth-share matrix once was used widely, but has since faded from popularity as more comprehensive models have been developed.

Some of its weaknesses are:

- Market growth rate is only one factor in industry attractiveness, and relative market share is only one factor in competitive advantage. The growth-share matrix overlooks many other factors in these two important determinants of profitability.
- The framework assumes that each business unit is independent of the others. In some cases, a business unit that is a"dog" may be helping other business units gain a competitive advantage.
- The matrix depends heavily upon the breadth of the definition of the market. A business unit may dominate its small niche, but have very low market share in the overall industry. In such a case, the definition of the market can make the difference between a dog and a cash cow.

While its importance has diminished, the BCG matrix still can serve as a simple tool for viewing a corporation's business portfolio at a glance, and may serve as a starting point for discussing resource allocation among strategic business units.

G. E. MULTI FACTORAL ANALYSIS

The GE matrix is an alternative technique used in brand marketing and product management to help a company decide what product(s) to add to its product portfolio, and which market opportunities are worthy of continued investment. Also known as the 'Directional Policy Matrix,' the GE multi-factor model was first developed by General Electric in the 1970s.

Conceptually, the GE Matrix is similar to the Boston Box as it is plotted on a two-dimensional grid.

In most versions of the matrix:

- The Y-Axis comprises *industry attractiveness* measures, such as Market Profitability, Fit with Core Skills etc. and
- The X-Axis comprises *business strength* measures, such as Price, Service Levels etc.

Each product, brand, service, or potential product is mapped as a piechart onto this industry attractiveness/ business strength space.

The diametre of each piechart is proportional to the Volume or Revenue accruing to each opportunity, and the solid slice of each pie represents the share of the market enjoyed by the planning company.

The planning company should invest in opportunities that appear to the top left of the matrix. The rationale is that the planning company should invest in segments that are both attractive and in which it has established some measure of competitive advantage.

Opportunities appearing in the bottom right of the matrix are both unattractive to the planning company and in which it is competitively weak. At best, these are candidates for cash management; at worst candidates for divestment. Opportunities appearing 'in between' these extremes pose more of a problem, and the planning company has to make a strategic decision whether to 'redouble its efforts' in the hopes of achieving market leadership, manage them for cash, or cut its losses and divest.

CONTRIBUTION MARGIN

In cost-volume-profit analysis, a form of management accounting, contribution margin is the marginal profit per unit sale. It is a useful quantity in carrying out various calculations, and can be used as a measure of operating leverage. Typically, high contribution margins are prevalent in labour-intensive tertiary sector while low contribution margins are prevalent in capital-intensive industrial sector.

APPLICATIONS

Contribution arises in Cost-Volume-Profit Analysis, where it simplifies calculation of Net Income, and especially break even analysis.

Given the contribution margin, a manager can easily compute breakeven and target income sales, and make better decisions about whether to add or subtract a product line, about how to price a product or service, and about how to structure sales commissions or bonuses.

Contribution margin analysis is a measure of operating leverage: it measures how growth in sales translates to growth in profits.

The contribution margin is computed by using a contribution income statement: a management accounting version of the income statement that has been reformatted to group together a business's fixed and variable costs.

Contribution is different to Gross Margin in that a contribution calculation seeks to separate out variable costs from fixed costs on the basis of economic analysis of the nature of the expense whereas gross margin is determined using accounting standards.

CANNIBALIZATION

IN RETAIL BUSINESS

In marketing and strategy, cannibalization refers to a reduction in the sales volume, sales revenue, or market share of one product as a result of the introduction of a new product by the same producer.

For example, if Coca Cola were to introduce a similar product, this new product could take some of the sales away from the original Coke. Cannibalization is a key consideration in product portfolio analysis.

A second common case of cannibalization is when companies, particularly retail companies, open outlets too close to each other. Much of the market for the new outlet could have come from the old outlet. The potential for cannibalization is often discussed when considering companies with many outlets in an area, such as Starbucks or McDonald's. Another example of cannibalization is when a retailer creates a promotion like 20% discount for one item. The tendency of consumers is to buy the discounted item rather than the other items with a higher price. However when the promotion event is over, the regular drinker of Coke will resume buying Coke. By this behaviour, there is a temporary cannibalization happening due to a promotion event.

Although business cannibalization may seem inherently negative, it can be a positive thing. It sometimes involves a carefully planned strategy, and it also forces a company to think outside the box in order to evolve with the changing needs of both the marketplace and the consumer. In the world of e-commerce for example, some companies intentionally cannibalize their retail sales through lower prices on their online product offerings.

Seeing these discounts on items, more number of consumers than usual would buy these items. Even though their in-store sales might decline, the company may see overall positive gains. In project evaluation, the estimated profit generated from the new product must be reduced by the earnings on the lost sales.

IN MAINTAINING OR BUILDING EQUIPMENT

In maintenance of mechanical or electronic equipment, "cannibalization" refers to the practice of obtaining the spare parts necessary to repair one device by removing them from another similar device, rather than from a pool of spare parts. The device used as a source of spare parts is often crippled as a result, if only temporarily, in order to allow the recipient device to function properly again. Cannibalization can usually occur only with devices that use interchangeable parts.

Sometimes, removing parts from old equipment is the only way for an individual to obtain some types of parts, either because they are no longer made, or can only be ordered in large quantities. At the end of World War II a large quantity of high quality, but unusable war surplus equipment such as radar devices made a ready source of parts to build radio equipment.

Cannibalization be a sign of extreme budgetary pressure that prevents the purchase of adequate spare parts, or some other emergency such as time constraints and physical distance from a source of spare parts. At other times, it is a reflection of a surplus of equipment relative to current needs or usage, making some devices unnecessary except as a source of parts for cannibalization.

An example of this is the many 30- and 40-year-old railway locomotives being run by small operators in the United Kingdom. These operators will often buy more locomotives than they actually require, and keep a number of them stored as a source of spare parts.

This is often the case in the military, and ships and aircraft, as well as other particularly expensive equipment. Such is the case with the aircraft carrier USS Kitty Hawk, the sole survivor of a class of three ships built during the early-1960s. The ship herself is over forty years old, and having manufacturers build individual custom replacement parts would be highly impractical, and thus decommissioned ships, such as the USS Independence, have been utilized for the necessary parts to keep the Kitty Hawk in operation.

Sometimes cannibalization can occur if the equipment in question is obsolete, with the manufacturer(s) of the device or the spare parts no longer in existence. For example, Union Pacific's 4-8-4 locomotive 838 is used as a spare parts source for 844 since the type has been out of production for decades and the builder itself is no longer in existence.

PRODUCT BUNDLING

Product bundling is the process of securing two or more necessary goods or services from a single vendor. This strategy usually provides several advantages, including saving a great deal of money. Long a practice among businesses, the concept of product bundling has expanded to include residential customers over the last twenty years, especially in regard to various types of communication services.

The basic nature of product bundling involves the willingness of a supplier or vendor to provide two or more services to a customer for basic rate. This rate normally provides significant savings over purchasing the products individually. For example, a communications company may choose to offer a cable TV bundle that allows the subscriber to enjoy cable television, local telephone service, and Internet access as a single product offering, rather than having to purchase three different services at a cumulative higher rate.

Along with saving money, product bundling also provides other benefits for the customer. One has to do with sheer convenience. Rather than having to deal with multiple vendors in order to have access to multiple products, the customer has one central vendor for all his or her needs. This concept of one-stop shopping means the client spends less time keeping up with payments to various vendors, and has one central pipeline when there is a need for customer support or if there is a question about one of the services.

Vendors also benefit from providing various types of bundled packages to their clients. In many cases, the cost and convenience created by product bundling go a long way toward promoting customer loyalty. This makes the client less likely to switch to another vendor for any of the services, especially if the price for the bundle is competitive. Product bundling also simplifies the billing process for the vendor, since all services and products are usually billed on one monthly invoice, rather than several different ones.

Product bundling is also a common strategy with software products. For example, office suites offered by different manufacturers will normally include a data processing prigramme, a spreadsheet prigramme, an email client, and presentation creation software, all in one package. This makes it much easier for customers, since they can purchase all these software options as part of one package, rather than paying for them individually. Depending on which software manufacturer is involved, the savings can be substantial.

The idea of product bundling is also used in other ways. For example, a local business that mows lawns as its main service many offer customers a bundled package that also includes shrub trimming and basic landscaping, for a small additional fee. Often, this is less expensive to the customer than purchasing the different services separately. Even businesses like delicatessens can use this basic approach of product bundling, such as offering an entrée along with two or three sides for a single price that is lower than buying the items separately.

9

Packaging and Labeling

CONCEPT

Packaging is the science, art and technology of enclosing or protecting products for distribution, storage, sale, and use. Packaging also refers to the *process* of design, evaluation, and production of packages. Packaging can be described as a *coordinated system* of preparing goods for transport, warehousing, logistics, sale, and end use. Packaging contains, protects, preserves, transports, informs, and sells. In many countries it is fully integrated into government, business, institutional, industrial, and personal use.

Package labelling or labeling is any written, electronic, or graphic communications on the packaging or on a separate but associated label.

PURPOSES

Packaging and package labeling have several objectives:

- *Physical protection*: The objects enclosed in the package may require protection from, among other things, shock, vibration, compression, temperature, etc.
- *Barrier protection*: A barrier from oxygen, water vapour, dust, etc., is often required. Permeation is a critical factor in design. Some packages contain desiccants or Oxygen absorbers to help extend shelf life. Modified atmospheres or controlled atmospheres are also maintained in some food packages. Keeping the contents clean, fresh, sterile and safe for the intended shelf life is a primary function.

- *Containment or agglomeration*: Small objects are typically grouped together in one package for reasons of efficiency. For example, a single box of 1000 pencils requires less physical handling than 1000 single pencils. Liquids, powders, and granular materials need containment.
- *Information transmission*: Packages and labels communicate how to use, transport, recycle, or dispose of the package or product. With pharmaceuticals, food, medical, and chemical products, some types of information are required by governments. Some packages and labels also are used for track and trace purposes.
- *Marketing*: The packaging and labels can be used by marketers to encourage potential buyers to purchase the product. Package graphic design and physical design have been important and constantly evolving phenomenon for several decades. Marketing communications and graphic design are applied to the surface of the package and the point of sale display.
- *Security*: Packaging can play an important role in reducing the security risks of shipment. Packages can be made with improved tamper resistance to deter tampering and also can have tamper-evident features to help indicate tampering. Packages can be engineered to help reduce the risks of package pilferage: Some package constructions are more resistant to pilferage and some have pilfer indicating seals. Packages may include authentication seals and use security printing to help indicate that the package and contents are not counterfeit. Packages also can include anti-theft devices, such as dye-packs, RFID tags, or electronic substance surveillance tags that can be activated or detected by devices at exit points and require specialized tools to deactivate. Using packaging in this way is a means of loss prevention.
- *Convenience*: Packages can have features that add

convenience in distribution, handling, stacking, display, sale, opening, reclosing, use, dispensing, and reuse.

- *Portion control*: Single serving or single dosage packaging has a precise amount of contents to control usage. Bulk commodities can be divided into packages that are a more suitable size for individual households. It is also aids the control of inventory: selling sealed one-litre-bottles of milk, rather than having people bring their own bottles to fill themselves!

PACKAGING TYPES

Packaging may be looked at as being of several different types. For example a transport package or distribution package can be the shipping container used to ship, store, and handle the product or inner packages. Some identify a consumer package as one which is directed toward a consumer or household. Packaging may be described in relation to the type of product being packaged: medical device packaging, bulk chemical packaging, over-the-counter drug packaging, retail food packaging, military materiel packaging, pharmaceutical packaging, etc.

It is sometimes convenient to categorize packages by layer or function: "Primary", "secondary", etc.

- Primary packaging is the material that first envelops the product and holds it. This usually is the smallest unit of distribution or use and is the package which is in direct contact with the contents.
- Secondary packaging is outside the primary packaging, perhaps used to group primary packages together.
- Tertiary packaging is used for bulk handling, warehouse storage and transport shipping. The most common form is a palletized unit load that packs tightly into containers.

These broad categories can be somewhat arbitrary. For example, depending on the use, a shrink wrap can be primary packaging when applied directly to the product, secondary packaging when combining smaller packages, and tertiary packaging on some distribution packs.

SYMBOLS USED ON PACKAGES AND LABELS

Many types of symbols for package labeling are nationally and internationally standardized. For consumer packaging, symbols exist for product certifications, trademarks, proof of purchase, etc. Some requirements and symbols exist to communicate aspects of consumer use and safety. Examples of environmental and recycling symbols include: Recycling symbol, Resin identification code, and Green Dot.

Bar codes, Universal Product Codes, and RFID labels are common to allow automated information management in logistics and retailing. Country of Origin Labeling is often used.

Shipping Ccontainer Labeling

Technologies related to shipping containers are identification codes, bar codes, and electronic data interchange. These three core technologies serve to enable the business functions in the process of shipping containers throughout the distribution channel. Each has an essential function: identification codes either relate product information or serve as keys to other data, bar codes allow for the automated input of identification codes and other data, and EDI moves data between trading partners within the distribution channel.

Elements of these core technologies include UPC and EAN item identification codes, the SCC-14, the SSCC-18, Interleaved 2-of-5 and UCC/EAN-128 bar code symbologies, and ANSI ASC X12 and UN/EDIFACT EDI standards.

Small parcel carriers often have their own formats. For example, United Parcel Service has a MaxiCode 2-D code for parcel tracking.

RFID labels for shipping containers are also increasing in usage. A Wal-Mart division, Sam's Club, has also moved in this direction and is putting pressure on its suppliers for compliance.

Shipments of hazardous materials or dangerous goods have special information and symbols as required by UN, country, and specific carrier requirements. Two examples are:

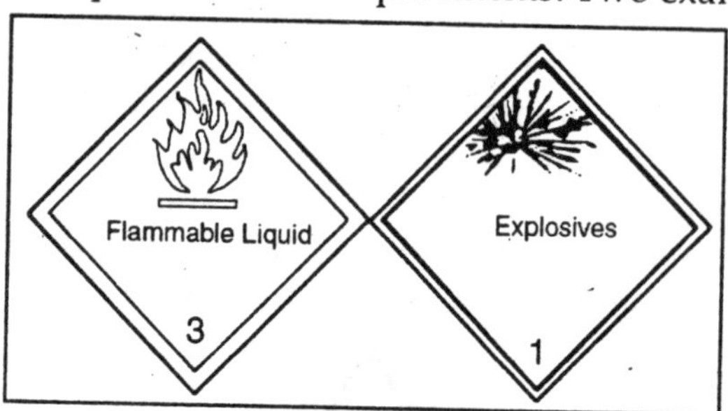

With transport packages, standardised symbols are also used to communicate handling needs. Some common ones are shown while others are listed in ASTM D5445 "Standard Practice for Pictorial Markings for Handling of Goods" and ISO 780 "Pictorial marking for handling of goods".

Fig. Fragile

Fig. Do not use Hand Hooks

Fig. This Way Up

Fig. Keep Away From Sunlight

Fig. Keep Away from Water

Fig. Centre of Gravity

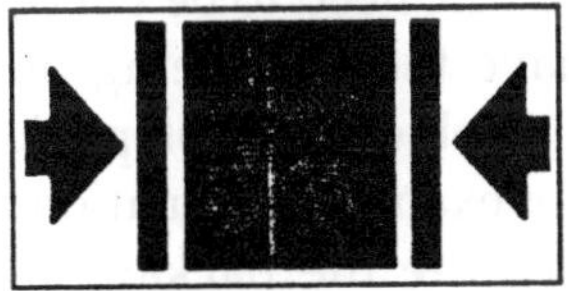

Fig. Clamp as indicated

Fig. Do not clamp as indicated

PACKAGE DEVELOPMENT CONSIDERATIONS

Package design and development are often thought of as an integral part of the new product development process. Alternatively, development of a package can be a separate process, but must be linked closely with the product to be packaged. Package design starts with the identification of all the requirements: structural design, marketing, shelf life, quality assurance, logistics, legal, regulatory, graphic design, end-use, environmental, etc. The design criteria, performance, completion time targets, resources, and cost constraints need to be established and agreed upon.

An example of how package design is affected by other factors is the relationship to logistics. When the distribution system includes individual shipments by a small parcel carrier, the sortation, handling, and mixed stacking make severe demands on the strength and protective ability of the transport package.

If the logistics system consists of uniform palletized unit loads, the structural design of the package can be designed to those specific needs: vertical stacking, perhaps for a longer time frame. A package designed for one mode of shipment may not be suited for another.

With some types of products, the design process involves detailed regulatory requirements for the package. For example with packaging foods, any package components that may contact the food are food contact materials. Toxicologists and food scientists need to verify that the packaging materials are allowed by applicable regulations. Packaging engineers need to verify that the completed package will keep the product safe for its intended shelf life with normal usage. Packaging processes, labeling, distribution, and sale need to be validated to comply with regulations and have the well being of the consumer in mind. Sometimes the objectives of package development seem contradictory. For example, regulations for an over-the-counter drug might require the package to be tamper-evident and child resistant:These intentionally make the package difficult to open.. The intended consumer, however, might be handicapped or elderly and be unable to readily open the package. Meeting all goals is a challenge.

Package design may take place within a company or with various degrees of external packaging engineering: independent contractors, consultants, vendor evaluations, independent laboratories, contract packagers, total outsourcing, etc. Some sort of formal Project planning and Project management methodology is required for all but the simplest package design and development prigrammes. An effective quality management system and Verification and Validation protocols are mandatory for some types of packaging and recommended for all.

Package development involves considerations for sustainability, environmental responsibility, and applicable environmental and recycling regulations. It may involve a life cycle assessment which considers the material and energy inputs and outputs to the package, the packaged product, the packaging process, the logistics system, waste management, etc. It is necessary to know the relevant regulatory requirements for point of manufacture, sale, and use.

The traditional "three R's" of reduce, reuse, and recycle are part of a waste hierarchy which may be considered in product and package development.

- *Prevention*: Waste prevention is a primary goal. Packaging should be used only where needed. Proper packaging can also help prevent waste. Packaging plays an important part in preventing loss or damage to the packaged-product. Usually, the energy content and material usage of the product being packaged are much greater than that of the package. A vital function of the package is to protect the product for its intended use: if the product is damaged or degraded, its entire energy and material content may be lost.
- *Minimization*: The mass and volume of packaging can be measured and used as one of the criteria to minimize during the package design process. Usually "reduced" packaging also helps minimize costs. Packaging engineers continue to work toward reduced packaging.
- *Reuse*: The reuse of a package or component for other purposes is encouraged. Returnable packaging has long been useful for closed loop logistics systems. Inspection, cleaning, repair and recouperage are often needed. Some manufacturers re-use the packaging of the incoming parts for a product, either as packaging for the outgoing product or as part of the product itself.
- *Recycling*: Recycling is the reprocessing of materials into new products. Emphasis is focused on recycling the largest primary components of a package: steel, aluminum, papers, plastics, etc. Small components can be chosen which are not difficult to separate and do not contaminate recycling operations.
- *Energy recovery*: Waste-to-energy and Refuse-derived fuel in approved facilities are able to make use of the heat available from the packaging components.
- *Disposal*: Incineration, and placement in a sanitary landfill are needed for some materials. Certain states within the US regulate packages for toxic contents, which have the potential to contaminate emissions

and ash from incineration and leachate from landfill. Packages should not be littered.

Development of sustainable packaging is an area of considerable interest by standards organizations, government, consumers, packagers, and retailers.

PACKAGING MACHINES

A choice of packaging machinery includes: technical capabilities, labour requirements, worker safety, maintainability, serviceability, reliability, ability to integrate into the packaging line, capital cost, floorspace, flexibility, energy usage, quality of outgoing packages, qualifications, throughput, efficiency, productivity, ergonomics, return on investment, etc.

Packaging machines may be of the following general types:

- Blister packs, skin packs and Vacuum Packaging Machines
- Bottle caps equipment, Over-Capping, Lidding, Closing, Seaming and Sealing Machines
- Box, Case and Tray Forming, Packing, Unpacking, Closing and Sealing Machines
- Cartoning machines
- Cleaning, Sterilizing, Cooling and Drying Machines
- Converting Machines
- Conveyor belts, Accumulating and Related Machines
- Feeding, Orienting, Placing and Related Machines
- Filling Machines: handling liquid and powdered products
- Inspecting, Detecting and Check weigher Machines
- Label dispensers Help peel and apply labels more efficiently
- Package Filling and Closing Machines
- Palletizing, Depalletizing, Unit load assembly
- Product Identification: labeling, marking, etc.
- Shrink wrap Machines
- Form, Fill and Seal Machines
- Other speciality machinery: slitters, perforating, laser cutters, parts attachment, etc.

ACTIVE PACKAGING

The terms active packaging, intelligent packaging, and smart packaging refer to packaging systems used with foods, pharmaceuticals, and several other types of products. They help extend shelf life, monitor freshness, display information on quality, improve safety, and improve convenience.

The terms are closely related. *Active packaging* usually means having active functions beyond the inert passive containment and protection of the product. *Intelligent* and *smart* packaging usually involve the ability to sense or measure an attribute of the product, the inner atmosphere of the package, or the shipping environment. This information can be communicated to users or can trigger active packaging functions.

Depending on the working definitions, some traditional types of packaging might be considered as "active" or "intellegent". More often, the terms are used with new technologically advanced systems.

MOISTURE CONTROL

For many years, dessiccants have been used to actively control the moisture in a closed package. A desiccant is a hygroscopic substance usually in a porous pouch, is placed inside of a package. They have been used to reduce corrosion of machinery and to extend the shelf life of moisture sensitive foods and drugs.

OXYGEN CONTROL

Oxygen scavengers or Oxygen absorbers help remove oxygen from a closed package. Some are small packets or sachcts containing powdered iron: as the iron rusts, oxygen is removed from the surrounding atmosphere. Newer systems are on cards or can be built into package films or molded structures.

ATMOSPHERE

With some products,such as cheese, it has long been common to flush the package with nitrogen prior to sealing:

the inert nitrogen is absorbed into the cheese, allowing a tight shrink film package. The nitrogen removes oxygan and "actively" interacts with the cheese to make the package functional.

More recently, other mixtures of gas have been used inside the package to extend the shelf life. The gas mixture depends on the specific product and its degradation mechanisms. Some package components have been developed that incorporate active chemistry to help maintain certain atmospheres in packages.

TEMPERATURE MONITOR

Some temperature indicators give a visual signal that a specified temperature has been exceeded. Others, Time temperature indicators, signal when a critical accumulation of temperature deviation over time has been exceeded. When the mechanism of the indicator is tuned to the mechanism of product degradation, these can provide valuable signals for consumers. Digital temperature data loggers record the temperatures encountered throuout the shipment. This data can be used to predict product degradation and help determine if the product is suited for normal sale or if expedited sale is required. They also determine the time of the temperature excess: this can be used to direct corrective action.

Thermochromic inks are sometimes used to signal temperature excess or change. Some are reversible while others have a permanent change of colour. These can be used alone or with other packaging functions such as bar codes.

The inks can also signal a desired temperature for consumers. For example, one type of beer can has ink that graphically shows when an ideal drinking temperature is achieved.

CONTROLLING PACKAGE TEMPERATURES

For critical vaccines, insulated shipping containers are passive packaging to help control the temperatures fluctuations seen even with a controlled cold chains. In addition, gel packs are often used to actively keep the temperature of the contents within specified acceptable temperature ranges. Some newer packages have the ability to heat or cool the product for the consumer. These have segregated compartments where exothermic or endothermic reactions provide the desired effect.

DISPENSING SYSTEMS

Some packages have closures or other dispensing systems that actively change the contents from a liquid to an aerosol. These are used for products ranging from precision inhalers for medications to spray bottles of household cleaners.

Some dispensing packages for two-part epoxy adhesives do more than passively contain the two components. When dispensed, some packages metre and mix the two components so the adhesive is fully functioning at the point of application.

RFID

Radio-frequency identification chips are becoming more common as smart labels that are used to track and trace packages and unit loads throughout distribution. Newer developments include recording the temperature history of shipments and other intelligent packaging functions.

SHOCK AND VIBRATION

Shock detectors have been available for many years. These are attached to the package or to the product in the package to determine is an excessive shock has been encountered. The mechanisms of these shock overload devices have been spring-mass systems, magnets, drops of red dye, and several others.

Recently, digital data loggers have been available to more accurately record the shocks and vibrations of shipment. These are used to monitor critical shipments to determine if extra inspection and calibration is required. They are also used to monitor the types of shocks and vibrations encountered in transit for use in package testing in a laboratory.

OTHER DEVELOPMENTS

Some newer packaging films contain enzymes, antibacterial agents, scavengers, and other active components to help control food degradation.

REGULATIONS

Active packaging is often designed to actively interact with the contents of the package. Thus extra care is often needed for active or smart packagings that are food contact materials.

Food packagers take extra care with some types of active packaging. For example when the oxygen atmosphere in a package is reduced for extending shelf life, controls for anaerobic bacteria need to be considered. Also when a controlled atmosphere reduces the appe

KEEP CASE

A keep case or poly-box is a type of DVD packaging. From the well-known brand Amaray, this type of case is often called *Amaray case,* creating a genericized trademark and ambiguities about the real manufacturer of the case.

Besides DVD-Video films, keep cases are used in most video games for the Xbox, Xbox 360, PlayStation 2, Nintendo GameCube and Wii, as well as PC titles and MP3-CD audiobooks.

ASEPTIC PROCESSING

Aseptic processing is the process by which a sterile product is packaged in a sterile container in a way which maintains sterility.

Sterility is achieved with a flash-heating process which retains more nutrients and uses less energy than conventional sterilization techniques such as retort or hot-fill canning. Aseptic food preservation methods allow processed food to keep for long periods of time without preservatives, as long as they are not opened. The aseptic packages are typically a mix of paper, polyethylene, and aluminum, with a tight polyethylene inside layer. Together the materials form a tight seal against microbiological organisms, contaminants, and degradation, eliminating the need for refrigeration.

The first aseptic filling plant for milk was presented in Switzerland in 1961. The Tetra Pak company later became one of the leading suppliers of processing and packaging equipment for dairies. Aseptic techniques were common in Europe and Asia before they were introduced in the United States in the 1980s.

Aseptic containers may range in size from a few fluid ounces to a nearly 8-million-gallon aseptic tank on an ocean-going ship. Aseptic processing makes worldwide export and import of new, economical and safe food products possible. Bag-In-Box technology is commonly used because it provides strong containers that are light weight and easy to handle prior to being filled. Other common package types are drink boxes and pouches.

In 1991, the Institute of Food Technologists rated the top 10 innovations in food technology. Aseptic processing and packaging ranked No. 1, ahead of juice concentrates, safe canning processes, freeze-drying and food fortification. In 2007 Dr. Philip E. Nelson received the World Food Prize in recognition for his pioneering work in aseptic processing and bulk storage.

AUTHENTICATION

Authentication is the performance of establishing or confirming something as *authentic,* that is, that claims made by or about the subject are true. This might involve confirming the identity of a person, tracing the origins of an artifact, ensuring that a product is what its packaging and labeling claims to be, or assuring that a computer prigramme is a trusted one. Authentication can also be used for identity delegation. Identity Delegation in IT network is an evolving field.

BAG-IN-BOX

In packaging, a Bag-in-Box or BiB is a type of container for the storage and transportation of liquids. It consists of a strong bladder, usually made of several layers of metallised film or other plastics, seated inside a corrugated fibreboard box. The bag is supplied to the 'filler' as an empty pre made bag. The 'filler' then generally removes the tap, fills the bag and then replaces the tap. The bags are available as singles for semi-automatic machines or as web bags, where the bags have perforations between each one. These are used on automated filling systems where the bag is separated on line either before the bag is automatically filled or after. There is now a technology available called FSF and pioneered by Scholle where equipment is supplied to the filler who manufactures the bags on-line from reels of film, then the FlexiTap is inserted then filled on the Scholle line.

Bag in a box packaging is liked by producers because it is inexpensive. Seen from the environmental perspective, a bag also has benefits. The bag allows a contents of 3-1000l, so that less packaging or labelling is required. The material it is made from is lighter than the alternatives, which reduces pollution caused by transport.

BATTLE BAG

The Battle Bag, or Mann Bag, is a lightweight load carrying system designed to allow the Combat Infantryman to carry enough ammunition and ancillaries such as medical supplies, spare batteries and radio equipment. There are a multitude of different suppliers for these, with the British Army having designed its own version for issue under the PECOC programme. The key compartments, or pouches, on the battle bag consist of the main compartment, 3 to 4 ammo pouches, an FFD pouch, and a radio pouch, which is usually mounted within the main compartment. Some designs of battle bags have MOLLE strips on them, to allow the user to accessorise the bag to their operational requirements. Others, such as the BlackHawk bag, have an internal map case.

The Battle bag was originally designed for use as a "grab bag", to allow drivers and vehicle-borne troops to grab essential supplies in a dismount for such functions as an ambush or the assault phase of a mechanised attack. From there, it has spread in popularity with troops due to its ability to be worn comfortably over Body Armour, as well as the fact that it can be rapidly removed from the wearer in a medical emergency, or to allow the wearer to crawl through "mouseholes".

BLISTER PACK

Blister pack is a term for several types of pre-formed plastic packaging used for small consumer goods.

The two primary components of a blister pack are the cavity or pocket made from a "formable" web, either plastic or aluminium - and the lidding, made from paper, carton, plastic or aluminium. The "formed" cavity or pocket contains the product and the "lidding" seals the product in the package.

BOTTLE CAP

Bottle caps, or Closures, are used to seal the openings of bottles of many types. They can be small circular pieces of metal, usually steel, with plastic backings, and for plastic bottles a plastic cap is used instead. A bottle cap is typically colourfully decorated with the logo of the brand of beverage. Caps can also be plastic, sometimes with a pour spout. Flip-Top caps like Flapper closures provide controlled dispensing of dry products. Bottle caps are often made of a different type of plastic than the bottle itself, and are often recyclable.

Bottle caps were originally designed to be pressed over and around the top of a glass bottle to grab a small flange on the bottleneck. The Crown Cork was patented by William Painter on 2 February 1892. It originally had 24 teeth and a cork seal with a paper backing to prevent contact between the contents and the metal cap. The current version has 21 teeth. To open these bottles, a bottle opener is generally advised, although some bottles incorporate a screw cap, eliminating the need for the opener.

Individuals have experimented with different ways of opening bottles, including using teeth or snapping them open across another surface. A separate interest to collecting bottle caps is that of interesting ways to open bottles.

The height of the crown cap was reduced and specified in the German standard DIN 6099 in the 1960s. This also defined the "twist-off" crown cap, now widely used in the United States and Australia. This bottle cap is pressed around screw threads instead of a flange. Such a bottle cap can be taken off merely by twisting the cap.

Bottle caps are also a way for bottlers to hold promotions, especially for soda companies. A message is printed on the inside of the cap and people with the right message may win a prize. Since the bottle must be purchased to determine the message and win, people usually purchase more of the drink to increase their chances of winning. The most common prize is a free soda from that company.

Some companies, such as Snapple, also print interesting facts on the inside of their caps. Mickey's Malt Liquor as well, prints riddles underneath the 24 and 40 oz. bottle caps. Usually this is done on wide-mouthed bottles that have large caps with enough printing area to put a short sentence.

BOTTLE CRATE

A bottle crate or beverage crate is a container used for transport of beverage containers. In the present day they are usually made of plastic, but before the widespread use of plastic they tended to be made of wood or metal.

Beverage crates began to be made of HDPE in the 1950s. Such crates can be surprisingly long-lived. In the 1980s in Sweden, a take-back campaign was organized, when 25-bottle crates were replaced by the more ergonomic 20-bottle crates. Some of the crates returned for recycling had been in use since the 1960s.

Because manufacturers avoid lead-based and cadmium-based pigmentations, in response to legislation and public opinion, they have had to resort to other methods of colouring HDPE crates. In Japan, since the early 1970s, HDPE bottle crates have been pigmented with a variety of perylene, quinacridone, azo condensation, and isoindolinone pigments. Japanese manufacturers have modified these in order to control nucleating behaviour, and have improved weathering performance and impact-resistance properties by making the light-stabilisization systems more efficient.

BOX SEALING TAPE

Box sealing tape or parcel tape is a pressure sensitive tape used for closing or sealing corrugated fibreboard boxes. It consists of a pressure sensitive adhesive coated onto a backing material which is usually a polypropylene or polyester film which is oriented to have strength in both the long direction and the cross direction.

Most often, the tape is 48 mm wide but it is also used in 72 mm widths.

A variety of backing strengths and calipers as well as adhesive formulations are available. It is often transparent or tan. Other colours and printing are sometimes available.

BOXTOP

A boxtop, in the context of being a proof of purchase, is understood to be the upper portion of a product box, detached, and mailed as part of a claim for a radio premium or other advertising offer. During the 1930s through 1950s, cereal boxtops were usually the most common proofs of purchase used to claim such premiums.

Popular cereal boxtops of the period were Wheaties, which sponsiored Jack Armstrong, the All-American Boy; Kellogg's Pep, which sponsored The Adventures of Superman; Ralston-Purina, which sponsored Tom Mix Ranston Straight Shooters; and various General Mills, particularly Cheerios and Kix, which sponsored The Lone Ranger.

CHILD-RESISTANT PACKAGING

Child-resistant packaging or C-R packaging is special packaging used to reduce the risk of children ingesting dangerous items. This is often accomplished by the use of a special safety cap. It is required by regulation for prescription drugs, over-the-counter medications, pesticides, and household chemicals. In some juridictions, *unit packaging* such as blister packs is also regulated for child safety.

The United States Consumer Product Safety Commission has stated in a press release that "There is no such thing as child-proof packaging. So you shouldn't think of packaging as your primary line of defence. Rather, you should think of packaging, even child-resistant packaging, as your last line of defence."

FAIR PACKAGING AND LABELING ACT

The Fair Packaging and Labeling Act is a US law that applies to labels on many consumer products.

It requires the label to state:

- The identity of the product;
- The name and place of business of the manufacturer, packer, or distributor; and
- The net quantity of contents.

The contents statement must include both metric and U.S. customary units.

Passed under Lyndon B. Johnson in 1966, the law first took effect on July 1, 1967. The metric labeling requirement was added in 1992 and took effect on February 14, 1994. The law is codified as 15 U.S.C. § 1451-1461.

There has been an effort by industry threatened by a European Union directive that would force metric-only labeling starting January 1, 2010, to amend the FPLA to allow manufacturers to use metric-only labeling. Forced metric-only labeling would lead to substantial added cost due to the forced necessity of producing two distinct package types. An amendment to delay indefinitely forced metric-only labeling was adopted by the European Commission September 10, 2007, approved by the European Parliament November 29, 2007, and by the European Economic and Social Committee December 12, 2007.

FOOD LABELING REGULATIONS

The law in the UK on food labeling is multifaceted and is spread over many reforms and parliamentary acts, making the subject complex. In the US, food labeling is mainly regulated by 21 CFR part 101 in accordance with 21 CFR 1.21, 74.705, Part 102, 104.20, 179.26 and FD&C. Codex Alimentarius also published a document on the food labeling which is supposed to be followed by the food industry internationally.

Nevertheless, there are general laws which should be implied on any food product:

- *Name*: Must also inform the customer the nature of the product. It may also be necessary to attach a description to the product name. However, there are certain generic names which must be only used for their conventional uses, for example: Muesli, Coffee, prawns.
- *Ingredients*: All ingredients of the food must be stated under the heading'Ingredients' and must be stated in descending order of weight. Moreover, certain ingredients such as preservatives must be identified as such by the label'Preservatives', a specific name, e.g."sodium nitrite", and the corresponding European registration number colloquially known as an"E number", e.g."E250".
- *Nutritional Information*: Although it is not a legal requirement to declare Nutritional information on the product, if the manufacturer makes claims that the product is'Low in Sugar', it must be supported with nutritional information. However, as a rule it is recommended to declare nutritional information as consumers more than ever are investigating this information before making a purchase. Moreover, there are two European nutritional labeling standards which must be adhered to if nutritional information is shown.
- *Medicinal or Nutritional Claims*: Medicinal and Nutritional claims are tightly regulated, some are only allowed under certain conditions while others are not authorized at all. For example, presenting claims the food product can treat, prevent or cure diseases or other'adverse conditions' are prohibited. While claiming the food is reduced in fat or rich in vitamins require the food to meet compulsory standards and grades, in addition, the terms must be used in a form specified in regulations.
- *Date Tagging*: *There are two types of date tagging*:

- *Use by Date*:'Use by date' must be followed by a day or/and month which the product must be consumed by. To be employed on perishable foods that usually would be kept cold, for example, fish, meat, dairy products and'ready to eat' salads.
- *Best Before Date*:'Best before date is used as an indicator of when the product will begin to degrade from optimal quality: this includes when the food becomes stale, begins to taste'off' or decays, rots or goes mouldy. There are also regulations on which type of best before date must be applied:
    a. Best before + Day for foods with a shelf life of up to 3 months.
    b. Best before end + Month for foods with more than a 3 month shelf life.
    c. Best before end + Year for food with more than an 18 month shelf life.

- *Storage Conditions*: If there are any particular storage conditions for the product to maintain its shelf life, these must be pointed out. However, as a rule it is recommended to always describe the necessary storage conditions for a food product.
- *Business Name and Address*: In addition to the business name and address, it is necessary to indicate the manufacturer or packager, if independent to the main business and the seller established within the European Union.
- *Place of Origin*: The food is required to specify its place of origin, especially if the name or trademark is misleading - such as if the product is called 'English Brie Cheese' when it is produced in France.
- *Instruction for Use*: This is only necessary if it is not obvious how to use or prepare the product, in which case the consumer's own initiative must be used.
- *Presentation*: The label must be legible and easy to read, also it must be written in English, however, the

manufacturer may also include other languages.

- *Batch identifier, such as Lot Mark or Batch Code*: It must be possible to identify individual batches with a lot mark or batch code - the code must be prefixed with the letter 'L' if it can not be distinguish from other codes, however, the date mark can be used as a lot mark. Manufacturers must bear in mind that the smaller the size of a batch, the smaller financial consequences in the case of a product withdrawal.
- *Sectioning*: All of the following must be in the same field of vision:
  a. Product name
  b. Date mark
  c. Weight
  d. Quantity
  e. Alcohol strength.
- *Standard specification:* Indicate the level of the standard compliances which the product are manufactured and packaging are completed against, and the specification limits if the standard is not publicly available, especially for those of
  a. Microbial limits
  b. Heavy metal limits
  c. The limits of pesticide residuals
  d. The limits of preservatives, artificial flavouring and colouring etc.
- Food additives - with a best practice, the items should be presented by their approved names, functional classes, and numbers of International Numbering System or equivalent.

However, there are many other Laws and European regulations for different types of food products.

PLASTIC BAG

A plastic bag or pouch is a type of flexible packaging made of thin, flexible, plastics film. Plastic bags are used for containing and transporting goods such as foods, produce, powders, ice, chemicals and waste.

Most plastic bags are heat sealed together. Some are bonded with adhesives or are stitched. A press-to-close zipper can be used to open and close the bag many times.

PHAMACEUTICAL PACKAGING

Pharmaceutical packaging has to be carried out for the purpose of the safety of the pharmaceutical preparations in order to keep them free from contamination and hinder microbial growth in the pharmaceuticals. Packaging is one of the most important tools in the pharmaceutical industry and various pharmaceutical preparations are being used.

PACKAGING GAS

A packaging gas is a gas used to pack sensitive materials in a modified atmosphere. It is usually inert, or of a nature that protects the packaged goods, thus inhibiting reactions such as spoilage. Some may also serve as propellant for aerosols like whipped cream.

For packaging food, various gases are approved.

Their E numbers are in parenthesis:

- argon (E938), used for canned products
- Helium (E939), used for canned products
- Nitrogen (E941)
- Oxygen (E948), used eg. for packaging of vegetables
- Hydrogen (E949)
- Carbon dioxide (E290, also propellant)

Specific kind of packaging gases are aerosol propellants:

- Dichlorodifluoromethane known as CFC (E940), rarely used because of the damage that it does to the ozone layer
- Nitrous oxide (E942), used for aerosol whipped cream canisters
- Butane (E943a)
- Isobutane (E943b)
- Propane (E944)

PACKAGING ENGINEERING

Packaging engineering, also Package engineering is a

broad topic ranging from design conceptualization to product placement. All steps along the manufacturing process, and more, must be taken into account in the design of the package for any given product. Package engineering includes industry-specific aspects of industrial engineering, marketing, materials science, industrial design and logistics. Packaging engineers must interact with Research and Development, Manufacturing, Marketing, Graphic Design, Regulatory, Purchasing, Planning and so on. The package must sell and protect the product, while maintaining an efficient, cost-effective process cycle.

Some packaging engineers have backgrounds in other science or engineering disciplines while some have college degrees specializing in this field.

Formal packaging prigrammes might be listed as package engineering, packaging science, packaging technology, etc. BS, MS, and PhD prigrammes are available. Students in a packaging prigramme typically begin with generalized science, business, and engineering classes before progressing into industry-specific topics such as shelf life stability, corrugated box design, cushioning, labeling regulations, distribution testing, project management, food safety, robotics, RFID tags, Quality management, package testing, packaging machinery, Tamper-evident methods, recycling, computer-aided design, etc.

PACKAGE TESTING

Package testing or Packaging testing involves the measurement of a characteristic involved with packaging. This includes packaging materials, packaging components, primary packages, shipping containers, and unit loads, as well as the associated processes.

Testing measures the effects and interactions of the levels of packaging, the package contents, external forces, and end-use.

It can involve controlled laboratory experiments, subjective evaluations by people, or field testing. Documentation is important: formal test method, test report, photographs, video, etc.

Testing can be a qualitative or quantitative procedure. Package testing is often a physical test. With some types of packaging such as food and pharmaceuticals, chemical tests are conducted to determine suitability of food contact materials. Testing prigrammes range from simple tests with little replication to more thorough experimental designs.

Package testing can extend for the full life cycle. Packages can be tested for their ability to be recycled and their ability to degrade as surface litter, in a sealed landfill or under composting conditions.

Purposes

Packaging testing might have a variety of purposes, such as:

- Determine if, or verify that, the requirements of a specification, regulation, or contract are met
- Decide if a new product development prigramme is on track: Demonstrate proof of concept
- Provide standard data for other scientific, engineering, and quality assurance functions
- Validate suitability for end-use
- Provide a basis for technical communication
- Provide a technical means of comparison of several options
- Provide evidence in legal proceedings: product liability, patents, product claims, etc
- Help solve problems with current packaging
- Help identify potential cost savings in packaging
- Predict, in a laboratory, the performance of a package during distribution and the acceptance by customers

Importance of testing

For some types of products, package testing is mandated by regulations: food. pharmaceuticals, medical devices, dangerous goods, ect. This may cover both the design qualification, periodic retesting, and control of the packaging processes. Processes may be controlled by a variety of quality management systems such as HACCP, statistical process control, validation protocols, ISO 9000, etc.

For unregulated products, the degree of package testing can be a business decision.

Risk management may involve factors such as:

- Costs of packaging
- Costs of package testing
- Value of contents being shipped
- Value of customer's good will
- Product liability exposure
- Other potential costs of inadequate packaging
- Etc

With distribution packaging, one vital packaging development consideration is to determine that a product will not be damaged throughout the entire process of getting to the customer from the manufacturer. A primary purpose of a package is to ensure the safety of a product during transportation and storage. If a product is damaged during this process, then the package has failed to accomplish its primary objective and the customer will either return the product or be unlikely to purchase the product altogether.

Package testing is often a formal part of Project management prigrammes. Packages are usually tested when there is a new packaging design, a revision to a current design, a change in packaging material, and various other reasons. Testing a new packaging design before full scale manufacturing can save time and money.

LABORATORY AFFILIATION

Many suppliers or vendors offer limited material and package testing as a free service to customers. It is common for packagers to partner with reputable suppliers: Many suppliers have certified quality management systems such as ISO 9000 or allow customers to conduct technical and quality audits. Data from testing is commonly shared. There is sometimes a risk that supplier testing may tend to be self-serving and not completely impartial.

Large companies often have their own packaging staff and a package testing and development laboratory. Corporate engineers know their products, manufacturing capabilities, logistics system, and their customers best. Cost reduction of existing products and cost avoidance for new products have been documented.

Another option is to use paid consultants, Independent contractors, and third-party test laboratories. They are commonly chosen for specialized expertise, for access to certain test equipment, for surge projects, or where independent testing is otherwise required. Many have certifications and accreditations: ISO 9000, ISO/IEC 17025, and various governing agencies.

PROCEDURES

Several standards organizations publish test methods for package testing.

Included are:

- International Organization for Standardization, ISO
- ASTM International
- European Committee for Standardization. CEN
- TAPPI
- International Safe Transit Association, etc.

Governments and regulators publish some packaging test methods. There are also many corporate test standards in use. A review of technical literature and patents also provides good options to consider for test procedures.

If a test is conducted with a deviation from a published test method, the test report must fully disclose that deviation.

MATERIALS TESTING

The basis of packaging design and performance is the component materials. The physical properties, and sometimes chemical properties, of the materials need to be communicated to packaging engineers to aid in the design process. Suppliers publish data sheets and other technical communications that include the typical or average relevant physical properties and the test method these are based upon. Sometimes these are adequate. Other times, additional material and component testing is required by the packager or supplier to better define certain characteristics.

When a final package design is complete, the specifications for the component materials needs to be communicated to suppliers. Packaging materials testing is often needed to identify the critical material characteristics and engineering tolerances. These are used to prepare and enforce specifications.

For example, shrink film data might include: tensile strength, elongation, Elastic modulus, surface energy, thickness, Moisture vapour transmission rate, Oxygen transmission rate, heat seal strength, heat sealing conditions, heat shrinking conditions, etc. Average and process capability are often provided. The chemical properties related for use as Food contact materials may be necessary.

10

Branding

CONCEPT OF BRAND

A brand is the identity of a specific product, service, or business. A brand can take many forms, including a name, sign, symbol, or slogan. The word brand began simply as a way to tell one person's cattle from another by means of a hot iron stamp. A legally protected brand name is called a trademark. The word brand has continued to evolve to encompass identity - in effect the personality of a product, company or service.

A brand is the personality of a product, service or company and how it relates to key constituencies: Customers, Staff, Partners, Investors etc. Some people distinguish the psychological aspect of a brand from the experiential aspect. The experiential aspect consists of the sum of all points of contact with the brand and is known as the brand experience. The psychological aspect, sometimes referred to as the brand image, is a symbolic construct created within the minds of people and consists of all the information and expectations associated with a product or service.

People engaged in branding seek to develop or align the expectations behind the brand experience, creating the impression that a brand associated with a product or service has certain qualities or characteristics that make it special or unique. A brand is therefore one of the most valuable elements in an advertising theme, as it demonstrates what the brand owner is able to offer in the marketplace. The art of creating and maintaining a brand is called brand management.

Orientation of the whole organization towards its brand is called brand orientation.

Careful brand management seeks to make the product or services relevant to the target audience. Brands should be seen as more than the difference between the actual cost of a product and its selling price - they represent the sum of all valuable qualities of a product to the consumer. There are many intangibles involved in business, intangibles left wholly from the income statement and balance sheet which determine how a business is perceived.

The learned skill of a knowledge worker, the type of mental working, the type of stitch: all may be without an 'accounting cost' but for those who truly know the product, for it is these people the company should wish to find and keep, the difference is incomparable.

A brand which is widely known in the marketplace acquires brand recognition. When brand recognition builds up to a point where a brand enjoys a critical mass of positive sentiment in the marketplace, it is said to have achieved brand franchise. One goal in brand recognition is the identification of a brand without the name of the company present. For example, Disney has been successful at branding with their particular script font.

Consumers may look on branding as an important value added aspect of products or services, as it often serves to denote a certain attractive quality or characteristic. From the perspective of brand owners, branded products or services also command higher prices. Where two products resemble each other, but one of the products has no associated branding, people may often select the more expensive branded product on the basis of the quality of the brand or the reputation of the brand owner.

BENEFITS OF GLOBAL BRANDING

In addition to taking advantage of the outstanding growth opportunities, the following drives the increasing interest in taking brands global:

- Economies of scale

- Lower marketing costs
- Laying the groundwork for future extensions worldwide
- Maintaining consistent brand imagery
- Quicker identification and integration of innovations
- Preempting international competitors from entering domestic markets or locking you out of other geographic markets
- Increasing international media reach is an enabler
- Increases in international business and tourism are also enablers

GLOBAL BRAND VARIABLES

The following elements may differ from country to country:

- Corporate slogan
- Products and services
- Product names
- Product features
- Positionings
- Marketing mixes

These differences will depend upon:

- Language differences
- Fifferent styles of communication
- Other cultural differences
- Differences in category and brand development
- Different consumption patterns
- Different competitive sets and marketplace conditions
- Different legal and regulatory environments
- Different national approaches to marketing

Local Brand

A brand that is sold and marketed in a relatively small and restricted geographical area. A local brand is a brand that can be found in only one country or region. It may be called a regional brand if the area encompasses more than one metropolitan market. It may also be a brand that is developed for a specific national market, however an interesting thing about local brand is that the local branding is mostly done by consumers then by the producers. Examples of Local Brands in Sweden are Stomatol, Mijerierna etc..

Brand Name

The brand name is quite often used interchangeably within "brand", although it is more correctly used to specifically denote written or spoken linguistic elements of any product. In this context a "brand name" constitutes a type of trademark, if the brand name exclusively identifies the brand owner as the commercial source of products or services. A brand owner may seek to protect proprietary rights in relation to a brand name through trademark registration. Advertising spokespersons have also become part of some brands, for example: Mr. Whipple of Charmin toilet tissue and Tony the Tiger of Kellogg's. Local Branding is usually done by the consumers rather than the producers.

Brand Identity

A product identity, or brand image are typically the attributes one associates with a brand, how the brand owner wants the consumer to perceive the brand - and by extension the branded company, organization, product or service. The brand owner will seek to bridge the gap between the brand image and the brand identity. Effective brand names build a connection between the brand personality as it is perceived by the target audience and the actual product/service. The brand name should be conceptually on target with the product/service. Furthermore, the brand name should be on target with the brand demographic. Typically, sustainable brand names are easy to remember, transcend trends and have positive connotations. Brand identity is fundamental to consumer recognition and symbolizes the brand's differentiation from competitors.

Brand identity is what the owner wants to communicate to its potential consumers. However, over time, a product's brand identity may acquire, gaining new attributes from consumer perspective but not necessarily from the marketing communications an owner percolates to targeted consumers.

Therefore, brand associations become handy to check the consumer's perception of the brand.

Brand identity needs to focus on authentic qualities - real characteristics of the value and brand promise being provided and sustained by organisational and/or production characteristics.

Visual Brand Identity

The recognition and perception of a brand is highly influenced by its visual presentation. A brand's visual identity is the overall look of its communications. Effective visual brand identity is achieved by the consistent use of particular visual elements to create distinction, such as specific fonts, colours, and graphic elements.

At the core of every brand identity is a brand mark, or logo. In the United States, brand identity and logo design naturally grew out of the Modernist movement in the 1950's and greatly drew on the principals of that movement–simplicity and geometric abstraction. These principles can be observed in the work of the pioneers of the practice of visual brand identity design, such as Paul Rand, Chermayeff and Geismar and Saul Bass.

Brand Parity

Brand parity is the perception of the customers that all brands are equivalent.

BRANDING APPROACHES

Company Name

Often, especially in the industrial sector, it is just the company's name which is promoted.

In this case a very strong brand name is made the vehicle for a range of products or even a range of subsidiary brands.

Individual Branding

Each brand has a separate name, which may even compete against other brands from the same company.

Attitude Branding and Lconic Brands

Attitude branding is the choice to represent a larger feeling, which is not necessarily connected with the product or consumption of the product at all. Marketing labeled as attitude branding include that of Nike, Starbucks, The Body Shop, Safeway, and Apple Inc.

"A great brand raises the bar — it adds a greater sense of purpose to the experience, whether it's the challenge to do your best in sports and fitness, or the affirmation that the cup of coffee you're drinking really matters.

Iconic brands are defined as having aspects that contribute to consumer's self-expression and personal identity. Brands whose value to consumers comes primarily from having identity value comes are said to be "identity brands".

Some of these brands have such a strong identity that they become more or less "cultural icons" which makes them iconic brands.

Examples of iconic brands are: Apple Inc., Nike and Harley Davidson.

Many iconic brands include almost ritual-like behaviour when buying and consuming the products.

There are four key elements to creating iconic brands:

1. *"Necessary conditions"*: The performance of the product must at least be ok preferably with a reputation of having good quality.
2. *"Myth-making"*: A meaningful story-telling fabricated by cultural "insiders". These must be seen as legitimate and respected by consumers for stories to be accepted.
3. *"Cultural contradictions"*: Some kind of mismatch between prevailing ideology and emergent undercurrents in society. In other words a difference with the way consumers are and how they some times wish they were.
4. *"The cultural brand management process"*: Actively engaging in the myth-making process making sure the brand maintains its position as an icon.

"No-brand" Branding

Recently a number of companies have successfully pursued "No-Brand" strategies by creating packaging that imitates generic brand simplicity. Examples include the Japanese company Muji, which means "No label" in English and the Florida company No-Ad Sunscreen. Although there is a distinct Muji brand, Muji products are not branded. This no-brand strategy means that little is spent on advertisement or classical marketing and Muji's success is attributed to the word-of-mouth, a simple shopping experience and the anti-brand movement. "No brand" branding may be construed as a type of branding as the product is made conspicuous through the absence of a brand name.

Derived Brands

In this case the supplier of a key component, used by a number of suppliers of the end-product, may wish to guarantee its own position by promoting that component as a brand in its own right. The most frequently quoted example is Intel, which secures its position in the PC market with the slogan "Intel Inside".

Brand Extension

The existing strong brand name can be used as a vehicle for new or modified products; for example, many fashion and designer companies extended brands into fragrances, shoes and accessories, home textile, home decor, luggage, glasses, furniture, hotels, etc.

Mars extended its brand to ice cream, Caterpillar to shoes and watches, Michelin to a restaurant guide, Adidas and Puma to personal hygiene. Dunlop extended its brand from tires to other rubber products such as shoes, golf balls, tennis racquets and adhesives.

There is a difference between brand extension and line extension. A line extension is when a current brand name is used to enter a new market segment in the existing product class, with new varieties or flavours or sizes. When Coca-Cola launched "Diet Coke" and "Cherry Coke" they stayed within the originating product category: non-alcoholic carbonated beverages. Procter and Gamble did likewise extending its strong lines into neighbouring products within the same category, dish washing detergents.

Multi-Brands

Alternatively, in a market that is fragmented amongst a number of brands a supplier can choose deliberately to launch totally new brands in apparent competition with its own existing strong brand; simply to soak up some of the share of the market which will in any case go to minor brands. The rationale is that having 3 out of 12 brands in such a market will give a greater overall share than having 1 out of 10.

In its most extreme manifestation, a supplier pioneering a new market which it believes will be particularly attractive may choose immediately to launch a second brand in competition with its first, in order to pre-empt others entering the market.

Individual brand names naturally allow greater flexibility by permitting a variety of different products, of differing quality, to be sold without confusing the consumer's perception of what business the company is in or diluting higher quality products.

Once again, Procter and Gamble is a leading exponent of this philosophy, running as many as ten detergent brands in the US market. This also increases the total number of"facings" it receives on supermarket shelves. Sara Lee, on the other hand, uses it to keep the very different parts of the business separate - from Sara Lee cakes through Kiwi polishes to L'Eggs pantyhose. In the hotel business, Marriott uses the name Fairfield Inns for its budget chain.

Cannibalization is a particular problem of a"multibrand" approach, in which the new brand takes business away from an established one which the organization also owns. This may be acceptable if there is a net gain overall. Alternatively, it may be the price the organization is willing to pay for shifting its position in the market; the new product being one stage in this process.

Private Labels

With the emergence of strong retailers, private label brands, also called own brands, or store brands, also emerged as a major factor in the marketplace. Where the retailer has a particularly strong identity this"own brand" may be able to compete against even the strongest brand leaders, and may outperform those products that are not otherwise strongly branded.

Individual and Organizational Brands

There are kinds of branding that treat individuals and organizations as the"products" to be branded. Personal branding treats persons and their careers as brands. The term is thought to have been first used in a 1997 substance by Tom Peters. Faith branding treats religious figures and organizations as brands. Religious media expert Phil Cooke has written that faith branding handles the question of how to express faith in a media-dominated culture. Nation branding works with the perception and reputation of countries as brands.

BRAND MANAGEMENT

Brand management is the application of marketing techniques to a specific product, product line, or brand. It seeks to increase a product's perceived value to the customer and thereby increase brand franchise and brand equity. Marketers see a brand as an implied promise that the level of quality people have come to expect from a brand will continue with future purchases of the same product. This may increase sales by making a comparison with competing products more favourable. It may also enable the manufacturer to charge more for the product. The value of the brand is determined by the amount of profit it generates for the manufacturer. This can result from a combination of increased sales and increased price, and/or reduced COGS, and/or reduced or more efficient marketing investment. All of these enhancements may improve the profitability of a brand, and thus,"Brand Managers" often carry line-management accountability for a brand's P&L profitability, in contrast to marketing staff manager roles to manage and execute. In this regard, Brand Management is often viewed in organizations as a broader and more strategic role than Marketing alone.

The annual list of the world's most valuable brands, published by Interbrand and Business Week, indicates that the market value of companies often consists largely of brand equity. Research by McKinsey and Company, a global consulting firm, in 2000 suggested that strong, well-leveraged brands produce higher returns to shareholders than weaker, narrower brands. Taken together, this means that brands seriously impact shareholder value, which ultimately makes branding a CEO responsibility.

PRINCIPLES OF BRAND MANAGEMENT

A good brand name should:

- Be protected under trademark law.
- Be easy to pronounce.
- Be easy to remember.
- Be easy to recognize.
- Be easy to translate into all languages in the markets where the brand will be used.
- Attract attention.
- Suggest product benefits or suggest usage
- Suggest the company or product image.
- Distinguish the product's positioning relative to the competition.
- Be attractive.
- Stand out among a group of other brands.

ONLINE BRAND MANAGEMENT

Companies are embracing brand reputation management as a strategic imperative and are increasingly turning to online monitoring in their efforts to prevent their public image from becoming tarnished. Online brand reputation protection can mean monitoring for the misappropriation of a brand trademark by fraudsters intent on confusing consumers for monetary gain. It can also mean monitoring for less malicious, although perhaps equally damaging, infractions, such as the unauthorized use of a brand logo or even for negative brand information from online consumers that appears in online communities and other social media platforms. The red flag can be something as benign as a blog rant about a bad hotel experience or an electronic gadget that functions expectations.

CORPORATE BRANDING

Corporate branding refers to a company applying its name to a product. The product and the company name become the brand name. The company can advertise several of its products under a single brand name in a practice referred to as *family branding* or *umbrella branding*.

By using corporate branding with a successfully marketed product, a company can familiarize consumers with its products and may create brand loyalty. If the public likes one product from this company, then they may seek out the brand name when buying other products. Corporate branding is usually only successful if the company is well known and sells reputable products with a positive image. One of the disadvantages of corporate branding is that the company can become identified with only one type of product.

To consumers, corporate branding represents a level of quality that they have come to expect from the company. They will expect every product with the same brand name to have the same level of quality that they are familiar with. The company can increase sales by comparing one of their more popular products with a similar product by another company. The value of the brand is determined by the profits the products have made. If profits are high, then the manufacturer is able to charge more for their product.

When applying corporate branding to a product or products, companies need to follow a few guidelines. A corporate brand should be easy to recognize and attract attention. It should also be legally protectable and suggest the company or product image.

Ideally, the brand should be easy to pronounce and easy to remember. A premier brand product typically costs more to purchase than an economy brand. Consumers are paying for the name and the quality of product that name guarantees.

There are a few extensions to corporate branding. One brand name may be used for a number of products in family branding, or all the products may be given different brand names in a practice called *individual branding*. When large retailers buy goods in bulk and then put their own brand name on them, this is called *store branding, label branding,* or *private branding. Co-branding* is when two or more manufactures combine to sell their products. When a company sells the right to use their brand name to another company for use in another location or for non-competitive purposes, this is called *brand licensing*.

Corporate branding has the ability to make a product very successful. If the brand name has a track record of a guarantee of quality, then there are huge amounts of money to be made by using the name. However, just one shoddy product under the brand name may cause bad word of mouth, affecting sales of all the other products under the same name and causing irreversible damage to the company.

FAMILY BRANDING

Family branding is a type of marketing tactic. It involves using one brand name to market multiple products. For example, a company may use one brand to market soap, lotion, hair shampoo, and nail polish. This differs from branding individual products, which involves giving each product its own name and image. For example, a company may sell lipstick and nail polish, giving each product line a separate marketing identity.

The idea behind family branding is that a company can make a wide range of products both desirable and profitable by giving them all one recognizable name. Then, by building recognition of this brand name, a company can also build customer loyalty. When the company introduces new products or even makes changes to existing products, it can depend on customer loyalty to ensure its market will purchase the new or altered product. Additionally, family branding, makes it possible to use an advertising campaign to successfully market a range of products instead of just one at a time.

Often, companies in the food industry use family branding techniques to market their products. For example, a company may make and sell bread, potato chips, frozen food, and condiments all under one highly recognizable name. This umbrella branding may mean such companies will sell more than they would with individual branding. Some consumers are more likely to choose a product with a familiar name over one that is less well-known, even if the known brand is more expensive.

There is a downside for companies that use family branding, however. In order to keep sales up, they have to maintain consistent levels of quality across their entire product line. If one of the products is perceived as being of lesser quality, this consumer perception could cause sales to drop for the whole family of products. Likewise, a brand that does have consistent quality could suffer if the company that makes it experiences bad publicity.

Interestingly, some companies use both family and individual branding. For example, a company may have a strong brand name, yet choose to market some of its products with individual branding. This may occur, for example, when a product is introduced to a new market. In such a case, individual branding can prevent problems for the family of products if the new product fails. Sometimes an individual brand may be more appropriate because the product is being introduced to another class of consumers; introducing a product designed for budget shoppers under the same brand intended for affluent shoppers may not produce the desired results.

INDIVIDUAL BRANDING

Individual branding is the marketing strategy of giving each product in a product portfolio its own unique brand name. This is contrasted with family branding in which the products in a product line are given the same brand name. The advantage of individual branding is that each product has an image and identity that is unique. This facilitates the positioning process.

TRADEMARK

Generally speaking, a trademark is a word, symbol, phrase or device which uniquely identifies a particular company or individual. There are many types of bottles used to contain soft drinks, for example, but only one with the distinctive logo and design of Coca-Cola. Each element of a Coca-Cola bottle- the shape, red imprint and name-could be considered a trademark of the Coca-Cola company. Because all of these elements have been legally registered with the United States Patent and Trademark Office, no other soft drink company can create a similar trademark.

This same philosophy holds true with distinctive slogans or brand names. A photocopying machine is not a trademark, but 'Xerox' is. Any product bearing the name Xerox implies the same level of quality as the original product. Sometimes a trademark becomes so popular that it replaces the generic description of the product. Consumers shop for Q-Tips instead of cotton swabs, for instance, even though the name 'Q-Tip' is a registered trademark of the Johnson and Johnson company. Other trademarks which have become universal include Jacuzzi, Band-Aid and Crayola.

A trademark should be registered with agencies such as the United States Patent and Trade Office for maximum legal protection. Trademark laws work much like copyright laws in the sense of first rights. Once a company or individual successfully registers a trademark, a circled "R" or the abbreviation "Reg. TM" can be legally imprinted on the product or slogan. There is no such condition as 'trademark pending', unlike applications for patents which may take years to process through the USPTO.

Sometimes the criteria for trademark registration can be challenging to understand. Companies and individuals cannot simply register ownership of common words or phrases, but they can turn a distinctive combination of words into a trademark. The Nike shoe company has a legal right to trademark the phrase 'Just Do It' because the words have become an identifiable slogan. The Nike swoosh, as simple as it may appear, is also a registered trademark. This doesn't mean, however, that another company can't use a stylized check mark, but it can't be readily confused with the swoosh logo owned by Nike.

Companies and individuals who have registered a trademark will pursue many legal avenues to protect it. Courts must decide if the unauthorized use of a trademarked slogan or product by others has caused actual damage in the marketplace. A local restaurant featuring fried chicken, for example, cannot use the image of an elderly man in a white suit as its official logo. This would create confusion with the registered trademark of Colonel Sanders owned by Kentucky Fried Chicken. But it would be legal for the local restaurant to say 'If Mr. Sanders ate here, he'd be a General.' Kentucky Fried Chicken's registered trademark does not protect individual words, just the entire phrase or symbol.

11

Pricing

INTRODUCTION

Consider a Belgian couple contemplating a shopping trip to London during the Christmas period. The cheapest way to cross the Channel would be to take a ticket on the ferry from Oostende to Ramsgate, which would amount to about Bfr. 1,500 per person. While they can afford this from a budgetary viewpoint, taking the boat would mean spending about five hours travelling, which would mean losing almost half of the 'available' weekend to hunt for interesting bargains in the London shopping area.

Taking the plane would drastically reduce travelling time, but the air fare of Bfr. 4,900 per person is not overly appealing. Friends recommend that they buy a combined ticket from the Belgian Railways and the Channel.

This seems to be the most interesting option, but unfortunately no more regular tickets are available for the morning of the Christmas weekend. The price of a first class-Railway/Channel ticket is prohibitive.

Ultimately, the couple decides to travel by Hovercraft, at a rate of Bfr. 2,200 per person. This example emphasises the complexity of consumer choices in the face of a variety of alternatives offered at different prices.

The mirror image of this problem is the pricing issue for firms offering the products or services to various types of customers: their pricing problem will be equally multifaceted and complex. To introduce the nature of the problem and the issues involved.

MEANING OF PRICE

In ordinary usage, price is the quantity of payment or compensation for something. People may say about a criminal that he has 'paid the price to society' to imply that he has paid a penalty or compensation.

They may say that somebody has 'paid for his folly' to imply that he suffered the consequences of his actions. Economists view price as an exchange ratio between goods that are exchanged for each other. In the case of barter of two goods in the quantities x and y, the price of a unit of the first good is the ratio y/x, while the price of a unit of the second good is the ratio x/y.

This however has not been used consistently, so that old confusion regarding value frequently reappears. The value of something is a quantity counted in common units of value called numeraire, which may even be an imaginary good. This is done to compare different goods. The unit of value is frequently confused with price, because market value is calculated as the quantity of some good multiplied by its nominal price.

Theory of price asserts that the market price reflects interaction between two opposing considerations. On the one side are demand considerations based on marginal utility, while on the other side are supply considerations based on marginal cost.

An equilibrium price is supposed to be at once equal to marginal utility from the buyer's side and marginal cost from the seller's side. Though this view is accepted by almost every economist, and it constitutes the core of mainstream economics, it has recently been challenged seriously.

There was time when people debated use-value versus exchange value, often wondering about the paradox of value. The use-value was supposed to give some measure of usefulness, later refined as marginal benefit while exchange value was the measure of how much one good was in terms of another, namely what is now called relative price.

RELATIVE AND NOMINAL PRICE

The difference between nominal price and relative or real price is often made. Nominal price is the price quoted in money while relative or real price is the exchange ratio between real goods regardless of money. The distinction is made to make sense of inflation.

When all prices are quoted in terms of money units, and the prices in money units change more or less proportionately, the ratio of exchange may not change much. In the extreme case, if all prices quoted in money change in the same proportion, the relative price remains the same. It is now becoming clear that the distinction is not useful and indeed hides a major confusion.

The conventional wisdom is that proportional change in all nominal prices does not affect real price, and hence should not affect either demand or supply and therefore also should not affect output.

The new criticism is that the crucial question is why is there more money to pay for the same old real output. If this question is answered, it will show that dynamically, even as the real price remains exactly the same, output in real terms can change, just because additional money allow additional output to be traded.

The supply curve can shift such that at the old price, the new higher output is sold. This shift if not possible without additional money. From this point of view, a price is similar to an opportunity cost, that is, what must be given up in exchange for the good or service that is being purchased. For example, if x=1 and y=2, the relative price of x in terms of y is 2, and the price of y in terms of x is 0.5.

The price of an item is also called the price point, especially where it refers to stores that set a limited number of price points. For example, Dollar General is a general store or "five and dime" store that sets price points only at even amounts, such as exactly one, two, three, five, or ten dollars. Other stores only have a single price point though in some cases this price may purchase more than one of some very small items.Price is relatively less than the cost price.

CONFUSION BETWEEN PRICES AND COSTS OF PRODUCTION

Technically, though, these are different concepts. Price is what a buyer pays to acquire products from a seller. Cost of production concerns the seller's investment in the product being exchanged with a buyer. For marketing organizations seeking to make a profit the hope is that price will exceed cost of production so the organization can see financial gain from the transaction.

Finally, while pricing is a topic central to a company's profitability, pricing decisions are not limited to for-profit companies. Non-profit organizations, such as charities, educational institutions and industry trade groups, also set prices, though this is often not as apparent.

For instance, charities seeking to raise money may set different"target" levels for donations that reward donors with increases in status, gifts or other benefits.

While a charitable organization may not call it a price in their promotional material, in reality these targets are prices since they specify a cost that must be paid by buyers in order to obtain something of value.

IMPORTANCE OF PRICE

When marketers talk about what they do as part of their responsibilities for marketing products, the tasks associated with setting price are often not at the top of the list. Marketers are much more likely to discuss their activities related to promotion, product development, market research and other tasks that are viewed as the more interesting and exciting parts of the job.

Yet pricing decisions can have important consequences for the marketing organization and the attention given by the marketer to pricing is just as important as the attention given to more recognizable marketing activities.

Some reasons pricing is important include:

- *Most Flexible Marketing Mix Variable*: For marketers price is the most adjustable of all marketing decisions. Unlike product and distribution decisions, which can take months or years to change, or some forms of promotion which can be time consuming to alter, price can be changed very rapidly. The flexibility of pricing decisions is particularly important in times when the marketer seeks to quickly stimulate demand or respond to competitor price actions. For instance, a marketer can agree to a field salesperson's request to lower price for a potential prospect during a phone conversation. Likewise a marketer in charge of online operations can raise prices on hot selling products with the click of a few website buttons.

- *Setting the Right Price*: Pricing decisions made hastily without sufficient research, analysis, and strategic evaluation can lead to the marketing organization losing revenue. Prices set too low may mean the company is missing out on additional profits that could be earned if the target market is willing to spend more to acquire the product. Additionally, attempts to raise an initially low priced product to a higher price may be met by customer resistance as they may feel the marketer is attempting to take advantage of their customers. Prices set too high can also impact revenue as it prevents interested customers from purchasing the product. Setting the right price level often takes considerable market knowledge and, especially with new products, testing of different pricing options.
- *Trigger of First Impressions*: Often times customers' perception of a product is formed as soon as they learn the price, such as when a product is first seen when walking down the aisle of a store. While the final decision to make a purchase may be based on the value offered by the entire marketing offering, it is possible the customer will not evaluate a marketer's product at all based on price alone. It is important for marketers to know if customers are more likely to dismiss a product when all they know

is its price. If so, pricing may become the most important of all marketing decisions if it can be shown that customers are avoiding learning more about the product because of the price.

- *Important Part of Sales Promotion*: Many times price adjustments are part of sales promotions that lower price for a short term to stimulate interest in the product. However, as we noted in our discussion of promotional pricing in the Sales Promotion tutorial, marketers must guard against the temptation to adjust prices too frequently since continually increasing and decreasing price can lead customers to be conditioned to anticipate price reductions and, consequently, withhold purchase until the price reduction occurs again.

STRATEGIC PRICING

One of the four major elements of the marketing mix is price. Pricing is an important strategic issue because it is related to product positioning. Furthermore, pricing affects other marketing mix elements such as product features, channel decisions, and promotion.

While there is no single recipe to determine pricing, the following is a general sequence of steps that might be followed for developing the pricing of a new product:

- *Develop marketing strategy*: Perform marketing analysis, segmentation, targeting, and positioning.
- *Make marketing mix decisions*: Define the product, distribution, and promotional tactics.
- *Estimate the demand curve*: Understand how quantity demanded varies with price.
- *Calculate cost*: Include fixed and variable costs associated with the product.
- *Understand environmental factors*: Evaluate likely competitor actions, understand legal constraints, etc.
- *Set pricing objectives*: For example, profit maximization, revenue maximization, or price stabilization.

- *Determine pricing*: Using information collected in the steps, select a pricing method, develop the pricing structure, and define discounts.

These steps are interrelated and are not necessarily performed in the order. Nonetheless, the list serves to present a starting framework.

MARKETING STRATEGY AND THE MARKETING MIX

Before the product is developed, the marketing strategy is formulated, including target market selection and product positioning. There usually is a tradeoff between product quality and price, so price is an important variable in positioning. Because of inherent tradeoffs between marketing mix elements, pricing will depend on other product, distribution, and promotion decisions.

ESTIMATE THE DEMAND CURVE

Because there is a relationship between price and quantity demanded, it is important to understand the impact of pricing on sales by estimating the demand curve for the product.

For existing products, experiments can be performed at prices above and below the current price in order to determine the price elasticity of demand. Inelastic demand indicates that price increases might be feasible.

CALCULATE COSTS

If the firm has decided to launch the product, there likely is at least a basic understanding of the costs involved, otherwise, there might be no profit to be made. The unit cost of the product sets the lower limit of what the firm might charge, and determines the profit margin at higher prices.

The total unit cost of a producing a product is composed of the variable cost of producing each additional unit and fixed costs that are incurred regardless of the quantity produced. The pricing policy should consider both types of costs.

ENVIRONMENTAL FACTORS

Pricing must take into account the competitive and legal

environment in which the company operates. From a competitive standpoint, the firm must consider the implications of its pricing on the pricing decisions of competitors.

For example, setting the price too low may risk a price war that may not be in the best interest of either side. Setting the price too high may attract a large number of competitors who want to share in the profits.

From a legal standpoint, a firm is not free to price its products at any level it chooses. For example, there may be price controls that prohibit pricing a product too high. Pricing it too low may be considered predatory pricing or "dumping" in the case of international trade.

Offering a different price for different consumers may violate laws against price discrimination. Finally, collusion with competitors to fix prices at an agreed level is illegal in many countries.

PRICE DISCOUNTS

The normally quoted price to end users is known as the list price. This price usually is discounted for distribution channel members and some end users.

There are several types of discounts:

- *Quantity discount*: Offered to customers who purchase in large quantities.
- *Cumulative quantity discount*: A discount that increases as the cumulative quantity increases. Cumulative discounts may be offered to resellers who purchase large quantities over time but who do not wish to place large individual orders.
- *Seasonal discount*: Based on the time that the purchase is made and designed to reduce seasonal variation in sales. For example, the travel industry offers much lower off-season rates. Such discounts do not have to be based on time of the year; they also can be based on day of the week or time of the day, such as pricing offered by long distance and wireless service providers.

- *Cash discount*: Extended to customers who pay their bill before a specified date.
- *Trade discount*: A functional discount offered to channel members for performing their roles. For example, a trade discount may be offered to a small retailer who may not purchase in quantity but nonetheless performs the important retail function.
- *Promotional discount*: A short-term discounted price offered to stimulate sales.

PRICING OBJECTIVES

Pricing objectives or goals give direction to the whole pricing process. Determining what your objectives are is the first step in pricing.

When deciding on pricing objectives you must consider:

- The overall financial, marketing, and strategic objectives of the company;
- The objectives of your product or brand;
- Consumer price elasticity and price points; and
- The resources you have available.

Some of the more common pricing objectives are:

- Maximize long-run profit
- Maximize short-run profit
- Increase sales volume
- Increase monetary sales
- Increase market share
- Obtain a target rate of return on investment
- Obtain a target rate of return on sales
- *Stabilize market or stabilize market price*: an objective to stabilize price means that the marketing manager attempts to keep prices stable in the marketplace and to compete on non-price considerations. Stabilization of margin is basically a cost-plus approach in which the manager attempts to maintain the same margin regardless of changes in cost.

- Company growth
- Maintain price leadership
- Desensitize customers to price
- Discourage new entrants into the industry
- Match competitors prices
- Encourage the exit of marginal firms from the industry
- Survival
- Avoid government investigation or intervention
- Obtain or maintain the loyalty and enthusiasm of distributors and other sales personnel
- Enhance the image of the firm, brand, or product
- Be perceived as "fair" by customers and potential customers
- Create interest and excitement about a product
- Discourage competitors from cutting prices
- Use price to make the product "visible"
- Build store traffic
- Help prepare for the sale of the business
- Social, ethical, or ideological objectives
- Get competitive advantage

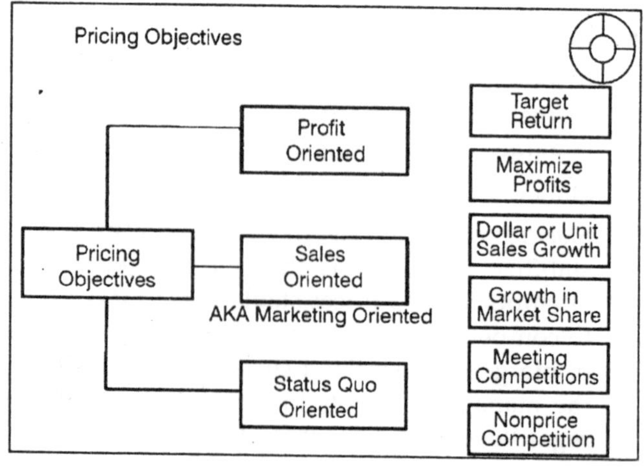

PRICE DETERMINATION

Determination of the prices depends internal and external factors. Pricing goals represents internal policy. Also, price policy should be aligned on several other factors.

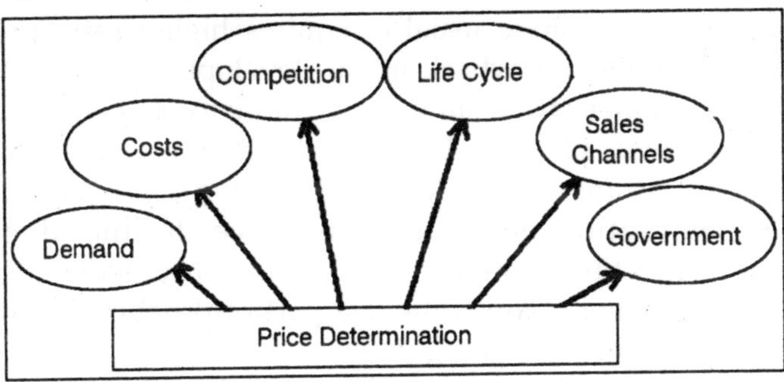

Demand is the key determinant for market oriented company. Demand is the starting point for all activities. Simply, the average customer will be demanding different product quantities, depending on price. Law of the market says that demand and price are counter proportional. Competition has a significant influence to price determination of market oriented companies. Prices need to be adjusted in order to address the competition. Every company should research market and competition, prior to launch of the new product. Survey should include direct competitors but also the substitutes. Based on market survey and the strength of the company the prices can be the same, lower or higher. Costs– While demand and competition are external factor, the costs are internal. The costs must be embedded in every stage of price determination process.

There are several methods of cost embedding into price:

- *Costs Plus*: Company calculates the costs and increase price for the specific profit.
- *Markup*: Price based on cost increased for amount of specific markup percentage.
- *Target Return Method*: Calculated required markup, in order to achieve return on investment.
- Profit Maximizing is the price where the marginal profit equals marginal cost.

- *Breakeven Analysis*: Is the number of units sold that generates profit that can cover cost. This point does not have profit nor lost.

Life Cycle pricing approach analysis the current phase of product life in market:

- Entering phase usually requires higher sales prices in order to payback initial development costs. Also customers are willing to pay more for a new product.
- Growth phase is bringing the market stabilization. Prices are more or less stabile.
- Saturation phase leads to price decline, due to competition entrance and loss of consumer's interest
- Declining phase is the last part of product life cycle. Prices are still going down.

Sales Channels have the different shopping occasion. Consequently the pricing is adjusted to sales channel. For example, the same products is cheaper in hypermarket than on petrol station.

Government is usually do not interfere into price determination. Exceptionally it may limit maximal prices for a certain products. Still, government is influencing pricing, since the taxes and custom duties are the part of the price.

PRICING STRATEGY VERSUS TACTICS

In the literature, the term 'pricing tactics' is subject to much confusion. In this text, we adhere to the viewpoint of van Waterschoot and Van den Bulte and Morris and Calantone, which is that pricing strategies determine longterm price structure and levels and their evolution over time in response to long-term environmental changes, while tactics refer to short-term price decisions to realise short-term objectives or respond to short-term environmental changes. Often, the same instruments are used for strategic and tactical purposes.

A temporary price cut, for instance, can be part of a random-discounting strategy, or intended to pursue an immediate goal like liquidating excess stocks. For many companies, discounting is 'correctional', in response to sudden changes in consumer demand, trading conditions, and operational inefficiencies. Concentrate on empirically observed effects of short-term price reductions or 'price promotions'. As the literature on promotions is extensive, we keep the discussion tractable by studying only price discounts in their purest form. Coupons, or other short-term marketing instruments such as gifts or extra quantities, are not considered here. Also, our discussion is based mainly on studies in the packaged-goods sector, which constitute the bulk of the promotion literature. We therefore analyse consumer and retailer promotions and trade promotions.

Index

R

S

T

U

V